RARE BIRDS

RARE BIRDS

The Extraordinary Tale of the Bermuda Petrel
and the
Man Who Brought It Back from Extinction

ELIZABETH GEHRMAN

BEACON PRESS, BOSTON

Beacon Press
Boston, Massachusetts
www.beacon.org

Beacon Press books
are published under the auspices of
the Unitarian Universalist Association of Congregations.

18 17 16 15   8 7 6 5 4 3 2 1

This book is printed on acid-free paper that meets the uncoated paper
ANSI/NISO specifications for permanence as revised in 1992.

Text design by Wilsted & Taylor Publishing Services

Bermuda map printed with permission of Bruce Adams
Flying petrel photo printed with permission of Chris Burville

Library of Congress Cataloging-in-Publication Data
Gehrman, Elizabeth.
Rare birds : the extraordinary tale of the Bermuda petrel and
the man who brought it back from extinction / Elizabeth Gehrman.
p. cm.
Includes bibliographical references and index.
ISBN 978-0-8070-1078-5 (paperback : alk. paper)
1. Bermuda petrel. 2. Rare birds. 3. Wingate, David, 1935– I. Title.
QL696.P665G44 2013
598.168—dc23   2012014237

For my parents

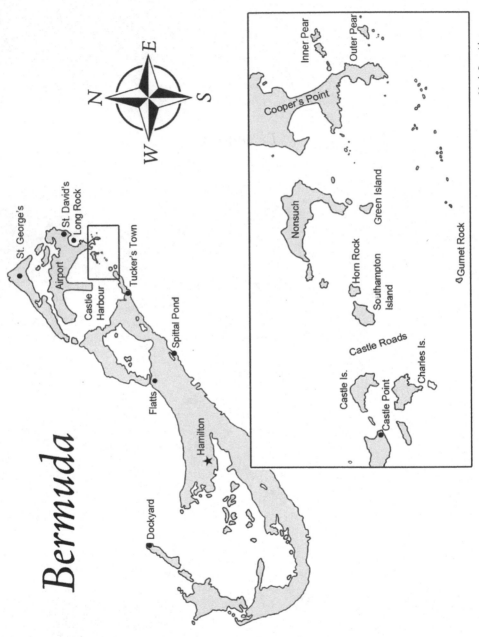

Bermuda

St. George's

St. David's

Long Rock

Airport

Tucker's Town

Castle
Harbour

Spittal Pond

Flatts

Hamilton

Dockyard

N E
S W

Cooper's Point

Inner Pear

Outer Pear

Green Island

Nonsuch

Horn Rock

Southampton
Island

Gurnet Rock

Castle Roads

Castle Is.

Charles Is.

Castle Point

Map by Bruce Adams

CONTENTS

Prologue

IN APRIL 2009, JUST two months short of four hundred years since the English ship *Sea Venture* wrecked on the jagged, shallow reefs encircling Bermuda and claimed the island for the Crown, I pounded over the choppy waters of Castle Harbour in a Boston Whaler Montauk with Jeremy Madeiros, the country's terrestrial conservation officer, to an island the early settlers called Nonsuch—pronounced *Nonesuch*—for its unparalleled natural beauty.

The land has changed so dramatically since the early seventeenth century that it's hard to say why Nonsuch seemed more breathtaking to untraveled British eyes than any of the 137 other islands that make up this 21-square-mile archipelago alone in the middle of the Atlantic Ocean. Two miles by boat from Tucker's Town, where today you can pick up a summer cottage for $20 million or so, the long, low mound of rocky coastline topped with scrubby vegetation would seem unremarkable were it not for what is happening there.

I had heard in passing about a bird called the cahow, or Bermuda petrel, during the half-dozen trips I'd made to the country since the previous summer, when I was sent there to write a travel story for a magazine. But, like most people who know of it—including, it seems, many Bermudians—I had only a vague notion that the cahow was somehow significant. I had no idea how fascinating its tale was, and how instructive a warning it provided of humankind's power over nature, for good or ill.

Madeiros gave me the condensed version as we disembarked at the island's concrete dock and set off toward a small cluster of white-peaked buildings painted, in the traditional style, a sunny pastel. The compound was once a quarantine hospital; Madeiros and his family now shared it with cockroaches, endemic skinks, and wolf spiders as big as your palm.

The cahow, he said, was believed extinct since the early 1600s, just a few years after Bermuda was colonized. Like its more famous kin the dodo, discovered in 1598 and last sighted less than a century later, the cahow had no significant predators until the arrival of man and his attendant rats, cats, dogs, and pigs. The trusting and docile birds were no match for the clubs and claws and teeth that bore down on them, and just eleven years after the wreck of the *Sea Venture*, the first known conservation legislation in the Western Hemisphere was issued for the cahows' protection—but as far as anyone could tell, the birds were already gone.

But imagine if a dodo were to suddenly stride out from under the forest canopy of the Indian Ocean island its ancestors once occupied. It was just as much of a jolt to the scientific community and the public when, in 1951, the cahow was rediscovered, clinging to survival on a few barren rocks in the only place on earth it calls home.

Accompanying the expedition that found the first live cahow seen in modern times was a fifteen-year-old Bermudian boy named David Wingate, who would grow up to devote his life to restoring Nonsuch to its virgin state and returning the cahow to its place in the world. For decades, Wingate alone worked to save the birds. He fought incredible odds in a race against time, more than once proving colleagues who called him crazy dead wrong. In an era before *conservation* became a household word, he had no template and virtually no government funding—but he gave the birds the chance they needed in their centuries-long fight for survival.

Madeiros, who took over the project when mandatory retirement forced Wingate to step down as conservation officer in 2000, led me to the artificial concrete burrows that dotted the ground a few steps from the backyard of his summer house, the only residence on Nonsuch. He removed the concave top of one to reveal what appeared to be a sooty, squirming, oversized cotton ball, and gently lifted Somers, as he called the bird—after Admiral Sir George Somers, Bermuda's founder—out of his dark, grass-lined nest and handed him to me.

Thus, on protected land that is as close an approximation of pre-Columbian Bermuda as can be achieved, I became one of only a few people in the world to hold the first cahow chick born on Nonsuch in almost four hundred years. Somers was the premier product of a translocation project started in 2005 that aims to move the birds off the rocky islets they now inhabit to an area less endangered by erosion and hurricanes, and more like the land they once so gregariously dominated.

The almost weightless bird sat placidly in my cupped hands, a coconut-sized ball of fluff with two stuffed-toy eyes and a beak the color of pencil lead. As I scratched the back of his neck with my thumb, Somers curled his head back in pleasure, revealing his reptilian roots in his exposed ear hole and the thin, wrinkled skin beneath his inches-thick gray down. He squeaked like a trapped mouse when I passed him back to Madeiros to be placed in a small canvas bag for weighing.

Encountering an untamed animal in the wild, as I had before on precious few occasions, is always a moving experience. This time it was made more so by the knowledge that Somers and the two-hundred-odd birds like him that constitute an entire species fought so hard to get here and remain locked in a daily battle to persist.

Before visiting Bermuda, I had never traveled to the same country even twice in a row, much less six times. But in that first week I learned enough about the island to know it was bursting with stories waiting to be told. Something about the place kept tugging me back, and in getting to know the residents, I heard about shipwrecks and treasures of gold, Civil War blockade runners and World War II U-boat patrols, unique cave species and millennia-old subaquatic cedar forests.

And then I met Somers. I had found the story I needed to tell.

CHAPTER ONE

The Bird Man of Bermuda

DAVID WINGATE WANTS TO see his birds. "This is cahow weather," he says, peering through the rain-splashed windshield of his white Suzuki Alto at treetops dancing violently in the wind. "We may be miserable, but the cahows are just yippee-happy right now. If we could go out to Nonsuch tonight, they'd be celebrating."

Just a handful of people have seen cahows in flight, and even fewer have witnessed the staggeringly graceful, scramjet-fast aerial courtship they perform on only the darkest fall and winter nights. Wingate, though, has spent enough time with the birds that he has felt their wings brush the top of his head as they darted past him in the blackened sky, gliding ever slower through the air before dropping to land like a cartoon anvil. But in the past few years things have changed, and troubles from bad knees to bad blood have conspired to keep him from the birds he calls his first love.

This week he's supposed to make his first trip to Nonsuch at night in two years. He'd been trying to get out there—or at least into the harbor in his boat—for a night watch once or twice every November since he moved off the island in 2003, but last year he didn't go because of the knee-replacement surgery that laid him up for six months and left six-inch vertical scars in the dead center of both his legs. Before that—well, it's a long story.

Mid-November is when the birds are most active, from a human perspective. It's when the returning fledglings arrive at Castle Harbour after as much as four years spent flying virtually nonstop, drinking seawater and sleeping on the wing. During that time a young cahow might travel thousands of miles a week, weaving in and out among the rolling waves and heaving swells of the open ocean, a lone feathered missile gliding and banking along the westerlies as it roams over millions of square miles of the Atlantic. Then, one day, a day like every other in the bird's life so far, some unknowable instinct kicks in; some primal urge tells it to head back to Bermuda to find a mate. And, like a high school senior hustling to Cancun for spring break, it does. And when it arrives, it lands within three yards of the tree or rock or sheer cliff wall from which it fledged. When it takes off again to get to the business at hand, it rises and dips through the night sky and calls to its new friends in low, spectral moans until that special someone answers and the sexual chemistry becomes so achingly clear that the other birds must roll their eyes and tell the pair to get a burrow.

Seeing that, to Wingate, is heaven, an adrenaline high like no other. But this week, as in Novembers recently past, the Fates are refusing to allow him his greatest thrill.

First, there's the weather, which is often unsettled in Bermuda this time of year. What the weather service describes as a "solid cloud deck" is hovering over the country; tomorrow it will combine with a low-pressure system from the south and the next day with the nor'easter created by what's left of Hurricane Ida as it charges up the coast of the United States, generating a mini perfect storm that will result in near-constant rain, winds gusting to 33 miles an hour, and a total of just a few hours of sunshine over the next three days. The small-craft warning that will be issued for each of those days would most certainly apply to Wingate's battered 17-foot Boston Whaler—not that that sort of thing usually keeps him out of the water.

Far worse than the weather, for Wingate, is that he threw his back out yesterday after having to bail his boat with a hand pump because the electrical system's on the fritz again. (Covering the boat while it's moored, he says, is "too much trouble.")

He turns into the parking lot of a bungalow-style pink building called Shorelands, which houses the Bermuda Department of Conservation Services, and slowly begins to extricate himself from his sardine can of a car, the smallest he could find in the country. He's here to go through two plastic storage containers full of old photographs to select some for a Canadian filmmaker who's in town shooting the cahows for a DVD series on the environment. But Wingate can't carry the bins. He can barely make it into the building. He hobbles up the sloping lawn and, once inside, leans on any available surface as he plods forward, wincing and groaning all the way.

"I've turned overnight into a doddering old man," he says, finally lowering himself into an office chair in a first-floor conference room, where he can spread out the pictures on an enormous laminated table. "This is not me, you'll see."

✦

At seventy-five, Wingate is a trim six feet tall and broad-shouldered, with a full head of uncombed white hair, thin lips, watery blue eyes, and the slightly crooked teeth of a British schoolboy. He has a short beard, also white, and his dress is emphatically casual, tending toward shorts, polo shirts, and boat shoes or Crocs for all but the most formal occasions.

"Whenever Dad had to come to something at school," his daughter Karen Wingate remembers, "my sister and I would be in agony. We knew he'd be late. And if he comes, what will he be wearing? Ripped shorts and a shirt covered in bird poop? He was always scruffy, with his hands bleeding and burrs clinging to him, because he'd be off in the bushes after a bird."

Like most Bermudians, Wingate speaks with a mix of accents—in his case, Scottish, handed down from his father's side, and English, from his mother's. Thus his nasally *cannot* becomes *canna* and *glasses* something like *glahshees*. Though most people pronounce the bird's name *ka-HOW*, as in "How now brown cahow," Wingate more often says *KA-how*, rhyming the first syllable with the vowel sound in the American pronunciation of *laugh*.

He had a skin-cancer scare last summer when he developed a persistent sore on his lip. Though a biopsy proved negative, just to be on the safe side he cut out a rectangular piece of cardboard and affixed it, dangling, to the back of his baseball cap with blue painter's tape. On cloudless days, he works the thing down over the bill of the hat, past his wire-framed aviator-style bifocals, and over his mouth, where it jumps slightly whenever he talks. When asked why he doesn't just use zinc oxide on his lips, he replies that he prefers a mechanical barrier. He's thinking about replacing the cardboard soon with a leather version, maybe in the shape of a handlebar mustache—"to look like Mark Twain," he says with a chuckle.

"I think everyone, even his best friends, would say he's, well, he's not certifiable, but he's certainly a genuine eccentric," David Saul says of Wingate. Saul, a former finance minister, former premier, bird lover, and raconteur, is no slouch himself in the eccentricity department, with a specially made steel coffin—guillotine-ended for easy opening—accumulating coral while it waits for him at the bottom of Devonshire Bay a quarter-mile from the backyard of his house.

Saul can't recall any particular anecdotes to back up this assertion.

"No, nothing that I—I wouldn't have even mentally recorded anything like that because everything about him was strange. You'd meet him and there'd be a bird in his pocket. You know, what could be unusual about that?"

A live bird?

"Oh, sure! To open up his car and—I am sure when he was conservation officer he carried birds, turtles, live and dead, many, many dead, scores, if not hundreds, dead, in his various vehicles. But this would not be considered to be, you know, you wouldn't go home and say, 'I just saw David Wingate, *guess* what!' Well, they'd say—" He shrugs. "If he was acting normal, we'd think he was ill."

Wingate was nicknamed Bird in grammar school, partly, he speculates, because of his prominent hooked nose. Saul dismisses this idea. "No, they'd've called him Hawky," he says. "It was because of his interest in birds, to the exclusion of everything else, probably even girls, at the time. Everyone in Bermuda who's over fifty still addresses him as Bird Wingate."

Saul, who is several years younger than Wingate and knew him only by reputation when they were growing up, maintains that Wingate took his childhood nickname as a badge of honor, but Wingate recalls it very differently. At a time in life when fitting in is the most essential tool of social success, he was openly different, and he remembers being teased and bullied for his unusual hobby. "I was very lonely," Wingate says of those days. "In fact, I had a bit of an inferiority complex."

Wingate may have felt he was being cruelly taunted by the other boys at the Saltus Grammar School, but he also admits he "disdained" the bullies for—ironically—their single-mindedness. The difference was that while they loved football and cricket, Wingate's pursuit was, literally, loftier. He has kept detailed diaries since 1950, and in the first few books, he repeatedly mentions his disinclination for mandatory after-school sports, even going so far as to note that "everything turned out well" the day he was sent to detention because it got him out of "games." In February of that year, two days after the first local newspaper article about him appeared in the *Royal Gazette*—"BOY BIRD WATCHER HAS IDENTIFIED FIFTY DIFFERENT SPECIES IN YEAR," reads the front-page headline, in 36-point type—comes the following entry:

> I was late for school, and found it a most miserable day, because the whole sixth form joked & laughed about my bird-watching as though it was a horrible crime.

By the next semester he seems to have toughened up a bit, as he mentions in passing "the perpetual annoyance and stupid name-calling such as 'Birdy' and 'Bird-Brain.'"

Wandering around with a notebook and binoculars, meticulously recording his sightings, he must have seemed hopelessly nerdy to the more sportive boys. But despite the mutual antipathy, he may even then have been beginning to earn their grudging respect, for in a place as small as Bermuda, it doesn't take long to make a name for yourself. By age fourteen, Wingate was presenting the neighbors with gifts of his ornithological lists and diaries and getting phone calls from adults all over the island—including at least one from someone at the Bermuda Biological Station—to come and identify unusual birds for them.

"If you ever had a sick bird," Saul recalls, "an owl that struck the electric cables or anything, you just took it to his house and dumped it. Don't even bother to ring, to knock the door. Just leave it there. And if it was dead, he would stuff it. I would imagine he stuffed half the birds at the aquarium museum. In the general population's mind, the man is synonymous with birds. You just say, 'You know that crazy birdman,' and they'd all say, 'You mean David Wingate?' 'Yes, David Wingate.'"

Just a few years ago, Wingate's daughter Janet met a man with a cat who, without knowing who she was, volunteered that the cat's name was Wingate because, the man said, "he looovvves de birds."

Wingate wasn't always obsessed with birds, but he was preoccupied with the natural world from the time he could walk. At age three, he collected a herd of wood lice that he called his *beesh*, for *beasts*. He kept them in a matchbox and took them to bed with him, until his mother found them crawling all over the pillow. Chastened not by her disapproval—his parents were tolerant of his diversions—but by the possibility that she might expel his pets from their new homes, he simply relocated his menageries, catching bugs of various sorts and stashing them under the bed instead of in it. Occasionally a spider would escape and build a web over him as he slept.

"When you're a kid," he says of his attraction to crawling things, "your nose is close to the ground."

Wingate's parents, a postal employee and a legal secretary, didn't seem to know where their "born naturalist" came from, but were willing to indulge him, particularly as he was the baby of the family for thirteen years, until his sister Katharine came along. After a brief flirtation with astronomy—abandoned when, as he wrote in 1950, "I could not get the same thrill as I did before I found myself making silly blunders in judging the stars"—at age eleven his interest in the natural world took a turn toward birds. His older brother, Peter, had started an egg collection, which was a fairly standard pastime for Bermudian boys at the time, despite laws meant to protect nests from poaching.

"Every kid in the English countryside had a bird-egg collection," Wingate says, "going way back to the 1700s. Interest peaked in the nineteenth century."

Bermuda has been heavily influenced by both the United States and Great Britain, and in the 1940s and '50s, when Wingate was growing up, Victorian England was not the quaint bit of ancient history it seems now, but a part of living memory that continued to influence culture and daily life in the colonies, just as the 1960s and '70s do in America today. The amateur study of natural history and a passion for collecting were *tres façonnable* in the mid- to late-1800s, and the fad was particularly pronounced in the United Kingdom, where both of Wingate's parents were raised. Connoisseurs of everything from seashells to beetles abounded in the middle and upper classes, and those who had the money would send emissaries to the far corners of the earth to obtain for them ever-rarer specimens.

Wingate's great-grandfather was among those caught up in the fascination for diversity and predilection for cataloging that characterized the time, though in a slightly different form. James Wingate was a noted collector of Scottish coins who wrote the definitive book on the subject in 1868 and sold his stash of ancient groats and testons seven years later for £3,263. The price, called "fabulous" in 1905 by the *Coin Collector*, was equivalent to about $1.75 million in today's dollars.*

Unlike his zealous ancestor, Peter Wingate grew bored with collecting when the opposite sex began to appeal. But David seemed to have inherited the accumulator's gene, and made sure his brother's lovingly amassed hoard didn't go to waste. He adopted the clutch and would eventually take his absorption with it several thousand steps beyond anything Peter could have imagined.

By age twelve, Wingate could distinguish a greater shearwater from a Cory's shearwater and a bay-breasted warbler from the blackpoll variety. He spent every spare moment exploring the forests and beaches and salt marshes of Bermuda, counting snowy egrets and white-eyed vireos and hoping for a glimpse of a migratory American avocet or a white ibis. In 1949, the American naturalist Richard Pough, who two years later would help found the Nature Conservancy, met Wingate on a visit to Bermuda, where Pough and his wife often spent their

---

* Bermuda used the English currency system and tied its values to the pound sterling until 1970, when it switched to Bermudian dollars, which are on a par with the U.S. dollar.

December wedding anniversaries. He sought out Wingate's parents to tell them the boy had potential.

"He advised them to buy me a *Peterson Field Guide*," Wingate recalls, "and then they got me a pair of binoculars. It was the best Christmas present ever." Wingate took off on his bike, and the family didn't see him for the rest of the holiday.

❖

The photos haphazardly thrown together in the plastic bins on the conservation department's conference table stretch back to the early 1940s. Maybe a tenth of them are from Wingate's personal life—him as a child, clean-cut in a white dress shirt; him in his twenties, laughing with his brother and sisters and parents on the manicured lawn of Aldie, the family home; several of his wife Anita looking serene on their wedding day. But most, floating loose in no particular order or in manila envelopes marked "On Her Majesty's Service," span his career as Bermuda's first conservation officer.

Though it took half a decade for him to get an official title, he started working at the position *de facto* when he returned home from college with a B.S. in zoology and a dream to save the cahow.

Even for a young man with great ambitions and an inevitable degree of naïveté, the challenge must have seemed overwhelming. The last known sighting of a live cahow had come around 1620; for 330 years, as far as anyone knew, the birds had been extinct, eaten into oblivion by the first settlers to Bermuda and the animals they'd brought with them. By 1951, when the American ornithologist Robert Cushman Murphy and Louis S. Mowbray of the Bermuda Aquarium stunned the world by announcing they had rediscovered the cahow, the bird had long since come to seem little more than a legend.

Wingate was fifteen and along for the ride when the two scientists made the extraordinary find. Rarely, outside of fiction, does a single moment change a person's life in so clear and defining a way, but when Murphy extracted a blinking, docile adult bird from deep in a rock hollow and held it up to the light, everything else fell away from

Wingate's field of vision. "All I knew was that I had a calling," he says. "Bringing back the cahow was what I was meant to do."

He says he doesn't remember wondering, even after college, how he'd make a living at the task he'd set for himself, or how long it might take to see success. "I don't think it mattered," he says, "because it was a lifetime commitment. I wasn't thinking of it as a project with a beginning and an end. I was seeing it as a way of life."

But it would be a life without a road map.

According to Stuart Pimm, the Doris Duke Professor of Conservation Ecology at Duke University's Nicholas School of the Environment, "No one—or very, very few people indeed—had ever tried anything like this before."

Prior to the founding of the World Wildlife Fund in 1961, the ever-increasing rate of species loss was not understood, nor was the fact that human beings could help restore what they had once destroyed. "David Wingate was one of the early pioneers," says Pimm. "The Society for Conservation Biology was founded in 1985. He started almost thirty years prior to that. That's what makes him such an iconic figure. He was out there in the middle of nowhere, and he had to just suss it out. There wasn't a manual. Not only wasn't there a manual; there wasn't even a literature. It wasn't as if he could have gone to scientific journals and found any advice on saving a species."

Even captive-breeding programs, Pimm adds, were in their infancy. Around the time of the cahow's rediscovery, the British ornithologist and conservationist Sir Peter Scott began working with the nene, or Hawaiian goose, which, like the cahow, had been decimated by humans and human-introduced mammal predators. In 1952, with only thirty nenes known to exist in the wild, Scott began breeding the birds in England and reintroducing them to their native Hawaii; today their population numbers around nineteen hundred. "Of course," Pimm adds, "the thing about the cahow is it's something you couldn't breed in captivity. There's no way you could do that with a bird like the cahow. The only thing you can do is nurse the wild population back."

Cahows presented other challenges as well. For one, they were an utter mystery. Some facts could be deduced from research on other petrels, but little was known about *any* petrel species. As pelagic birds, petrels spend up to 90 percent of their lives in the most remote parts of the open ocean. They are rarely seen except during the breeding season, and in the 1950s the technology to track their movements the rest of the year had not yet been imagined, much less invented.

Vexing schedule aside, there was the inconvenience factor. Petrels are part of the order *Procellariiformes* and the family *Procellariidae*; both words derive from the Latin for "a storm or violent wind." Because they use the wind's energy to conserve their own, the birds are most active during the worst weather, when humans, scientists included, prefer to tuck up indoors beside a cozy fire. When they're not flying, cahows and most other species of petrel shelter deep in earthen burrows or rock crevices, as far from civilization as they can manage. And cahows are nocturnal; artificial light disorients them, and they shy away even from bright moonlight.

How could Wingate protect something he couldn't even see?

He picks up a black-and-white photograph of a Bermuda street scene—more of an unpaved-road scene, really. In it, vegetation is bursting over the low stone walls and towering rock cuts on either side of the road, which curves away into a shadow that falls from cedars so high and broad they almost touch one another overhead. An open buggy is grinding through the crushed-coral surface of the road up a slight incline with a bicyclist hanging onto either side of it, the horse straining against the added weight. "People would tie on going up the hill," Wingate says. "This is the way I grew up, pedaling my bike home from school." He flips the picture to check the date on the back. "Nineteen forty-eight. I was, what, twelve."

Bicycles are called "push-bikes" or "pedal-bikes" in Bermuda, to distinguish them from the sputtering, spewing motorbikes that have become inseparable from the national character. Two years before this picture was taken, the Motor Car Act was passed, allowing the "general use" of automobiles. Today there are more than 47,000 vehicles on the road here, giving the country one of the highest traffic densities in the world, with more than 2,300 cars, trucks, and motorbikes per square mile.

Though he's seen them many times before, Wingate remains fascinated by the photographs. "Oh gosh, makes me weep," he says, "to see how much it's changed."

Though tourism had been growing steadily at least since Mark Twain first visited in 1867, it essentially halted during World War II, when British and American servicemen swarmed the island. But the war brought the country to the attention of a lot of people who'd never given it a thought, and as early as the summer of 1946, according to a "Letter from Bermuda" published in the *New Yorker*, about six hundred American tourists were arriving every week, with thousands more already reserving space for the following fall. The price of a room had risen by 30 percent, from $12 just five years earlier to $16 or $17. "The friendly invasion of uniformed visitors and the abnormal boom they have brought may mean the end of life's leisurely pace here," the story predicted. "There is a general feeling of acceleration."

The resident population, which was less than 20,000 at the time of Bermuda's first census, in 1911, had grown to 37,403 by 1950, the year before the cahow's rediscovery. Flush with wartime cash and unregulated by a government anxious for greater employment and ever-more tourist dollars, developers started throwing up houses and hotels like children collecting Monopoly pieces. The country almost completely lacked conservation laws, and the ones that existed were rarely enforced.

When Wingate returned from college in 1957, it was to an island changed. Few people in Bermuda knew about the cahows and even fewer cared. If development continued at its current pace, he feared, the dozen or so birds left would be buried under a heap of concrete. He knew his only hope was to turn back time.

✢

For more than three centuries, cahows had been cloaked to mankind by darkness and isolation. Predatory brown rats on Castle Harbour's larger islands had relegated the few birds still clinging to existence to five satellite islets that people rarely if ever visited, particularly during the hours the cahows might have been visible.

"In those days no one in their right mind would have thought of landing on those islands at night," Wingate says of the years just after rediscovery.

The islets are composed almost completely of eolianite, a porous, thorn-sharp rock formed by the gradual cementation of windblown, wave-hardened beach sand. Their landscape is as jagged as an EKG readout, and the water churns around them in all directions and continually crashes against their sides and across their low-lying areas. Castle Harbour is in Bermuda's lee, but that's small comfort when unchecked ocean winds sweep over the nearly flat archipelago as though it didn't exist. The harbor is also open to the south shore, so tremendous tidal currents surge through twice a day as they flow onto the Bermuda Platform and then off again. Even a mild breeze running against the currents can turn the water to a chaotic plane of chop.

As a cahow habitat, the few craggy acres scattered about the harbor were far from ideal. First, the birds had only the rocks' natural crevices in which to incubate their young—what little soil there is sits on the islets like a toddler's kippah on a bald man's head—and were competing for scarce nesting sites with white-tailed tropic birds, which would trample and peck cahow chicks to death and take over while the adults were out fishing. But even more worrisome, the islets, whose total area is less than one-four-thousandth the size of the cahow's original breeding ground, are crumbling into the ocean due to erosion, hurricanes, and the action of several species of clionid—a boring sponge that dissolves rock just below the tide line, undercutting cliff faces to such a depth that the limestone above eventually comes crashing down.

Wingate knew he had to get the birds off the islets and onto more stable ground, but there weren't many options for habitat relocation. Since the Revolutionary War, Bermuda had been an important military site for Great Britain and the United States, and in the early 1940s, the latter had connected Long Bird and Cooper's islands to St. David's Island to make room for an airport. Charles and Castle islands were too close to the mainland to keep mammalian predators away, and Southampton was so difficult to land on that monitoring the birds without permanent shelter would be next to impossible.

Then there was Nonsuch. A vaguely boomerang-shaped hump of land about a hundred yards from where the birds were found in 1951, it was isolated enough from the mainland that predators could be controlled, and at fifteen acres and forty feet above sea level, it would provide the cahows with enough soil to someday nest in the thousands. It would make a nice habitat for Wingate, too, with a handful of ramshackle buildings that were once the site of a yellow-fever hospital.

By the time he started to think seriously about moving to the island in 1958, he knew that to save the cahow, he had to give it a proper habitat. He hadn't worked out quite what that meant, though, until he noticed the skinks.

"They were abundant on Nonsuch," he says of the Bermuda rock skink, a critically endangered seven-inch-long lizard that is found nowhere in the world but here. "There were forty times as many as on the mainland, where feral cats prey on them and they get trapped by the litter on roadsides. So it dawned on me that hey, this island, because of its isolation, is a sanctuary—not just for banner species like the cahow, but for a whole lot of other facets of our heritage. Why not capitalize on this and make it a living museum of precolonial Bermuda? In other words, take a holistic approach and restore everything together in its original context."

The first, most major challenge for Wingate would be reforesta-tion. "Without the forest, none of the other flora or fauna could come back," he says. But the forest on Nonsuch had been wiped out by a botanical blight that had hit the entire country several years earlier. "Every tree on the island had been killed, and there were about a dozen goats living over there, which had grazed away the rest of the vegetation so that the birds had disappeared too. There was virtually nothing left."

A photograph from the time, except for having been taken in broad daylight rather than against the backdrop of a scabrous full moon, looks exactly like the stereotypical illustration of a haunted house: You're standing at the bottom of a gently winding path that leads to a huddle of stone buildings atop the distant hill. On either side of the path is a lumpy collection of sparse green scrub no more than knee-high, and about thirty defoliated cedars fill the frame. The ones to your left have broken off and their tops have blown away; the ones to your right arch over the walkway at nearly 90-degree angles, their kyphotic stance created by years of battling those same harsh winds in a fruitless scrabble toward the sun. The trees' ghostly gray limbs might grab you at any moment, you fear, as you imagine the sound of a lone wolf howling in the distance.

There were no wolves on Nonsuch, but it's almost amazing they never made their way to the island. For the history of invasive species crowding out the plants and animals that belong in Bermuda, if it weren't so tragic, would read like a Keystone Kops episode of good intentions gone awry.

The earliest invasives, of course, arrived aboard the first ships to land on Bermuda's shores. Then, "increased communication with the outside world resulted in a new wave of faunal and floral introductions during the Victorian era," Wingate wrote in a 1985 paper. "But most of these were relatively benign and their impact on surviving native species was cumulative rather than catastrophic."

True catastrophe came when an American industrialist with the improbable name of Carbon Petroleum Dubbs moved into a 12,000-square-foot house on Grape Bay Drive in Paget Parish, just across Hamilton Harbour from the capital city. He decided the home's fourteen-acre grounds weren't quite the showpiece he'd envisioned, and brought in some plants from the United States to spiff them up a bit. Among the nursery stock that was shipped to him from California around 1943 were some junipers.

In the middle of the twentieth century, seventeen indigenous plants could be found in Bermuda, giving it, as one visitor wrote, its "unique but monotonous loveliness." The most dominant plant, by far, was the Bermuda cedar, which is actually a type of juniper called *Juniperus bermudiana*. It is an evergreen with a thick trunk, gnarled branches, flat leaves that form a soft-needle fan, and reddish wood that is sweet-smelling and exceptionally hard. The trees were once used to make houses, ships, furniture, tchotchkes for the tourists, even coffins. They were burned as fuel and prized as natural privacy fences. In the absence of predators, they can live two hundred to three hundred years, and inland cedars can reach a height of fifty feet. They are hardy, well-adapted to growing in Bermuda's shallow soil, impervious to sea spray, and unparalleled as a windbreak. In the early 1940s, between two hundred and five hundred Bermuda cedars stood on every one of the country's thirteen thousand acres.

The American naturalist Addison Emery Verrill, writing about Bermuda in 1902, remarked that the cedar was "very little affected by insects." That changed quickly when the trees were colonized by the scale pest *Carulaspis minima*, which probably wouldn't have survived a water crossing but arrived alive and well on C. P. Dubbs's junipers thanks to the advent of air transport on the island a few years before.

The voracious bugs multiplied rapidly and spread across the country with shocking efficiency, perhaps in part because of the anole lizards that had been imported from Jamaica in the early 1900s to control the Mediterranean fruit fly, which had somehow got to Bermuda and was ravaging the citrus crops. Fruit flies, it was soon noticed, turned out to be among the anoles' least favorite treats, but over the four decades they'd been on the island the lizards had significantly decreased the populations of other beneficial insects that might have eaten the cedar scale.

The scale looked like a harmless dusting of snow, but it could strip a tree bare within six months of colonizing it, and in the end it destroyed 95 percent of the country's forest cover, including all but one cedar on Nonsuch. It was helped along in its devastation by the oyster-shell scale *Lepidosaphes newsteadi*, which probably arrived in the 1930s on plants imported for the Castle Harbour Hotel development in Tucker's Town, just southwest of Nonsuch, though its exact provenance was never discovered.

The Department of Agriculture's first response to arresting the destruction was to spray the trees with insecticide, but this proved impractical because it endangered drinking-water supplies. Biological control was the only way.

So between 1947 and 1953, twenty or thirty species of ladybugs—known in Bermuda as ladybird beetles—were introduced from various parts of the world, and an entire subdepartment of government sprang up to oversee their breeding and distribution. The project was started too late to have an immediate impact, though, and anyway, says Wingate, "the anoles would jump on the boxes of ladybirds placed in the field and eat them as they were coming out."

To control the anoles, kiskadees, small but aggressive yellow-breasted birds that attack in packs, were imported from Trinidad in 1957. Also known as tyrant flycatchers, they didn't make much of a dent in the anole population, since the lizards breed year-round, replacing their losses even in situations of high predation. But they did kill nestling vireos, catbirds, bluebirds, and cardinals, baby skinks, and the Bermuda cicada, which is now extinct largely because of them. As a newly minted college grad, Wingate says, "I recommended vehemently against bringing in the kiskadees on the basis that most island introductions—especially of omnivores that are unpredictable in their effect—were a disaster. Not only did the kiskadees kill other birds and the cicadas, but they also spread a lot of invasive plants that might not have been spread without them.

"I jokingly suggested at the time, 'Let's introduce tigers to control the kiskadees.'"

Surprisingly, no one took him up on the offer.

✦

After a visit to the doctor and a few days lying in a recliner in his living room popping painkillers and muscle relaxants—a practice to which he submits out of only the most desperate need—Wingate is feeling, if not back to his usual bouncy self, at least well enough to make the trek out to Nonsuch.

The bad weather is finally moving on, but its tail is still dragging through the area, blowing enough to raise the surf and continuing to pelt the mainland with soaking rains two or three times a day. Wingate gathers up his cardboard-rigged hat and the forest-green Swarovski binoculars he is never without, and gingerly folds himself into the Alto. As he rounds a curve of Harrington Sound Road going toward the public wharf in Tucker's Town Bay, where he has been mooring his various boats since 1958, he pulls the car over as far as he can—the roads here have no shoulders—and gets out to check for common terns, which like to perch on buoys in the sound waiting for bait fish to pass beneath them.

"It's a hell of a place to stop because the motor traffic's always honking at you," he says, unfazed by the backup he's causing. "But then to hell with them."

Once he makes it to the wharf, he realizes Penny Hill, the slim, silver-haired retired librarian he lives with, was right when she said there wouldn't be enough gas in the boat, so he doubles back to the house to retrieve his extra tank. Then, of course, the little Whaler—called *Rare Bird*, it's chipped and faded by the sun, with worms of rust in the anchor well, a cracked windshield and ripped seat cushion, and an orange life vest hanging from a forward cleat to act as extra bumper—needs a good twenty minutes of bailing. But once he's finally underway, Wingate is in his element, pointing out the Castle Harbour forts, where militia and soldiers were garrisoned for two hundred years beginning in 1612, a folly built on the old Frick property at the end of Castle Point, and Charles Island, which in 2003 had a 20-foot notch gouged out of its middle by Hurricane Fabian, the worst storm to hit the country in decades. "Pretty soon, these little islets will be gone and this will be a channel," he says, segueing into a capacious overview that touches on Bermuda's geology, currents, weather, history, and, his favorite topics, flora and fauna.

"Ninety-five percent of the plants in the country are invaders," he says as the boat bangs along the surface of the water in spine-jarring rhythm, losing distance on a mountain of gray cloud rolling in from the west. "The continents are more resilient to invasive species than an island like Bermuda because larger landmasses have more niches filled with species that evolved to fill them. But oceanic islands often have huge numbers of vacant niches, because only a few species get out to them. Which is why invasives can completely take over."

Just as a few fat raindrops begin to fall, he reaches the island, tying the boat to the skeletal remains of a barge that once supplied Bermuda's Royal Naval Dockyard with water and was brought here in the 1930s to act as a breakwater. Wingate takes damp shelter in the caretaker's cottage he lived in for a few years after his retirement. "I can call Penny and find out if there's an end to this storm," he says. "If not, we'll just have to ride it out."

To Wingate, nothing could be more natural than being stranded on an uninhabited island in a punishing downpour. "We had two children," he recalls of the early 1960s, when he and Anita moved to Nonsuch. "Janet was two and a half, and Karen was less than a year old. In storms we would essentially be marooned, with no telephone or other communication, not even a marine radio. My parents, on the mainland, had no idea how we were faring. But I'd been doing crazy things long enough that they knew I wouldn't risk my family."

When a hurricane hit, the island made an excellent observation post. "It's better if you like birds," he concedes. "They get trapped in the eye and dumped on land. In Emily, in 1987, the eye was fourteen miles wide, and the wind changed a hundred and eighty degrees in the course of two hours when it went over. Sargassum weed and little fish were sticking to the windows the next morning."

After today's storm passes, he roams the lush, still-dripping island ripping invasive plants out by their roots and talking about the Brazilian pepper and asparagus fern whose seeds are carried to Nonsuch by wind or birds or on the feet of visitors. Enough of the seeds take root that they make the task of maintaining the native forest truly Sisyphean. "I worry because holding off the invasives is like putting your finger in a dam, trying to stop the flood," he says, reiterating his persistent theme that certain elements of the project he began have been loosely managed since his retirement. "Things that make this a holistic approach—and it really needs to be one—are being neglected."

At the bird hide he built in the mid-1980s beside the island's man-made freshwater pond, his concerns seem well-founded. A scrum of cattails and bulrush lining the shore obscure the water completely, and not a single bird is visible.

"The pond has been left so long now it would be a huge job to clear it, and my back is too bad," he says. "I could organize volunteers."

In Bermuda, civil servants must retire at age sixty-five, and since 2000, the year of his life-altering birthday, Wingate has had to watch from the sidelines as others—notably his former protégé, Jeremy Madeiros—have done things their own way instead of his. It has not been easy, since for Wingate, handing off the baton meant giving up much more than just a job.

"His interests were narrow in some ways," says Walwyn Hughes, a former senator and former agriculture-department head who was Wingate's first boss. "He was focused so entirely on that island and on the cahows. They were his life."

The transition to Madeiros didn't go smoothly, and now, almost a decade later, Wingate is still hurt and angered by the events that took place. But in the hide, his grousing eventually gives way to nostalgia.

"This used to be my Discovery Channel," he says, looking out toward the pond from the little building's pleather-upholstered bench. "The window is like a television screen, but it's the real world. All the land birds come in to get a drink and bathe, and the waterbirds stop by on their migrations. I never knew what I would see—sora rail, bitterns?"

Suddenly he starts clapping, then makes a high-pitched *kak kak kak kak kak kak kak kak kak kak* sound followed by a susurrant *psh psh psh*.

"A flock of barn swallows? A dozen or so would roost on the cattails at night. It was amusing because the more that land on the cattail stem, the more it sags, and then they all slide off. Sandpipers, plovers, things that breed in the Arctic tundra and winter in South America. Wild ducks, herons. Moorhens, I guarantee."

One thing he never saw near the hide, or anywhere else on Nonsuch, was a cahow. But as he sits here trying in vain to attract some avian attention, he gets the call he's been waiting for all day: Chris Burville, a twenty-eight-year-old photographer and former dive instructor, is taking his boat out to attempt to capture some cahows in flight—an endeavor that would have been inconceivable just a little more than a decade ago. The first sighting of a cahow at sea didn't occur until 1993; the first photograph of one in flight came in 1996. Together, these events warranted an eighteen-page paper, "Identification of Bermuda Petrel," in *Birding* magazine.

Wingate heads back to the barge, unties his boat, and motors around the peninsula at the southern tip of Cooper's Island to St. David's, where he's to meet Burville at the pier behind the Black Horse Tavern, a restaurant that serves hamburgers, fried everything, and a few traditional dishes, including a fish chowder that uses, like something poured from Dan Aykroyd's Bass-o-matic, heads, tails, and whatever else happens to fall into the pot. It's considered good luck to get an eye.

After ordering a fish sandwich and a Corona, Wingate sees the thirty-two-foot Century *Options* pulling in to dock and heads down to greet her. He steps over the gunwale amid excited chatter about the birds. Already onboard are Burville and his girlfriend Sarah Lagan, a reporter for the *Bermuda Sun* newspaper; Burville's cousin Jeffrey Porter, a former Bermuda Aquarium employee; and Russell Whayman, a retired businessman who lives in St. David's and has been letting Burville keep the boat at his house.

It's late afternoon, and the birds should be starting to gather far offshore. Once out of the harbor, Burville opens the engine to about twenty-five knots—not too fast, since the receding storm has left the water roiling with twelve-foot swells. As the boat approaches the edge of the reef shelf, less than two miles offshore at a depth of two hundred and twenty feet, Wingate yells, "*Cahow!*" He points over the starboard bow. "There he is! There he is!" Immediately, the boat's motor is cut and Burville, Porter, and Lagan start stumbling around after the lights and reflectors.

"Bird off to the side!" says Whayman. "There's two of them! There's two of them!"

"Oh oh oh yeah! Yup! Yup!" cries Burville, bracing himself against the hydraulic billowing of the deck. "Sarah, where's the light?"

"He's coming back! He's coming back!" says Porter, aiming some high-powered strobes over the starboard side.

There could hardly be more excitement if a unicorn had been spotted sipping a mai tai in a shaded pool float.

"Christ!" yells Wingate.

"The other one's right there," says Burville. "Right there! Nine o'clock!"

The birds, oblivious to the uproar, are hard to track. Spot one and the next time you see it it's five hundred yards away, behind the boat one minute and in front of it the next, dipping to the water and soaring up again, coming impossibly close but never seeming to touch the surface. They rarely flap their wings yet speed across the waves like weightless gymnasts—ethereal, delicate, effortless. A hawk, by comparison, seems anchored to the thermal, and a peregrine falcon, clocked at 200 hundred miles an hour, appears a clumsy dead weight plummeting from sheer gravity.

When the two birds start wheeling away toward the open sea, Burville hands Whayman a plastic liter bottle of fish oil to spill from the stern as he pushes the throttle forward to get the boat moving again. The cahows reappear instantly, and Burville, reaching for his camera, swears as he slips on the deck's slick surface.

Wingate, meanwhile, is counting birds. "One, two, three, four . . . five, I think," he says. "If you're lucky, you might hear their courtship calls. *Ooooo-eek! Ooooo-eek!*"

"I definitely see four," says Whayman. "Five, five. There's four behind the boat and two out there. That's six!"

"Did I not tell you guys that David was the best lucky charm for cahow-watching?" Burville says, his shutter clicking incessantly.

The commotion dies down after the first couple of sightings, but Burville keeps at it, trying until the sun reaches the sea to get a shot of a cahow against the baby-aspirin-pink sky.

"That was great stuff," he says as he reluctantly starts to pack up his gear. He points toward the horizon. "There's still one over there. That fish oil really works."

"Yeah, until they find out there's no fish," Porter points out.

"That was just about as good as we've ever had it. I think they recognize David. Every time David comes out in the boat with us we get more."

"They're my babies," Wingate replies. "Can you imagine what it would have been like four hundred years ago? They would have been all over the place."

CHAPTER TWO

The Spoyle and Havock
of the Cahowes

NO ONE REALLY KNOWS what a cahow rookery looks—or sounds—like, but one thing is almost certain: If the birds' harrowing shrieks had never filled Bermuda's night skies, Bermudians would be speaking Spanish today.

Europe in the Middle Ages was ruled by superstition, and sailors were mostly poor and uneducated, drawn from the ranks of the working classes. But even the gentlemen explorers seeking adventure in the unimaginably foreign world they would encounter during the age of discovery can be forgiven for ascribing its many wonders and terrors to the supernatural forces they felt pressing in all around them. Given the constant uncertainty and peril of life at sea—not to mention the frequent imagination-fueling tedium—it's no wonder that virtually every maritime culture believed evil spirits resided there, from imps and demons that would drag down men and ships to devils that appeared as fish, conch shells, seals, and birds.

Thus it is said that in 1503, when Juan de Bermúdez, a navigator born in the Andalusian port town of Palos de la Frontera, drew near a chain of low, rocky islands in the mid-Atlantic, far from any landmass, his terrified men refused to anchor because of the cacophony of eerie, high-pitched cries that emanated from its shores at night.

Cahows perform their aerial courtships in moonless darkness, and their mating call is a long, uneven moan punctuated by high yelps and extended shrieks; think of a gale-force wind whistling through a broken window or the muffled screech of a car skidding out of control on a fog-shrouded road. The birds' compatriots, nocturnal Audubon's shearwaters, were also plentiful here before colonization, and sound a bit like a small machine getting stuck in the wrong gear, with a drawn-out, throaty note sung at a slightly higher pitch that Wingate describes as being "more witchlike."

Imagine those sounds multiplied by the million or so birds that are believed to have inhabited the islands at the time of Bermúdez's voyage and you'll have some idea of the overwhelming clamor that greeted sailors steeped in religion and only recently habituated to the occasional whoosh of a breaching whale. They dubbed the land that would take their captain's name "Isla de Demonios," or Devils' Isle, and for a century or more, the epithet stuck.

No doubt at least in part because of this reputation—bolstered by the treacherous reefs that all but prohibited safe passage to Bermuda's shores—Spain made no serious attempt to colonize the island, though the country had effectively claimed it in the naming and was clearly granted rights to it according to the 1494 Treaty of Tordesillas, which divided all of the world's newly explored territories between Spain and its neighbor Portugal.

Sixteenth-century documentation regarding Bermuda is sparse, but later writings suggest an oral tradition heavily influenced by the tales of demons. A 1610 chronicle by Englishman Sylvanus Jourdain notes that "the Ilands of the Barmudas, as every man knoweth that hath heard or read of them, were never inhabited by any Christian or Heathen people, but ever esteemed, and reputed, a most prodigious and inchanted place," while the explorer Captain John Smith, drawing on the first-hand accounts of others, writes in his 1629 *Generall Historie of Virginia, New England, & the Summer Isles* that the island "hath beene to the Spaniards more fearefull then an Utopian Purgatory, and to all Sea-men no lesse terrible then an inchanted den of Furies and Devils, the most dangerous, unfortunate, and forlorne place in the world."

In Spain, this impression was not diminished until 1603, when a galleon was careened off Bermuda for repairs, its fleet having dispersed in a storm. Captain Diego Ramirez anchored his crippled ship close to shore in a relatively protected area now known as Spanish Point, and it is from him that we have the earliest description of the cahow:

The headlands are undermined at water level with the haunts of certain nocturnal birds which during the day remain in their caves but at night come out to feed on fish, especially on squid of which there are great numbers. These birds come out from their caves at nightfall with such an outcry and varying clamor that one cannot help being afraid until one realizes the reason. This bird resembles an "ave fria" white and web-footed, longish beak with a white saw-like edge in it. This beak is very strong and is curved at the tip.

Ramirez goes on to recall the first night of his stay, when he and some crewmen took a small boat to an inlet to look for fresh water.

At dusk, such a shrieking and din filled the air that fear seized us. Only one variety of bird makes this noise but amidst the outcries some few clearly called "Diselo, Diselo!" ("Tell 'em, Tell 'em!"). One seaman said to me: "What is this devil trying to tell me? Out with it! Let's hear what it is!" I replied: "A la! A la! These are the devils of Bermuda which they say are hereabouts. The sign of the cross at them! We are Christians!"*

Though Ramirez appears to have been the first Spaniard to realize the true source of the demonic wailing, there is evidence that assorted landings were made in the century that separated his journey from Bermúdez's—presumably when the birds were at sea, and hence the "demons" quiet. Whether these visits were accidental or intentional is unclear, but at least one of them resulted in the introduction of the first real predator the cahow would ever know.

At the time, it was common practice for Spanish sailors exploring the New World to leave a few adult pigs or goats on the islands they encountered so that the animals would breed during the ships' journey

---

* Ironically, the cahows may also at one time have been believed to be angels. According to Irish legend, a monk called St. Brendan the Navigator made a seven-year journey across the Atlantic Ocean in the sixth century A.D. He and his men supposedly came to an island far from all others, where they met birds that talked to them and sang of God's glory. Some have interpreted the island to be Bermuda.

onward and provide a ready supply of fresh meat for the return trip or in case of shipwreck. "Pigs and goats were familiar food items," says Wingate one day over dinner at the Speciality Inn, a place that, if Bermuda had chain restaurants, might be a Friendly's, with kids fussing in booths beside their oblivious parents and a menu laden with comfort foods in generous portions. "It probably took a little bit of courage to kill and eat the first turtle."

Wingate suspects the hogs also acted like miners' canaries in these strange and possibly lethal lands. "A pig was a valuable asset," he says. "The sailors would come back and see whether the pigs were fat or not. If a pig can live on an island, so can a human."

A pig-drop was attempted as early as 1515 in Bermuda, called "the farthest of all the Ilands that are yet found at this day in the world" in a first-hand account of the trip by the Spanish historian and writer Gonzalo Fernandez de Oviedo y Valdés. But the effort, according to Oviedo, was frustrated by a "contrary winde" that kept the ship from coming closer than a bowshot from shore.

No one is quite sure when the pigs arrived or exactly how, but by Ramirez's 1603 visit they had clearly had the run of the place for some time. "There are great droves of hogs in the island," the captain wrote, "which have over-run it and trodden wide paths like well-traveled roads to the watering places. Along these trails there are palms worn in two-fingers' lengths where they have scratched themselves."

It's likely that breeding stock was left in 1563 by the explorer Pedro Menéndez de Avilés, who had been sent westward by King Philip II of Spain to colonize Florida and had been granted permission to look for his shipwrecked son during the voyage. It is said that on his way to founding St. Augustine, Avilés stopped to search in Bermuda, leaving the animals that would inspire the image for the first English colonial coins—one shilling pieces and two-, three-, and six-pence, all called hogge money, which circulated until the mid-seventeenth century and in turn lent their name to a popular Hamilton pub called the Hog Penny. The coins were reintroduced in 1988 as one-cent pieces with a much friendlier looking pig on the obverse than was stamped onto the originals.

The pigs on organic grower Tom Wadson's farm, purchased from a conservation herd at Virginia's historic Mount Vernon, are direct descendants of the animals left by Spanish explorers. One look at them tells you how simple it would have been for them to search out cahows, which at the time nested mostly in burrows under partly exposed tree roots and in the thick humus that lines the forest floor. The pigs are obviously intelligent, trotting over with ears flapping and tails twitching to greet any visitor who might be bearing edible gifts and deftly pushing aside a fence to get at the few blades of grass beneath it. Their long, wrinkly snouts call to mind Alf, the furry puppet whose eponymous NBC sitcom was an inexplicable hit in the 1980s, except that there's little cuddliness to be found here. The smooth-haired black pigs weigh upward of two hundred pounds, and almost constantly have their noses pressed flat to the ground, where they inhale with the dedication of a Dyson sucking up an area rug and nuzzle divets into the sandy loam until their faces are caked in dirt. They can detect odors in the tens of parts per billion and under several feet of soil.

According to early accounts, the berries of the Bermuda palmetto tree made up the bulk of the original hogs' diet in season. Once the berries were gone, the pigs would have moved on to grasses and barks, lizards and land crabs, and any tasty eggs or juveniles they could find, be they cahow, skink, or sea turtle. The first Englishman to walk Bermuda's shores came aboard a French ship that lost half its crew when it wrecked on the reefs in 1593, and his brief account of his nearly five months on the island suggests that at certain times of year the pigs, which have a territory range of about ten square miles, or half the country, actually ate themselves out of food. "In the south part of this Island of Bermuda there are hogs," writes Henry May, "but they are so leane that you cannot eat them, by reason the Island is so barren."

Feral hogs can be ruthless in their quest for sustenance. They've been known to take down baby farm animals and even weakened adults, so it's easy to imagine the Spanish pigs clearing the 14-square-mile main island of cahows and driving the birds to larger outer islands like St. David's and Somerset, which today are connected to the mainland by bridges and causeways.

Wingate estimates that before the arrival of the hogs, a landmass the size of today's Bermuda could have supported a population of up to a million nesting cahows and shearwaters. Early accounts suggest that in the four or five decades the hogs ran wild over the island, they killed anywhere from 50 to 90 percent of the birds. But it would take the arrival of man to finish the job.

✦

In June 1609, the 98-foot barque *Sea Venture* departed Falmouth Harbour on England's southwest coast to lead her fleet of six merchant ships and two pinnaces on an eight-week journey across the Atlantic. Round-hulled, with a large cargo hold, three masts, and high castles at both ends, she was ferrying 150 men and women to their new lives in America's two-year-old Virginia Colony. Fortunately for historians, as flagship the *Sea Venture* carried the most important and well-educated passengers, including two who chronicled the voyage in detail, Sylvanus Jourdain and William Strachey.

For seven weeks the seas were calm, and optimism for the future remained high. Then, just a week short of landfall, a hurricane struck, and the *Sea Venture* was separated from the other vessels and pushed southwest toward the Caribbean then helplessly northeast again. For three bloodcurdling days, the ship was lashed by walls of water and stung by nails of windblown rain that, "like whole Rivers did flood in the ayre," according to Strachey. The winds, he writes, "spake more loud, and grew more tumultuous and malignant," than he had ever before seen them, despite having been caught in several previous storms on his journeys around the Middle East and North Africa. "There was not a moment in which the sodaine splitting, or instant over-setting of the shippe was not expected."

As if the weather alone weren't bad enough, early in the storm the ship sprang a leak. Though the crew jettisoned extraneous cargo, weapons, and equipment, and, alongside passengers, pumped and bailed constantly, by the time the skies began to clear the *Sea Ven-ture*'s hold was full to the brim, and her top deck had basically become a raft. It was then, on the morning of the fourth day—after all on-board had "commend[ed their] sinfull soules to God [and] committed the shippe to the mercy of the Sea"—that Admiral Sir George Somers sighted land and began the slow limp toward it, striking bottom and coming to rest about a half mile off what is now known as St. Cath-erine's Point in St. George's.

All of the passengers made it safely to shore in longboats and, after a brief but well-earned rest, set about stripping the *Sea Venture* of her spars and rigging, rescuing any stores and livestock that remained on-board, erecting rudimentary shelter, and locating fresh food and water.

Both of the ship's scribes go to pains to correct the error in the name Devils' Isle. In fact, writes Jourdain, Bermuda had turned out to be "one of the sweetest Paradises that be upon the earth."*

In the nearly ten months the stranded colonists stayed on the is-land, food was plentiful. They tried gardening using seeds brought from England, but the effort wasn't successful, and was hardly neces-sary in any case. Unlike their countryman Henry May, the *Sea Venture* survivors found the island dense with vegetation; they relied particu-larly on palmetto hearts and berries, prickly pears, and cedar berries, which made a "pleasant" fermented drink. On their second day ashore, they discovered the wild pigs when one strayed into the herd that had come onboard the ship, and began penning and feeding them with their own. The men soon started bringing in, by both line and net, all sorts of exotic fish—five thousand of which, Strachey tells us, could be taken in one haul. The settlers trapped birds from buntings to hawks, and oysters, crabs, spiny lobsters, and land snails were also abundant. The flesh of any animal not put to immediate use was dried and salted with crystals extracted from boiled seawater.

---

* Most scholars believe Shakespeare's *The Tempest* was inspired by the legends of Bermuda's enchantment and the story of the *Sea Venture* wreck recounted in the works of Strachey and Jourdain, which circulated privately in England as early as 1610, around the time the play is believed to have been written.

As the seasons changed so did the menu. The hogs were fattest when the berries were at their best, August through November, and they were slaughtered for food when the weather was bad and fishing dangerous. In February, when the hogs thinned as the fruits grew scarce, turtles were captured in large numbers; one could feed fifty people, Jourdain points out, but forty were sometimes taken in a day. And in the fall, as temperatures began to cool and many of the migrating birds departed on their southerly routes, by lucky coincidence a new species came along to take their place.

Strachey describes the cahow at some length:

A kinde of webbe-footed Fowle there is, of the bignesse of an English greene Plover, or Sea-Meawe, which all the Summer wee saw not, and in the darkest nights of November and December (for in the night they onely feed) they would come forth, but not flye farre from home, and hovering in the ayre, and over the Sea, made a strange hollow and harsh howling. . . . [T]hese gather themselves together and breed in those Ilands which are high, and so farre alone into the Sea, that the Wild Hogges cannot swimme over [to] them, and there in the ground they have their Burrowes, like Conyes in a Warren, and so brought in the loose Mould, though not so deepe: which Birds with a light bough in a darke night (as in our Lowbelling), wee caught. . . . There are thousands of these Birds, and two or three Ilands full of their Burrowes, whether at any time (in two houres warning) wee could send our Cock-boat, and bring home as many as would serve the whole Company.

Thus it is also from Strachey we get the first inkling of what lay in store for the cahow.

✦

By May 1610, the *Sea Venture*'s crew and passengers had finished the daunting task of constructing two new ships in which they could complete their voyage. Under the supervision of Sir Thomas Gates, who was to have been governor of Jamestown, and Admiral Somers, the *Deliverance* and the *Patience* had slowly taken shape. The former, built mainly with salvage from the *Sea Venture*, was a 40-by-19-foot pinnace with two masts and castles fore and aft. The latter, built entirely, but for a single iron bolt, of Bermuda cedar—including painstakingly whittled dowels used in place of nails—was a barque with a 29-foot keel and a 15½-foot beam. She carried thirty tons, exactly a tenth as much as the *Sea Venture*, but she made a significant difference in both comfort and safety on the 710-mile voyage to Virginia.

And so, ten months after they had set sail from England, about twelve dozen castaways put to sea again. During their extended stopover, a baby boy, named Bermudas, had been added to their number, but they had also lost eight of the original survivors, including one who was murdered by a fellow sailor, another who was shot for treason, and three more who stayed behind for a life of leisure and to keep dibs on the island for king and country.

When the two small ships reached Jamestown thirteen days after setting sail, the *Sea Venture* colonists were shocked to find the town desolate. Of the approximately 350 settlers John Smith had left in America just eight months before, only 60 were still alive in James Fort; the rest had succumbed to disease or starvation, victims of a successful plan by the region's Indians to rid themselves of the interlopers by refusing to trade and attacking them whenever they left their compound to hunt or fish.

Having departed Bermuda expecting to encounter a flourishing society across the water, Somers, Gates, and company had brought enough provisions for the voyage, with just a little to spare. There's no record of exactly what was onboard, but the survivors probably carried dried hearts of palm and cedar-berry beer, perhaps a few loggerhead or green turtles, and a passel of hogs. An excavation recently conducted at Jamestown found checkered nerite and flamingo-tongue snails, both native to Bermuda; a pipe stem and cobbles of Bermuda limestone; a signet ring bearing William Strachey's family crest; and two cahow bones.

The dried birds and whatever salted fish and pork remained onboard when the castaways landed were enough to feed them and the few skeletal figures left at Jamestown for three weeks, at which point the entire party decided to abandon the colony and head for a settlement in Newfoundland.

Almost miraculously, just two days into their trip to Canada, the four vessels that sailed from Jamestown met with a boat bringing news that 150 new colonists and a year's worth of supplies were en route, along with orders to return to the pestilential fort. Not everyone was delighted by this directive, but it was followed and the colony was saved.

Despite the timely infusion of stores, fresh meat was still lacking, so Somers volunteered to return to the fecund little island he had come to love to stock up on fish, fowl, and hogs. He set off in the *Patience*, with a crew that included his nephew Matthew Somers, in May of 1610, and, finding his three former crewmen fat and happy on his arrival, became more convinced than ever that Bermuda must become part of the British Empire.

Somers was not to see his wish fulfilled. He died that November at age fifty-six, but not before instructing Matthew to return to England to raise money for the establishment of a colony on his cherished island. Somers's body was shipped back to his estate in Lyme Regis, but his heart was buried in Bermuda.

✦

Bermuda was not the only island chain that was completely unspoiled at the dawn of the age of exploration. The most famous example of the arrival of Europeans on territory previously uninhabited by humans is the Galápagos, which achieved immortality when Charles Darwin used them as a laboratory in which to refine his nascent theory of evolution. The type of genetic isolation that occurs in such secluded areas—and that gave Darwin his galvanizing finches—creates what's known as endemism, which is simply the emergence of species that are found nowhere else. Since islands are by definition surrounded by water, and sometimes hundreds of miles of it, man is often the first terrestrial mammal to set foot on them; and because the survival of endemic species depends upon a single population and the stability of a specific ecosystem, such species are particularly vulnerable to the transformative influences of human habitation.

Perhaps the best known extinction of an endemic species took place on Mauritius, an island nearly as far from the Madagascar coast as Bermuda is from the East Coast of the United States. When Dutch sailors arrived there in 1598, they found flying-fox bats, keel-scaled boas, and a strange, flightless bird with short, bunched tail feathers and a large hooked bill. It stood three feet high and, as a member of the dove family, had a placid temperament. Settlers called it the dodo, and it was described in an early account as "superb and proud" and "very jaunty and audacious of gait."

Unlike the cahow, the dodo was said to have had, with the exception of its breast and belly, tough flesh with an oily flavor, so it was not the first choice for meat when other sources were available. This, and the fact that Mauritius is nearly forty times the size of Bermuda, probably helped to keep the species going several decades longer than the tasty cahow. Nonetheless, the dodo was extinguished by the second half of the seventeenth century—like the cahow by introduced mammals and overhunting.

History is brimming with tales of the abundance of virgin seas and forests. It has been said of cod, whales, and salmon that one could walk across the water on their backs; for bison, simply substitute the word *prairie* for *water*, and you will find writers making the same claim. Mussels and oysters were supposedly so plentiful on some coastlines that they accreted like reefs, posing navigational hazards, and flocks of passenger pigeons, geese, and other birds once cast great moving shadows on the ground and clogged waterways so that ships had difficulty passing through. In all such cases, man arrived on the scene, chronicled the teeming masses, and then quickly set about exterminating them. It seems that enough was never enough when too much could easily be had.

There can be little doubt that every seaman who fetched up on Bermuda during the cahows' nesting season—they begin to arrive in mid-

October, and the young fledge by June—from the early 1500s on used
the birds for food. Ramirez, who stayed for less than a month in 1603,
writes that once he and his men had "finally . . . solved the mystery" of
the supposed demons inhabiting the islands, they brought more than
five hundred of the birds to the ship and cooked them in hot water.

> [A]nd they were so fat and good that every night the men went
> hunting and we dried and salted more than a thousand for the
> voyage, and the men ate them all the time, and they are so plenti-
> ful that four thousand could be killed at the same spot in a single
> night.

Jourdain, Strachey, and Nathaniel Butler, Bermuda's governor
from 1619 to 1622, also rhapsodize over the sweetness of the plump
cahows. The birds' eggs, they note, looked and tasted almost exactly like chicken eggs; and as for catching cahows, nothing could be
simpler.

"Our men found a prettie way to take them," Strachey writes,
"which was by standing on the Rockes or Sands by the Sea-side, and
hollowing, laughing, and making the strangest outcry that possibly
they could." The birds would come flocking to the noise, "and settle
upon the very armes and head of him that so cryed, and still creepe
neerer and neerer, answering the noyse themselves." The hunter would
then choose the heaviest among the birds, catching as many as "three
hundred in an houre."

But cahows weren't singled out among bird species. Jourdain writes
that the white herons on Bermuda were "so familiar and tame, that
wee beate them downe from the trees with stones and staves." The
sooty tern was similarly dispatched, as, he continues, "using neither
sticke nor stone-bow, nor gunne, wee tooke them up with our hands
as many as we could, that every one of the company were to have some
three, some foure a peece."

The permanent settlers, too, made profligate use of the birds from
the beginning. "It is a night bird," Butler writes of the cahow,

> and all the daye long lies hidd in holes of the rocks, whence both
> themselves and their young are in great numbers extracted with

ease, and prove (especially the young) so pleaseinge in a dish, as ashamed I am to tell, how many dosen of them have bin devoured by some one of our northern stomacks, even at one only meale.

One might suppose, therefore, that the cahow—which, like the other creatures on the island, had experienced no major predation until the arrival of the hogs, and had certainly never learned to fear humans—would eventually have disappeared from the islands even without the extenuating circumstances that were soon to appear.

✦

The country's first governor, Richard Moore, decided the site of the stranded *Sea Venture* explorers' bivouac was ideal for more permanent habitation. It was on the lee side of St. George's—then called King's—Island, which forms the northern border of Castle Harbour. Protected to the northeast by high hills and along the harbor by Paget, Smith's, and St. David's islands, the town, also called St. George's, is situated at the end of one of the two natural channels that gave easy access to larger vessels. Castle Roads, which comes into Castle Harbour on the opposite side, was the wider of the channels, but St. George's Channel, at the northern tip of St. David's, was enough at the time to allow merchant ships to enter St. George's Harbour, helping to make the town a thriving commercial center in the decades to come.

Governor Moore immediately put the settlers to work raising basic shelters and erecting a church. He gave every man a plot of land and ordered that food crops be set, but events conspired in their neglect.

First, the colonists failed to account for the island's generally shallow, unfertilized soil, the unreliability of rain in a land with so little fresh water, and the effects of salt spray. "One good winter gale could strip bare a potato field and kill it completely," Wingate says. Tobacco, sent back to England as a tax payment to the Virginia Company, which had chartered the colony, also took up valuable space that might otherwise have been devoted to food. But most important, Moore's desperation to finish his defense projects took all the male colonists away from their planting. Amid repeated rumors from England that Spain intended to attack, Moore constructed an impressive array of forts in less than two years. He trained the men to fight and kept them all on St. George's, "whence they wer not to part upon paine of death," according to Butler—except, of course, to commute to Southampton and Castle islands, where construction was heaviest. Once on the islands, the workers no doubt feasted on cahows and their eggs in season for breakfast, lunch, and dinner, even as they labored to destroy one of the birds' few remaining habitats.

Company ships were bringing more and more settlers—six hundred in the first three years of Moore's administration—but crops were failing, and the provisions delivered with the immigrants were hardly enough to maintain the growing population. Finally, Moore was forced to release most of the men from their work on the forts, advising them, says Butler, "to provide for themselves, by fishinge, birdinge, and such like."

Thus it was relief, not dread, that greeted a Spanish warship—piloted by an Englishman—that appeared around this time. Daniel Elfrith was a privateer who had made off with his well-stocked prize after his former captain had seized her in the Amazon and trustingly put Elfrith in her command. The hold of the frigate, which anchored in February 1614 and would stay in Bermuda even after Elfrith took his leave on an outgoing passenger ship, was filled with grain that could be traded for Bermudian goods to make the first bread the colonists had seen in months.

Unfortunately, along with the welcome cargo came a stowaway: *Rattus rattus*. In a section headlined "The Countrey Neere Devoured with Rats," John Smith recounts the rodents' quick spread across the archipelago. "[S]ome fishes have beene taken with rats in their bellies, which they caught swimming from Ile to Ile," he writes. "[The rats'] nests they had almost in every tree, and in most places their burrowes in the ground like conies: they spared not the fruits of the plants, or trees, nor the very plants themselves, but ate them up. When [the settlers] had set their corne, the rats would come by troupes in the night and scratch it out of the ground."

The men laid traps, trained their dogs to hunt the rodents, and used "many other devices . . . to destroy them." But nothing helped to control the animals, and the colonists simply "could not prevaile, finding them still increasing against them."

The governor sent the ship *Edwin* off to request more aid, but "[w]hilst this Pinnace was on her way for England, scarcetie and famine every day more and more prevayle[d] upon the sickly colony," writes Butler. In 1615, hoping to alleviate the problem on St. George's, Moore sent 150 of the "most ancient, sick, and weake" to live on 77-acre Cooper's Island, at the southeast edge of Castle Harbour. Their hunger could be relieved by the cahows, which, according to John Smith, still nested there in "infinite numbers."

The Reverend Lewis Hughes, a minister who came in the early days of settlement, spent some time on Cooper's Island and writes that on his first night there,

> I saw in every Cabbin, Pots & Kettles full of birds boyling, and some on Spits rosting, and the silly wilde birds coming in so tame into my Cabbin and goe so familiarly betweene my feet, and round about the Cabbin, and into the fire, with a strange lamentable noyse, as though they did bemoane us, and bid us take, kill, roaste, and eate them.

In 1615 Governor Moore was relieved of his duties. The following year tough-minded Daniel Tucker, who had overseen the Virginia colony's stores and trade, arrived and promptly began to put the Bermuda settlement in order.

His plan to control the rat population was to systematically burn the entire archipelago, starting with the smaller islands before attacking the mainland. This did little to arrest the rats, which simply jumped in the water and swam to cooler accommodations, but it did destroy many acres of cahow habitat that had so far been spared from construction and agriculture.

The conflagrations ended in part because of an uprising led by Hughes against the governor's plan—the men didn't like to see valuable cedar going to waste—but mostly because as quickly as they came, the rats simply disappeared. Though early writers attribute their demise to a sudden cold snap, it is more likely that disease or starvation got them. "The rats crashed," says Wingate, "as all new invasive species will after an initial population explosion. They starve, get diseases. They didn't die out altogether, simply reached their balance."

Few specifics are given about how the famine ended, but it may be supposed that the simple change of seasons was enough to replenish stores somewhat. And with fewer colonists to feed—in addition to the famine, a disease, perhaps scurvy, killed dozens—there might now have been enough to go around.

Among the first official acts of Tucker's administration was to issue a series of general assizes, in which petty criminals were brought to trial and legislation enacted. In the second of these courts, writes Butler, no "matter of note" was handled except for the reading of a proclamation "against the spoyle and havock of the cahowes, and other birds, which wer almost all of them killed and scared awaye very improvidently by fire, diggeinge, stoneinge, and all kind of murtheringes."

Unfortunately, as Butler notes, the protection came "overlate."

CHAPTER THREE

Seeking the Invisible

WALKING AROUND A NATURE reserve in Bermuda with David Wingate is kind of what it must be like to stroll through Asbury Park, New Jersey, with Bruce Springsteen, if he were moonlighting as a polymathic college professor.

"That's a Japanese pittosporum," Wingate's saying as he descends from the parking lot toward Spittal Pond, the centerpiece of a popular protected area owned by the government and the Bermuda National Trust. "It is an invader, but it's actually beneficial because it's similar to the endemic olivewood. Plants like that are called 'native compatible.' They don't outcompete the natives."

A man comes up and hands him a camera. "The plover?" asks the man, who turns out to be something of a celebrity in his own right, the Bermudian landscape painter Otto Trott.

Wingate squints at the LCD screen. "No, the killdeer." He delivers a short lecture on the bird's migration habits, and Trott shows him what else he's photographed in recent days. The two compare notes for a while and eventually move on. As Wingate makes his way down the main path into the reserve, a man he doesn't know nods and mutters, "Mr. Wingate" as he passes by, and a hundred yards later a woman with a group of children on a scavenger hunt bounds up breathlessly. "You're not Wingate, are you?" she asks. "You are? Cool!" She and her friend stay and chat enthusiastically for a few minutes, but fall short of asking him for an autograph.

Spittal Pond has special meaning to Wingate, for it was here, before the land was officially protected, that he first began to discover the natural world in a systematic way. He had known the name of the place since he was a young boy, having narrowly missed a kindergarten field trip here when he flipped over the handlebars of his bike en route and ended up in a nearby church parking lot with a concussion. He rediscovered the area on his own several years later, as he recounts in some 1949 notes that were the precursor to the bird-watching diaries he began the following year. "It was three years ago, in July, during one of my rambles about our fair island," he wrote self-consciously at age fourteen.

> I was riding by the sea-side, admiring the weather torn coast, when suddenly, through the trees, I noticed a pond. Being anxious to know more about it, I left my bicycle and walked down through the shady canopy of trees. Little then did I know, or imagine what beauty, what adventure, was to be revealed to me, only so very few paces ahead.

A note in the margin reads "SPITTAL POND," the very one he'd been meant to see on his school field trip. "I spoke little of the pond that day," he continues in his 1949 reminiscence, "but I felt there was something great behind my find. That night, memories of the pond haunted my mind, and there was a growing urge in me to revisit it." When he returned to the pond before sunrise the next day, he saw, for the first time in his life in this country with almost no fresh water, what looked like a stream—a low area where the sea flows inland during rough weather. There were swallows flying overhead.

> I remembered that I hadn't seen them the day before. Perhaps they had just finished migrating.... Perhaps it was the hand of this marvelous mistery ... which had cast these beautiful birds at this spot, where there beauty might blend with the beauty of its surroundings. My imagination went wild. When I left the pond that day I was keen-keen on birds. I had seen more than just the beautiful birds, I had seen a cloudy and mysterious world beyond them ... that I was compelled to learn more about.

Known until the 1890s as Peniston's Pond—there is no record of the reason for the name change—Spittal Pond itself is about a quarter-mile long and narrows in the middle like an hourglass. The land that surrounds it was originally a series of private parcels, most of which were too flood-prone to develop. In 1946, just around the time Wingate came across the valley, one of the landowners gave a few acres to the Historical Monuments Trust, the forerunner of today's National Trust; over time, more and more of the lots were acquired, mostly through donation or at deeply discounted prices.

The pond has brackish water and is not a destination for migrating birds, but it is an important refueling station for those that are blown off-course or simply wearied by their flight. Though Bermuda is six hundred miles off the coast of the United States, it is in the center of a straight line between Nova Scotia and Brazil. "We're on the Atlantic flyway for millions of migratory birds," says Wingate, taking shelter under a palmetto as a flash rainstorm passes through. "So every time I came here I'd notice some weird new bird. The pond turned me on to bird-watching. It just kept drawing me back." Most of the wetlands in Bermuda are hidden—the tidal marshes by mangrove and the inland swamps by peat—so Spittal Pond is the only open pool in what must seem from the air like an oasis of dry land in a desert of water.

Wingate spent enough time at the pond as a child that by 1950 he had set up a rudimentary bird-watching blind there. Even more than ten years after his first visit, the place so transported him that his diary entry for December 31, 1959, contains a half page of notes on Spittal Pond before the single line, "Fieldwork unavoidably limited because I got married to Anita Morrison today!"

"I never did live that one down," he says.

The area still excites him just as much today as it did then. "There's a coot," he says of a ducklike bird bobbing on the water, "just fresh in from prairie pothole country. He's exhausted." Wingate marks it in one of the small notebooks he always carries, to be transferred later into his diary, just as a merlin falcon shoots past, nearly grabbing a panicked sparrow. "They catch birds unawares in flight," he says. He points out a giant land-crab burrow, some native hackberries, a chunk gouged from the seaside rocks where Hurricane Igor left its mark. A snowy egret chases a tricolored heron past a tree branch deposited into the pond by Hurricane Fabian. "It makes a great bird perch," he says, dropping the binoculars back to his chest so he can jot down three grebes, two blue-winged teals, four night herons roosting in the marsh grass, and an American robin—"*the* bird of the day," he says, since they're not common in Bermuda and it's unusual to see them so early in the season. "I've never had a boring trip here."

✦

Plenty of unlikely birds were turning up at Spittal Pond, but the cahow had passed into the realm of mythology. And Bermuda, the land of sunken treasure ships, labyrinthine cave systems, and a supposed airplane-eating triangle, has always been reluctant to give up its missing. There were rumors the bird still haunted the night skies, a ghost on the wing, but no credible scientific sightings. Or at least none documented by a proper British gentleman.

Until the American military enlarged it in the early 1940s to make way for the now-decommissioned Kindley Air Force Base, St. David's Island was a bayonet-shaped parcel of more than five hundred acres at the far eastern end of Castle Harbour. It was accessible only by boat, and Bermudians have always considered it a place apart. Its people, having descended largely from a mix of escaped African and West Indian slaves brought here beginning in 1616, Irish and Scottish indentured servants, and American Indians taken captive after King Philip's War in the late seventeenth century, looked different from mainland Bermudians and had their own way of speaking. Many St. David's islanders lived off the sea, and they told of birds that came around in winter called the pimlico and the Christmas bird, or cahow. Portuguese fishermen, who began arriving in 1849 from the island of Madeira, also spoke of the bird.

At eighty-three, Richard Thorsell resides in an assisted-living facility in Brevard, North Carolina, surrounded by mementos of his birding days. He is hard of hearing and has macular degeneration, and, more often than not, a thin oxygen tube circles his face. But, he says with a laugh, "I still drink. I still smoke. And if the girls are young enough I can still pinch them in the fanny."

And he can still remember, vividly, the few months he spent in Bermuda nearly sixty years ago, working with the newly rediscovered cahows. During Thorsell's first trip to the country, in 1954, he stayed with Louis S. Mowbray and his wife, Nellie. He says he was treated with "nothing but kindness" by the couple.

"I couldn't get over what fine hosts they were," he says, digging into a crab cake at the trendy Jordan Street Cafe, a few miles from his tidy one-bedroom apartment. "There was only one time the Mowbrays, especially Nellie, scolded me. I went out on a toot one night and ended up at a Portuguese social club. I had a good time, but the Mowbrays were incensed that I had mixed up with the Portuguese."

Bermuda was a very stratified society in the 1950s, and Portuguese fishermen would have been looked upon with caution or even contempt by upper-middle-class whites like the Mowbrays. But his "slumming" that night taught Thorsell something that Mowbray never could have learned. "I found out these Portuguese fishermen were well familiar with the cahows," he says. "They would go out at night and hear them. They just accepted that it's always been that way." The fishermen at the bar, who at the time would often have been out overnight looking for deepwater snapper, precisely imitated the cahows' call, and Thorsell was dead certain the men could be talking about no other species. "They were quite used to hearing these birds," he says, "and you can quote me on that."

The Portuguese fishermen and St. David's islanders probably hadn't read the seventeenth-century accounts of the cahow's disappearance, and so hadn't convinced themselves that the birds could not have survived. The British officers who began arriving on Bermuda in the middle of the nineteenth century, on the other hand, were so certain the bird had died off that it remained invisible to them.

"Bermuda had so many forts built during and after the American Revolution it became known as the Gibraltar of the West," says Wingate. "And in the mid-1800s, naturalism was reaching its peak in Great Britain. The garrisoned British officers were the scientists of the time, the people who wrote and published articles about birds and left a record. And they were so aloof from the fishermen that they didn't take them seriously." Savile Reid, a captain of the Corps of Royal Engineers and a member of the British Ornithologists' Union, aptly summarized the attitude of the ruling classes when he wrote, in 1883, "As to believing a word the good-natured colored people tell you about the extraordinary birds they see, it is simply impossible."

Not only were many of the officers sure the cahow did not exist, but more than one of them concluded it had never existed at all as a distinct species.

John L. Hurdis, who for a time was comptroller of customs and navy laws in Bermuda, had read of the "singular" bird in the accounts of John Smith and Samuel Purchas, whose 1625 history compiled many sources, and went with a friend to find it. They left the Ferry House in St. George's in a four-oared cutter on June 28, 1847, putting in at several of the Castle Harbour islands, and "were pleased to learn from persons there resident," Hurdis writes, "that the Cahow was still known by its old name, which was described to us as an imitation of its peculiar note *cao-hoo*, and that it still continued to breed in that locality. A boy assured us that he had recently caught two of those birds on Cooper's Island, and described them as 'brown or whitish,' and about the size of a duck."

Hurdis was eager to visit Gurnet Rock, a small, sheer cliff rising out of the sea a half mile off the south shore, because as a known breeding ground for terns, he thought it might also appeal to cahows. High winds kept him from crossing the harbor on June 28, but a few days later he dispatched a St. George's man, Salton Smith, to the rock to obtain specimens. Smith returned empty-handed, having lost some birds, a small pile of eggs, and, nearly, the boy who fetched them for him when his boat capsized. But the birds he found in any case would not have been cahows, since the cahows would have been somewhere off the coast of Ireland or Nova Scotia or the Azores at the time of his search.

Two years passed before a couple of captains from the 42nd Royal Highlanders Regiment managed to land on Gurnet (which Hurdis also mistakenly calls Black Rock) and take, by hand, two seabirds sitting on their nests, along with an egg. Hurdis examined the speci-

mens and determined them to be dusky shearwaters, now known as
Audubon's shearwaters. He decided this was the bird the early writers
called the cahow. "This discovery is highly interesting," he writes.

> The larger species, *Puffinus cinereus*, or Wandering Shearwater, of
> Audubon, is rarely met with in the Bermudas, and certainly does
> not breed upon their shores. It is, therefore, beyond all doubt that
> the cahow, described by Governor John Smith, in 1629; by Pur-
> chas, in 1738 [*sic*]; and by the native islanders of the present day,
> is identical with *Puffinus obscurus*, or the Dusky Shearwater, dis-
> covered on Black Rock, by Captains Orde and McLeod. Whether
> the dusky shearwater continues to frequent the rocky coast of the
> Bermudas during the winter months, I am unable to state.

Audubon's shearwaters were called pimlicos by fishermen, and the
cahows were so consistently confused with them that it's sometimes
hard to tell what was actually observed. But "the reason we know that
none of the specimens that were collected around that time were cahows," Wingate says, "is because they were all one species. If they had
gotten a cahow it would have been totally different from a shearwater.
The difference just would have jumped out at them."

John Tavernier Bartram seems to have been the only naturalist of
the time who had a hope of sorting things out.

Bartram was an infantryman who had come to Bermuda from
England with the 30th Regiment of Foot but eventually used a St.
George's doctor's money to buy his way out of the army. In exchange,
Bartram farmed the doctor's holdings for life, sharing the profit. He
lived with his wife, who by then had come from England, at the far
end of Stokes Point, a little polyp of land just a few hundred feet by
water from St. David's. The only access to his solitary cottage was a
carriage trail that cut roughly through steep hills, water, beach, and
brambles. He was such a successful farmer that he later bought land
of his own, including a rocky acre in St. George's Harbour now known
as Banjo Island.

Bartram was, even by Bermuda's relaxed standards, an oddball. As
he became more interested in natural history, he spent more and more

time alone, eventually separating from his wife. "Ultimately," Wingate writes in a 1964 issue of the *Bermuda Historical Quarterly*, "even his personal appearance began to suffer and he withdrew completely, like a hermit, into his own little realm." He greeted visitors in a dressing gown, wore his gray hair long, and kept his beard triple-plaited.

Bartram made a common-law marriage with a black woman who worked on the farm, and he amassed hundreds of live birds and other pets, stuffed birds, seashells, rocks, and whatever else struck his fancy—a collection large enough to merit its own "museum" on the property. His stature as a naturalist was the only thing that saved him from being an outcast, and indeed, Wingate writes, he eventually became "revered" for his knowledge, showing his diverse assemblage to those who exhibited true interest and not, as the English travel writer Baroness Anna Brassey noted in 1885, to "folks who put their heads in at the door and then went away, saying that they had seen B[a]rtram's collection and knew all about it!"

Bartram left copious, if somewhat stream-of-consciousness, notes, including an ornithological journal, and also a fifty-six-page book called *The Cage Birds of Bermuda*, both of which Wingate has spent hours parsing. It was "through his long association with the country people and their folklore," Wingate concludes, "that [Bartram] was able to penetrate the mystery surrounding the legendary Cahow and 'Pimlico.' None of the more transient naturalists even came close to achieving this."

In his notebooks, Bartram does, like all the naturalists of the time, confuse the cahow and the pimlico, though he seems more aware of his befuddlement than most and is certainly less arrogant. "I have spent a good deal of time in striveing to clear up the mistrey hanging over the cahow, the christmafs bird of the fishermen and the Pimleco of Baileys-bay, but up to this day 2nd November 1862 all remains as much in the dark as it was before I commenced."

But Bartram did identify the cahow.

[T]here is a bird that will answer to Purchas's description, but I cannot find anyone that has ever caught it or seen more than the outline of it, whilst sitting in thir boats fishing, at night, having their attention roused by its noise over head, and that the fishermen have given it the name of Christmas bird that being the time it is moast frequently heard, it to is nocturnal and is never seen or heard in daylight, and this is the bird that Purchas mistook for the Cao-hoo, the name Cao-hoo is local given by the inhabitants, because the sound in some measure resembles part of its call, but the bird evidently belongs to the familey of Petrel's.

There is no explanation for Bartram's leap from knowing no one who had ever caught or even really seen the cahow to the following, startling sentence: "I have the speciments now before me male female and young and egg." A later entry, in which he describes finding a bird and some eggs that were buried in a cliff fall, may help to clarify where he got at least one of these specimens. He describes the animal in detail, unwittingly confirming it to be a cahow, then writes:

[W]as this bird a stragler come here by acident, or do thay breed here year after year, I have never heard of them before unlefs it was this same bird found by Capte Orde, and McLeod ... the dead bird we found, is it *Puffinus obscura* or is it the broad billed Petrel (*Prion vittatus*) or the fishermen's Christmafs bird, it is just posable that it is one and all of them.

After Bartram's death in 1889, whatever cahow specimens he had, along with the rest of the birds in his museum, were sold in two lots: one to a Mr. J. R. Duerden for £35, according to a brief notice in the *Royal Gazette*, and the other to Harley James of St. George's. James kept the birds he purchased on display in various locations around the east end until they deteriorated too much for public consumption, and then stored whatever could be salvaged in the basement of a St. George's mansion. The house changed hands in 1952, and some of the moth-eaten birds subsequently turned up in an antiques shop in Paget Parish. On the second day the shop was open, March 17, 1953, Wingate went in to investigate, having heard of it less than twenty-four hours earlier from his friend and birding companion Charlie Zuill.

He found a black tern, a grebe, a short-eared owl, a night heron, two catbirds, a spotted sandpiper, male and female scarlet tanagers—and a cahow.

✦

By the time A.E. Verrill came along at the turn of the twentieth century, the idea of finding live cahows was considered anywhere from unlikely to ludicrous. In his book *The Bermuda Islands*, Verrill, Yale University's first professor of zoology and a prolific writer on everything from cephalopods to human parasites, examined the historical literature and correctly debunked Hurdis's shearwater theory, but then went even further astray by maintaining the cahow must have been a kind of auk—a bird that prefers cooler weather, "flies" underwater to prey on fish, and looks a bit like a penguin, though the two species are not closely related. "[The cahow] is not a shearwater, [and] not like any other member of the petrel family," Verrill concluded, under the definitive heading "The 'Cahow' of the Bermudas, an Extinct Bird."

It was around Verrill's time that tourism and science began to converge on Bermuda. Princess Louise, one of Queen Victoria's nine children and the wife of the Marquess of Lorne, who served five years as Canada's governor general, bestowed her benediction on the island when she wintered there in 1883. The Princess Hotel quickly rose on Front Street, Hamilton's main drag, to take advantage of the moment, and steamship lines began regular service from Quebec and New York. Mark Twain, perhaps the era's biggest celebrity, had been coming since 1867, remarking in a letter written on his last trip, just before his death in 1910, "You go to heaven if you want to, I'd druther stay [in Bermuda]." More and more of the moneyed elite poured into the country in the wake of the two famous visitors.

Meanwhile, naturalism continued its ascendancy as a favorite pastime of the new merchant class that burgeoned in the United States after the Civil War, and a fervid interest in undersea life had already taken hold of the general public. The first "fish house" opened in 1853 at the London Zoo, followed by aquaria in Paris, Hamburg, Naples, Washington, Boston, and New York. P.T. Barnum sent an assistant to Bermuda to bring back specimens for the aquarium he ran on Broadway from 1856 to 1865, and the forerunner of today's glass-bottomed boats came to the island in the form of glass-bottomed boxes held by visitors over the sides of locals' dinghies for a peek at the teeming reefs.

Verrill was one of the better known naturalists to arrive around this time, as were Alexander Agassiz, curator of the Harvard Museum, and Harvard's president, Charles William Eliot. Professors from New York University and Harvard officially established the regular presence of biologists on Bermuda when they arrived in 1897 to set up a summer base camp on White's Island in Hamilton Harbour. A few years later the operation moved to the grand Frascati Hotel in Flatts Village, where a picturesque inlet allowed quick access to open water and the Middle Road provided an easy route to Hamilton.

Partly in response to all this activity, the Bermuda Natural History Society was founded in 1901, bankrolled by the Carnegie Foundation and the rum merchant Goodwin Gosling and other flush Bermudians. One of its aims was to build a natural history museum and aquarium, and two years after a 1902 speech in which governor Sir Henry LeGuay Geary exhorted the assembly to begin thinking of new ways to entertain the tourists, the Biological Station Act was passed, providing government funds for a research center at Flatts and an aquarium on Agar's Island in Hamilton Harbour, where old military ammunition bunkers large enough to hold fish tanks already stood.

Louis L. Mowbray, the father of Louis S. Mowbray, was chosen as the curator of the new aquarium, which would move to Flatts, where it remains today, in 1926. Born in St. George's in 1877, Mowbray was a photographer of portraits and postcards who had always been interested in the waters around Bermuda. A self-taught naturalist, he displayed the sea slugs, anemones, corals, and fish he collected in the back room of his studio, and soon came to be considered a source of knowledge about all things aquatic. His appointment marked the beginning of science as a profession in the island nation.

On February 22, 1906, Mowbray went out into Castle Harbour in search of Audubon's shearwaters, probably for a museum somewhere in the States or Great Britain. "This was the age of specimen collecting," says Wingate, "before conservation. The rarer the bird, the more they sought after the specimens, which often enhanced the rarity of the bird."

A strong southwesterly gale had swept over Bermuda the day before, so when the curator found a strange-looking seabird tucked into a crevice in a Castle Island cliff, he brought it back to the mainland, assuming it to be a storm-driven vagrant blown off the course of its migration by the harsh winter weather. When it died a few days later, he sent its corpse to the Smithsonian Institution, which he believed would have other specimens with which to compare it as well as researchers more qualified than he to identify it. "Mowbray was mainly a fish man," says Wingate, "so he would have depended on ornithologists for that kind of information."

The U.S. scientists, he continues, "couldn't imagine a cahow had survived" and, having little to compare it with after all, labeled the bird a Peale's petrel, known today as a mottled petrel, from New Zealand. "That didn't make any sense," says Wingate. "A New Zealand petrel would never have been prospecting a nesting crevice in a different ocean on the other side of the world." It was recorded as the first instance of a Peale's petrel in the Northern Hemisphere.

Mowbray made another pivotal discovery the following year, near the newly unearthed entrance to one of Bermuda's extensive cave systems.

Bermuda rose up out of the sea about 100 million years ago as a volcano along the Mid-Atlantic Ridge, the underwater seam in the earth's crust that separates the Eurasian and African tectonic plates from the North and South American. Around 34 million years ago, the volcano erupted a second time and then died, its two mouths, or calderas, eroding into what would one day come to be called Castle and Hamilton harbors. Coral reefs accumulated around the volcano as sea levels rose in between ice ages, building a cap of limestone about three hundred feet thick.

Caves develop in limestone when rainwater falls on it, creating fissures and crevices that slowly enlarge. Most of Bermuda's 150 or so known caves, which began forming a million years ago, were dissolved out of the chalky rock during the low sea stands of the ice ages, when the whole Bermuda Platform was exposed and the island extended more than 200 square miles. Today, only the upper reaches of these caves are above sea level; pools of glass-clear saltwater fill their depths.

It was into one of these subterranean worlds that two twelve-year-old boys stumbled on a spring day in 1907 when the ball they were playing with went into the bushes and down a hole. One of the boys returned to the cave a few days later to collect some dripstones, which he brought to Mowbray at the museum in hopes of selling them. Mowbray, thus alerted, went to see the cave for himself. He swam across its crystalline waters and found, a few inches deep in calcite, the leg bones of a bird. Further digging turned up more bird bones, a rat skull, a bat skull, and three feathers embedded about an eighth of an inch into the rock.

He immediately recognized the find as significant, in part because he knew some of the bones he uncovered were from the shearwater, and the others were markedly different. "I have found the bones of the Cahow," he wrote to Verrill. But of course, he had no way of verifying this.

It wasn't until almost a decade later that the bones made their way to Robert Wilson Shufeldt, an avian osteologist and paleontologist living in Washington, D.C., who is known as much today for his virulent racism as for his brilliant ornithological work. Somehow the American Museum of Natural History had obtained the bones and the director thought Shufeldt should have a look. Shufeldt carefully examined and cataloged the remains, comparing them with the bones of other petrels and shearwaters and staying in touch with Mowbray as his work progressed.

While Shufeldt was meticulously preparing the paper that would lay his claim as the first to describe the new species, Mowbray beat him to the punch. In an April 1916 article published in the *Auk* with

John T. Nichols of the American Museum, Mowbray describes the fossils he initially found, as well as other bones he subsequently discovered, "some about a half mile from where the [1906 specimen] was taken." Nichols and Mowbray write that they had examined the remains and determined them to be "unquestionably distinct."

They declared the 1906 bird the "type specimen," or individual that defines the scientific name, of "a new race."

Shufeldt's paper appeared in the *Ibis* that October, and in it he writes that "the famous 'Cahow' proved to be a new Petrel instead of a well-known species of Shearwater; and the material examined by me to prove this was so perfect and so abundant, that it left not a scintilla of doubt on the subject." He called the bird *Aestrelata vociferans*; *Aestrelata* was the name of the genus at the time, and *vociferans* is Greek for *screaming*. In 1856, the French ornithologist Charles Lucien Bonaparte—Napoleon's cousin—had proposed *Pterodroma*, meaning "winged runner," for dark-colored birds of the genus, retaining *Aestrelata* for those with white bellies. Over time *Pterodroma* came to be applied to all gadfly petrels, as the genus is known in English.

For the species, Nichols and Mowbray's *cahow* stuck since it was the first name to make it to print. But whatever name it ended up with, Shufeldt was very clear on one point: The bird, only so recently caught alive, was quite extinct.

✦

That being settled, little more was said on the matter for the next two decades, and the cahow was forgotten, at least in part because of the world war raging in Europe. Not only were many of the globe's brightest scholars lost in the fighting, but most of those who remained turned their attention to industrialization, military innovation, and medical advancement, and away from the naturalism that had reigned in the previous century. Science became more professionalized and more driven by politics than personal interests. "[World War I] saw the destruction of the old European structure of science," according to a 1975 paper in the *Proceedings of the Royal Society of London*. "[F]rom now on Britain looked rather to America."

Accordingly, in the winter of 1935—the year Wingate was born—an article appeared in the bulletin of the New York Zoological Society. "The resurrection of a living creature, which is supposed to be extinct, is of far greater dramatic interest and actual scientific value than the mere naming of a new species," it began hyperbolically, with a backhanded slap to Nichols and Mowbray. "The 1935 Bermuda expedition of the Zoological Society was fortunate enough to make such a discovery."

The writer was William Beebe, a socialite naturalist from New York who had arrived in Bermuda in 1928—along with his wife, his girlfriend, several research assistants, a pet monkey, and a couple of black goats—to set up a laboratory on Nonsuch. He fell in love with the island and published a lyrical book about his explorations there called *Nonsuch: Land of Water*. By the time the book came out, in 1932, Nonsuch was famous for having been Beebe's home when he ushered in the era of deep-sea exploration by making the world's first bathysphere dive from about ten miles offshore. Starting in 1930, when they reached a depth of 803 feet, Beebe and his partner, Otis Barton, undertook a series of dives, setting a long-standing record of more than a half mile in 1934.

But Bermudians knew Beebe was interested in more than just diving, so, as they had with Bartram and later would with Wingate, they often brought him unusual finds. On June 8, 1935, a boy rode his bicycle to New Nonsuch, the mainland house Beebe had bought in 1932, carrying a package that contained a freshly dead petrel of a type Beebe had never before seen. The bird had been sent by the lighthouse keeper at St. David's, who had found it at the foot of the light, dashed senseless during a storm.

Since Beebe didn't keep an extensive ornithological library in Bermuda, he had one of his assistants stuff the animal and send it to Robert Cushman Murphy, who at the time was curator of oceanic birds at the American Museum of Natural History and, as Mowbray would write of him in a 1951 article in the *Bermudian*, "unquestionably the world's leading authority on oceanic birds."

"[E]xcited word came back," writes Beebe, "that it was the second known specimen of the real cahow or Bermuda shearwater." Murphy, noting the bits of down among the plumage, told Beebe it was a fledgling only "a few days out of the burrow." That meant one thing: The birds had to be nesting somewhere.

Another cahow was found in the early 1940s, having died when it struck a telephone wire. A short newspaper story said it was stuffed as a specimen, but there was no follow-up, and even Wingate doesn't know what became of the bird.

Still, even as hope renewed for the cahow, history was marching toward what would seem to be the bird's final death blow. The United States entered World War II in 1941 after Japan launched a surprise attack on its naval base in Pearl Harbor, Hawaii. The same year, Britain leased a portion of Bermuda's east end to the U.S. military to build an airbase.

Until then, the only air transport into and out of the country was by seaplane; the hilly terrain and narrow geography didn't allow for anything larger. But the United States had never let a little thing like Mother Nature stand in its way; if there wasn't room for an airport, it would make room.

A large portion of Castle Harbour was filled in to allow for the three runways, officers' quarters, hospital, barracks, mess hall, school, theater, bowling alley, tennis courts, and other structures that are needed to build what amounts to a self-contained city. Long Bird and several other islands were leveled, and Cooper's Island—where the cahow had last been seen in significant numbers, in 1615—was connected to St. David's. "Over the next four years a vast section of St. David's and the small isles of Castle Harbour were bulldozed into the sea and buried under dredged fill," Wingate later wrote. "Ugly wireless aerials and bright lights soon sprang up to replace the forest, and the peace was shattered by waves of transient military aircraft."

Another bird that breeds seasonally in Bermuda, the longtail, had been raising its young in Castle Harbour for thousands of years. "It was reported when the islands were destroyed for the airport the longtails came back and flew around wondering what happened to their islands," Wingate says. "They tried to colonize the suction-dredge barges in their confusion."

All of this building inevitably stirred up a large population of both the black rats that had come in the first few years of settlement and the brown rats that had arrived aboard late-nineteenth-century ships. Stray dogs, too, "overran the east end, killing seabirds and even crabs in broad daylight," Wingate wrote, as offended as if the mutts were Times Square muggers picking his own pockets.

A few American officers explored what wild areas remained around the base. The only true naturalist among them was Fred T. Hall, a captain in the Coast Artillery who would later become curator of the Davenport Public Museum in Iowa and director of the Buffalo Museum of Science. Hall "heard a lot of talk about the cahow around Bermuda," according to a story in the *Davenport Daily Times*, so he was already on the alert for the birds when, in March 1945, an American navigator and former biology teacher named Sam Ristich brought him a carcass he'd found washed up in the surf while out jogging on the beach at Cooper's Island. Hall did some exploring, once bringing along Ristich, assistant director of the Bermuda Biological Station Hilary B. Moore, and an unidentified British naval officer. They found the remains of five more birds, still partly intact and with the feathers attached. Rats had gnawed on the bones.

In letters written in 1951, Hall mentions that from the end of Cooper's Island he once heard "cries from the outer islands," and that "one of the British Naval officers, somewhat of an ornithologist, saw two birds flying near [Idol] Island at night on the last day of February, 1945." In neither case was Hall able to identify the birds in question.

In 1948 he sent his six specimens to the Smithsonian, and avian paleontologist Alexander Wetmore concluded they were Audubon's shearwaters—and cahows. Wetmore encouraged Hall to publish his findings, but Hall seems to have been a bit of a procrastinator. The only word of the find that ever made it to print was the *Daily Times* story, headlined "Davenport Public Museum Director Tells of Rediscovery of 'Extinct' Cahow Bird." It states that Hall's specimens merited the cahow an entry in the revised edition of Harvard ornithologist James Lee Peters's *Birds of the World*, which had previously listed the bird as extinct. Beyond this, though, a few bits of skin and bone could hardly be called a rediscovery.

✦

The observations of Hall and his colleagues were intriguing, but to many of the people who followed these kinds of things, it seemed the specimens they found were probably the end of the line, that the species could not have survived the onslaught of the American military. But there were a few who still believed.

Word of the cahow had by then made its way to Wingate, who was reading everything he could find about the birds of Bermuda and had begun hanging around the aquarium's new curator, Louis S. Mowbray, who had taken over from Louis L. in 1943. Wingate had the kind of childhood that no longer exists: After school or upon finishing his chores, he would say good-bye to his parents—perhaps—and disappear until sunset or well past it, riding his bike for miles, swimming, snorkeling, climbing cliffs, and poking around in tidal pools, taking heedless risks and never being questioned or corralled.

On one of those days, out on his own miles from home, he went to rummage around in Tom Moore's Jungle, a wooded area separating Harrington Sound from Castle Harbour on an isthmus known as the Walsingham district, after one of the *Sea Venture* survivors. The "jungle," a favorite haunt of the Dublin-born Romantic poet Thomas Moore, who spent three months in Bermuda around the turn of the nineteenth century, was "one of Bermuda's last wildernesses where nobody stopped you from trespassing," Wingate recalls. "You could get thoroughly lost in there. And there was the challenge of poison ivy, which would keep people from exploring it too thoroughly, so we all grew up thinking there was something around the corner and over the next hill that we had never discovered."

By this time, quite a collection of fossils had accumulated at the aquarium, and it was known that cahow bones were the most common type in the caves that honeycombed Walsingham. "I think because I was alone that day the cahow, and fossil bones, were on my mind," Wingate says. "I thought, Well, I'm going to search for bones. The whole expedition was a conscious effort to find my own cahow bones."

He had read the Shufeldt paper and knew what to look for. He knew, for example, that the hooked upper bill, or culmen, was a hard bone that survived very nicely and was often found fossilized, and that cahows had long, straight wing bones that were distinct from those of longtails and other birds common to Bermuda. He chose a cave whose mouth looked out onto Castle Harbour, and went in a few hundred feet—far enough that he could no longer see the entrance. He was shining his flashlight on the ground the whole way, looking into hidden corners and digging through the talus, until finally he felt in the debris a few hard objects, long and curved and covered with sediment. As soon as he shone his light on them, he knew.

When he came out of the cave to examine the bones more closely, he found himself looking out onto the Castle Harbour islands. "It was a very emotional moment of inspiration," he says, "coming from the silence and blackness of a cave that symbolized death and extinction into the sunlight and green vegetation and bird song outside."

He remembers it as an epiphany. "I thought, There's a damn good likelihood they're still out there," he says. "I've got to get out and look for myself." The hair stood up on the back of his neck as he held the cahow bones and looked across the harbor, wondering if the birds could still be alive somewhere.

Wingate didn't know it at the time, but someone else was thinking the same thing. Richard Pough had learned of the 1945 finds through Hilary Moore and had contacted Fred Hall in December 1947 about mounting an expedition to eradicate the rats from the Castle Harbour islands and search for further evidence of cahows. Hall didn't seem to share Pough's sense of urgency, though, and for the next two years, Pough became increasingly annoyed with the Iowan's endless delays; letters from him were slow in coming, and in each he made clear that though he would like to get back to Bermuda, his job and family responsibilities made it impossible.

By 1949, Pough was discussing the matter with Childs Frick, the son of the coal and steel baron Henry Clay Frick. Frick, a paleontologist, was a trustee and generous benefactor of the American Museum, and he had a house at the farthest reaches of Tucker's Town, where the land juts out into Castle Harbour in the direction of Nonsuch. Pough was convinced some birds were still alive in Castle Harbour, despite the disruptions caused by the American military. "I continue to be very much interested in the Bermuda petrel," he wrote to Frick in 1949, "and feel it would be a crime to let it become extinct now after it so miraculously pulled through the long period when it was so regarded."

It appears that Pough, getting nowhere with Hall, put the bug into Robert Cushman Murphy's ear about an expedition, too. As a seabird expert, Murphy, who had identified Beebe's 1935 find, knew petrels were often nocturnal, frequently burrowers, and almost always easy to miss. He had discussed the possibility of the cahow's survival with several of his colleagues. "Probably only two individuals in Bermuda, namely the Messrs. Mowbray, father and son, had even a suspicion that cahows survived today," Murphy wrote in a 1951 letter to Albert E. Parr, director of the American Museum, where Murphy had been appointed Lamont Curator of Birds two years previously.

> Dr. William Beebe wrote me recently that a rediscovery would be a "miracle." Admiral Sir William Tennant, an ardent ornithologist and late commander of the British Atlantic fleet, with headquarters at Bermuda, assured me that the cahow had gone the way of the passenger pigeon. The average resident of the Colony regarded it as something considerably farther from the modern world than a present-day Bostonian regards the heath hen.*

---

* The North American passenger pigeon is as much a symbol for destruction at the hands of man as the dodo. The pigeons numbered in billions east of the Rockies as late as the mid-nineteenth century, and were probably the most numerous bird in the world until commercial hunting introduced them as a cheap source of meat for booming East Coast cities. Millions of birds were killed every year, until their population could withstand no more slaughter. The last passenger pigeon, a female named Martha, died in the Cincinnati Zoo in September 1914. The heath hen has its own sad and dramatic story, similar to the cahows' and perhaps precautionary. The bird, a subspecies of prairie chicken whose mating sounds could be heard a mile away, was once common from Massachusetts to Maryland. Plump and easy to kill, heath hens became such a popular food for impoverished colonists that, despite legislation enacted in 1791 for their protection, by 1870 only three hundred remained—all living on Martha's Vineyard, just as the cahows had been pushed to Cooper's Island. Heath hen numbers continued to dwindle through hunting by feral cats

In 1950, Murphy wrote to Hall to ask for any information that might help in his search. Wingate, meantime, was hatching his own scheme. By January of that year, he and his friends Henry and Charlie Zuill, identical twins who lived a half mile from Aldie, Wingate's family home, had built a kayak. "We kept it somewhere around Tom Moore's," says Charlie Zuill, a retired art teacher, at his seaside condo in St. George's. "We got some scrap lumber and made a frame. I think my father may have given us some guidance. We built this frame, which we then covered with canvas. I'm not sure how we fastened it on, but we caulked it with sealant and painted it." By February, according to Wingate's diary, the kayak also had a mast, a boom, and a 4½-foot-tall sail. When the boat got damaged, the boys patched it with rubber glue and Scotch tape.

"We used to go out at night, on the rocks," Zuill says. "It was a two-man kayak, so only two could go at a time. We'd come back quite late, maybe as late as eleven or midnight, but our parents didn't seem too worried about us. We'd go out between Cooper's and Nonsuch, and there was usually quite a sea rolling. We'd ride the waves up and down. Once you got into Castle Harbour, in the lee, it wasn't too bad, but if we'd ever got snagged on a reef, we probably would have had to swim to Nonsuch and spend a rather miserable night."

Wingate knew that Mowbray had visited the islands to look for the cahow, and he was determined to use his kayak for the same purpose. He recalled the trip many years later on the American news show *Nightline*.

> I paddled out here, scared as hell, because I knew nothing about boats at that time. And this was really remote. And I mean, when

---

and poachers until, in 1908, a 600-acre preserve was established on the Vineyard for the last fifty wild birds. In it they thrived, and in just seven years, their population climbed to almost two thousand. But disaster struck, again and again. In 1916 a forest fire wiped out more than 90 percent of the birds. Following a harsh winter, an unusually large number of predatory goshawks appeared; and finally, blackhead disease, caused by the protozoan *Histomonas meleagridis*, made its way to the reserve, destroying the birds' livers and killing them. The last heath hen sighting came in 1933, when a male named Booming Ben was spotted searching for a mate.

you were out here, you were alone in those days. And I wanted to land on these islands so bad. But you saw the spiky rocks here, and the surge was washing over it. And I knew that if it punched at my kayak, I was finished.

Not long after that first harrowing attempt, Wingate retired the idea of going out to search on his own, not least because the boat wasn't seaworthy enough to try again. But when he recorded his goals for 1950, the first thing on his list was "Identify the Cahow bird." He wouldn't have long to wait.

CHAPTER FOUR

Unraveling the Mysteries

MURPHY AND HIS WIFE, Grace, arrived in Bermuda on January 23, 1951. They settled in at Frick's luxe home in Castle Point, but the first few days of their stay were frustrating because bad weather made the water too rough to attempt crossing the harbor. Instead, they went, sometimes with Mowbray and sometimes not, to visit several caves and quarries on the mainland and, with a U.S. Air Force guide, reconnoitered American-occupied Cooper's Island, where "superficial digging with pick and shovel" yielded no trace of the once-sizable population of cahows, according to a July 1951 paper Murphy and Mowbray published in the *Auk*. They did find a cache of bullets from small arms, however; soldiers had been using Cooper's and several of the islets for target practice for almost a decade.

Wingate, as he mentions in his diary on January 1 of that year, was now "fifteen and 3 months," and he was already becoming known in the big leagues. Murphy had heard about the boy from Fred Hall, who had learned of him from a Bermuda businessman who knew Wingate's father. It was pure luck for Wingate that the weather didn't break until the fifth day of the Murphys' stay in Bermuda—January 28, a Sunday. Since he didn't have school, he was just about to leave on his usual rounds of weekend-afternoon bird-watching when he got a surprise call from Mowbray. He and the Murphys were going to the Castle Harbour islands. Would Wingate like to come along?

"They thought I might be useful at climbing cliffs and finding nest holes," says Wingate, who began his diary entry that evening with the words, "Got up into what I judge to be the most important day of my Ornithological career."

He pedaled furiously to Flatts, and he and Mowbray took the

aquarium boat to pick up the Murphys. They crossed the Castle Roads channel and motored out to Gurnet Rock, but "waves lashed at its base," according to the diary, making landing impossible. Next they tried Green Island, a craggy half-acre triangle off the southeast end of Nonsuch. There they were able to land and found a few deep crevices that might have made good burrows, but, Wingate writes, "absolutely no sign of life."

Seen from the air, Inner Pear forms a lumpy, sideways semicolon on the far side of Cooper's Point, and Outer Pear a nearby comma. They are so small they can hardly be called islands; they're more like the exposed tips of reefs, and, since they not only have little soil but also are at the most seaward edge of the country, almost nothing grows on them but the prickly pear cactuses for which they were named. Landing on them, as on most of the Castle Harbour islets, is a perilous process that involves backing the boat up to as flat a rock as can be found and jumping when the waves are at their peak. Beebe described the operation, speaking of a trip he took to Green in a fruitless search for the cahow:

> I leaped from the stern of a small boat as it balanced upon the summit of a rising swell, and swarmed up a cliff composed of effectively arranged, serried ranks of pins, daggers, needles, half-opened scissors, knives, nails, fish-hooks, arrows and bits of broken glass. It proved, after all, to be only a cliff of aeolian sand, dissolved and re-fused and tempered to marble hardness, and sculptured and whetted to razor sharpness by the waves: but to hands and feet it was all the rest.

Somehow the Murphys, Mowbray, and Wingate all managed to make it onto Inner Pear without being impaled. The four split up and canvassed the island for clues of avian habitation.

Petrels are well known among birders for their strong musky scent, a bouquet that correspondents of Cornell University ornithologist Arthur Cleveland Bent described in a 1922 bulletin from the Smithsonian as "disagreeable," "horridly smelling," and having a "peculiar pungence comparable to no other odor." It arises from an effective defense mechanism wherein some species vomit an amber-colored or reddish oil when they are distressed that is so strong it comes to permeate their eggs, the skins of specimens, the clothes of researchers, and even the rocks on which the birds nest. Some petrels "can squirt this fluid with great precision for a distance of six or eight feet," Bent relays, and it "renders their discovery . . . easy."

The intrepid group on Inner Pear were disappointed they didn't get even the slightest whiff of this unforgettable fragrance. But a few feathers and bones were turning up, and there were large holes in the red clay stripes deep within the limestone. "Fresh earth at the entrances revealed neither scratches nor footprints," Murphy and Mowbray write in the *Auk*, "but there were soft patches of green and whitish excreta such as are characteristic of squid-eating seabirds."

Wingate and the Murphys were hard at work searching for more telltale droppings when Mowbray, on the other side of the rock, suddenly yelled, "Discovery!" Everyone rushed over to find him shining his flashlight on a bird nestled in a burrow about six feet long and "large enough to accommodate a man's head and shoulders," according to the Murphys' *Natural History* article. The tunnel didn't start until five feet into a horizontal limestone crevice, however, and it quickly narrowed so much that even Wingate couldn't have navigated it.

Mowbray fashioned a catch pole out of a length of bamboo and a thin line that had been thrown into the launch, and spent hours lying between layers of limestone trying to get the loop around the bird's neck. Twice he almost succeeding in pulling the creature out, but he was hindered by a mound of sand the bird had piled up in the tunnel during burrowing. "It was not until we tied a piece of wood on as a rake, and raked out a lot of the sand, that we eventually got him out," Wingate writes.

Murphy held the bird up to the light and spread its wings. Wingate says he'll never forget the ornithologist quietly marveling, "By gad, the cahow!"

The bird struggled at first. It "bit the hands that grasped it but only half-heartedly," the Murphys write in *Natural History*. "Within a moment it became completely unresistant, allowing itself to be stroked, tickled, and passed from hand to hand. During the whole period of badgering, extraction, and handling, it had neither uttered a sound nor ejected oil from its throat or nostrils." It remained "docile, dry, and fluffy, as well as practically devoid of odor."

Wingate's diary entry, filled with underlined sentence fragments and double exclamation points, is long enough to demand a special insert of extra notebook pages. "I could think of nothing better than to hear the song, and watch the courtship and actions of this almost unknown bird," he wrote. A lifelong obsession had been born.

✦

They found three more burrows that day on Inner Pear. Two of them were too curved to see into, but in the third they spotted another nesting bird. Mowbray was sure it was a cahow but decided they should spend a night on the island so they could get a better look when it came out to be spelled by its mate. "Daddy says that I can take a day or two off from school for this purpose," Wingate told his diary.

They reluctantly left Inner Pear to move on to Outer Pear, where they found some shearwater bones and four shearwater burrows, but no more cahows.

The next day Wingate's father picked him up from school to take him to the aquarium so he could be at the boat by four. He and Mowbray stopped by Frick's place to get the Murphys, and they rode across calm seas—a relative term in Castle Harbour—back to Inner Pear.

January in Bermuda is not always pretty, and spending the night with no shelter on a rock in the middle of the ocean never is. Added to that, a cold front moved in that night with showers and increased wind by dawn—and once clothes are soaked with salt spray, you can expect them to cling to you until you take them off. "What I remember most," says Wingate, "is how long and bitterly cold it was staying on that tiny islet all night with no place out of the wind to sleep. My thoughts were that this scientific expedition stuff can be tough, but I better not show my discomfort to give a good impression. That covers the long part of the night when nothing much happened."

Luckily, the few minutes when something did happen were enough to make the misery worthwhile. Initially, all four explorers stationed themselves outside the first burrow they'd found the day before. They heard a few faint calls and saw a murky streak flashing over their heads at 7 P.M. Then, "at approximately half past eight," Wingate writes in his diary, a bird "began flying low over the hole again in quick succession till at last it dropped into the cave mouth. Mr. Mowbray, in an advantageous position, grabbed it. It made absolutely no sound whatever, and when we picked it up it didn't even bother to struggle. It looked about casually while we confirmed it as a cahow—there was no difference whatever in the sex—and then put it down. Immediately it scuttled, snake fashion, along the edge of the hole and into its mate."

When ashore, cahows waddle on pink and black webbed feet. Though they're actually proportionately a little longer than a duck's legs, cahows' legs appear shorter because the birds tend to shamble along on their tarsi, which are the equivalent to a human's tibiae, or calf bones. The birds are about the size of a small pigeon, and their wings, brownish gray above with white undersides boldly outlined in black, are twice the length of their bodies and rather thin—more like those of a drone aircraft than those of, say, a whooping crane. Adult birds have a rounded, almost chubby head and a prominent forehead above their scimitar-shaped beaks, and their eyes are black buttons surrounded by a cowl of soft gray feathers.

The birds that were nesting that night had probably been expecting for about a month, as cahows lay their single eggs in early January. But since the chick had not yet arrived to make demands on their alone time, the pair were still acting like honeymooners. "The birds made no audible sound," write Murphy and Mowbray, explaining that they shone their flashlights down the burrow entrance at frequent intervals,

> but they expressed mutual satisfaction or affection in many other ways. The beam of light apparently created no disturbance. They could be seen nibbling at each other's beaks and necks and then launching into an "ecstatic" turn-around in the small chamber,

puffing up their plumage and shuffling about each other on flat tarsi. At such times it was not always possible to discern whether one remained on the egg or whether the latter merely lay in the middle of the melée.

Seeing this courtship ritual was just one of the moments that night that Wingate remembers as "exhilarating." "It was the first sightings of birds in flight and the first calls attributable to the cahow heard by any of us," he says. "I remember being stunned by their speed and maneuverability in the darkness. While each of us pretended to be scientific and unemotional on the surface, our minds must all have been racing with the implications, for the real significance of that night was that this time we had found the actual breeding sites and could begin to do something about helping the birds."

Mowbray and the Murphys—with Wingate along for another night watch or two, despite a paternal ban on missing any more school—located seven nesting pairs on two islets by February 10, when the Murphys returned to their home in Setauket, Long Island. They banded five of the birds and located ten more burrows, whether occupied or not they didn't know.

Early in the course of their fieldwork the first week, Murphy and Mowbray write, "[W]e learned that the likelihood of finding Cahows was in inverse ratio to the prevalence of rats. . . . [T]here was no trace of living birds here or in any other locality discovered to be occupied, or to have been occupied, by rats."

Naturally, the first order of business, given this situation, was to get rid of the rats on whatever islets were found to have burrows. Pough had recommended this years before when Fred Hall had discovered the rat-eaten remains washed up onshore. "Rats are the mortal enemies of ground nesting birds like the petrels," Pough wrote to Hall in 1948. "Something should be done and done promptly to eradicate the rats." But at the time, Mowbray was against any intervention that might bring attention to the birds; he had no doubt picked up this attitude from his father, who felt that publicity of any sort might bring disruptive curiosity seekers or, worse, murderous specimen collectors. "Two [shearwater nesting] localities are, I believe, known to Mr. Mowbray alone," Shufeldt wrote of Louis L. in 1916. "He proposes to keep the secret, and allow these much-persecuted birds to breed in peace and safety."

It is likely that Hall was referring to Mowbray *fils* when he wrote back to Pough, saying, "A few [Bermudians] seemed to feel that secrecy was the best protection—but it didn't keep the rats away." He scattered warfarin on the offshore islets he believed the birds might be colonizing. "I caused some ill feelings by trying to protect those birds," he wrote.

Murphy's attitude toward revelation was quite the opposite; he believed the more publicity, the better, since it would more or less force the Bermudian government to safeguard the Castle Harbour islands so far left alone by the U.S. military. As soon as he returned to New York, Murphy held a press conference announcing the historic find. The story made papers from the *New York Times* to the Lubbock, Texas, *Morning Avalanche* and from the *Times* of London to the Kingston, Jamaica, *Daily Gleaner.* The only concession Murphy made to secrecy was not publishing the names of the islets on which burrows had been found, instead calling them simply A, B, and C.

✦

In 1954, Richard Thorsell was a twenty-six-year-old recent college graduate—World War II had intervened in his education—visiting New York City for the weekend. He had been birding since around the age of nine, and had recently seen what he thought to be a red phalarope near his home in Morristown, New Jersey. "I wanted verification on it," he says, "because it was accidental in New Jersey"—that is, rare enough that there had been only five or fewer records of it in the state. He'd stopped in at the Museum of Natural History and was trying to sweet-talk the guard into letting him behind the scenes to see the collection of skins when in walked Richard Pough, now the museum's chairman of conservation and general ecology.

"I had known Dick since '42," Thorsell says. "He was the Audubon warden at Cape May, which was a great birding spot." Thorsell and another teenager had apparently impressed Pough that year when they mentioned they'd ridden their bikes 165 miles to reach the cape. "He spent the day with us and gave us good information on places we could bird."

Pough and Thorsell were in Pough's office catching up when the phone rang. "He said, 'Well, I have a young man in the office right now. Let me talk to him,'" Thorsell recalls. "Right place, right time." On the other end of the line was Harold Anthony, chairman of the mammalogy department and a friend of Childs Frick. Anthony was calling to say Frick was looking for someone who could go to Bermuda and work with the cahow, and to ask whether Pough knew of any candidates. The next thing Thorsell knew, he was at the Bermuda airport shaking hands with Louis Mowbray.

When the Murphys had left in February 1951, four nests were known to have contained incubating eggs. There was a feeling of hopeful anticipation when Mowbray had found, in March, that all four had hatched. But instead of fledging, all four were dead within the month. When their bones were later collected, they were found among those of generations of chicks. With an apparent 100 percent mortality rate, at least in recent years, how could the cahow have survived at all? And there was some indication that rats weren't the only killers. "Mr. Mowbray . . . found longtails in the cahow burrows in which one could see," Wingate writes in 1952, "and the only young bird visible, the longtail had killed! What a disaster, so the longtails are the trouble makers after all!"

White-tailed tropicbirds are so closely linked with the coming of spring that Bermudian men call the female tourists, who start descending on the island around the same time, "longtails" after the birds' nickname. Though they nest on tropical islands worldwide, longtails' main breeding colonies in the western Atlantic are Bermuda, the Bahamas, and the Antilles, and for many years—until the cahow took the honor in 2003—the longtail was regarded as Bermuda's national bird. They are satiny white pelagic birds with straight orange bills, splashes of black on their wings and around their eyes, and graceful, droopingly elongated dual tail feathers. Slightly bigger than a cahow but with about the same wingspan, longtails, too, come ashore only to breed, arriving in Bermuda in mid-March, just around the time the helpless cahow chicks are first left alone while their parents go out to feed.

A longtail's legs are stubbier than the cahow's, and they're so far back on the bird's body that it cannot walk. It uses them as paddles in the water and, on land, pushes itself along with them and its wings to inch forward on its belly, flying into and dropping out of the cliff-side crevices in which it nests—crevices the cahows now used too, since they had lost their original habitat to predators and human encroachment. And while cahows land only at night, longtails are diurnal, giving them the perfect opportunity to raid unprotected nests while the adult cahows are away.

One pair of longtails nesting in a cahow burrow hardly signified a trend, but still, the development bore watching. And since Mowbray was too busy to do it, with his full-time job at the aquarium, two American graduate students selected by Murphy and paid by Frick went down to help out.

Robert Perkins and Paul Shepard were in the first graduating class of Yale University's master's program in conservation. During the winter holidays each of their two years of study, the men spent several weeks in Bermuda, staying at the Biological Station in the daytime and on the cahow islands at night. They were ferried back and forth by Mowbray and had been asked to simply observe the birds, in part to learn more about the predation on chicks. Neither of them gathered much data, though.

"We would lie on our backs and look at the sky and watch to see if there were birds flying around," recalls Melba Shepard, who was married to Paul Shepard at the time and spent a week in Bermuda with him in 1952. "There was only once that Paul thought a bird flew into one of the burrows, and he didn't take a picture because he didn't want to frighten it. There was no other activity." Shepard made "fences" of drinking straws in front of the burrow entrances and set up a camera that would trip automatically if a cahow came in after he'd drifted off. "He did that every evening for two weeks," says Melba Shepard. Nothing.

"Shepard and Perkins came during the Christmas holidays," explains Wingate, who often accompanied the two students out to the islands. "Their visits coincided with a prelaying exodus that lasts six weeks. The birds leave in late November or early December and don't come back until early January to lay. But nobody knew there was an exodus, so they misinterpreted the lack of cahows as being due to the shock of rediscovery scaring them away."

Shepard, who went on to become an environmentalist and author, detailed the rat problem in *Natural History* magazine. "What had happened to the birds that had managed to breed there until very recently?" he wrote. "The answer depends on further study of Bermuda rats."

But despite Shepard's conviction, the case was building against the longtails. One January day Wingate notes that he and Perkins were finally able to land on Gurnet Rock, where they encountered numerous longtail feathers but no sign of rats. After Perkins left Bermuda, Wingate took it upon himself to continue monitoring the islands, often taking a friend's kayak (not homemade) to look for cahows. In February, after seeing a broken egg at the end of a burrow, he writes that on Inner Pear, "[e]very single burrow was occupied by a longtail. . . . I bet that was the culprit which broke the Cahow's egg."

By the end of the 1952–53 breeding season, the evidence seemed clear enough that Murphy, Pough, and Frick had begun looking for someone to do something—no one was quite sure what—about the tropicbirds. Thorsell came down for seven weeks beginning in early March, around the same time as the longtails. About every third night, he stayed with the Mowbrays, but for the most part he had a much less commodious sleeping arrangement, on a shelf on the main cliff of Inner Pear. "The cubicle we dug on the side of the cliff was slanted," he recalls at his home in North Carolina. "It was only a couple feet from a cave, and when the sea was rough the sand would fall on you all night long, and the whole thing would shake from the waves coming in. Wind would blow round the clock. And there was no communication—no walkie-talkie, no radio. I didn't have a telephone in my pocket." He laughs at the implausibility of modern technology. "I don't know what I did all day but look at longtails." On March 10, after his first night on the island, a southeasterly gale arose and Mowbray had difficulty reaching Thorsell to get him back to the mainland. "It might be worth noting that the seas were so rough that the seams of the 'Chub' were split," Thorsell writes of Mowbray's motorboat.

On March 12, he and Mowbray returned to Inner Pear to find a longtail sitting at the mouth of a cahow burrow, the cahow chick alive and apparently well behind it at the back of the tunnel. Over the next two days, more than twenty longtails appeared, quickly colonizing every other burrow. The chick looking on from backstage did not in the end survive, nor did any others that spring.

There was no longer any question that the longtails were a much more imminent threat than rats, which were rarely if ever seen on the cahow islets. It had been decided that to prevent further predation, Thorsell should begin screening every burrow during the daytime and destroying all the longtails that landed. This plan, needless to say, proved impractical. First, it would require someone to live on each of the islands with cahow burrows during the entire nesting season, since bad weather often made crossing Castle Harbour impossible. Second, there was the issue of the killing itself. "Elimination of longtails from the location of cahow nests," Thorsell writes in his report, "in essence implies extermination of long-tails from [Bermuda]."

This might be especially difficult since longtails, it turned out, were particularly hardy creatures. "Most birds you can suffocate by holding them tight enough to push all the air out," Thorsell explains. "Not that I'm a killer of birds, but. Longtails were too tough. You had to wring their neck. I'd grab their heads, get their bills, wring their necks, and throw them over." Thorsell wasn't troubled by this, since he felt he was doing it for the greater good, but the residents of Bermuda were. "They put an article in the paper about the longtails floating up, and it's a shame they didn't know what was killing them," he says with a devilish grin.

It wasn't until April 8 that Thorsell decided, while continuing along with Plan A, to try adding a Plan B first suggested by Pough. "Placed a board with a 2.75 inch hole at the entrance of burrow No. 8," Thorsell writes in his report. He put a stockade of grass blades across its opening so he would know in the morning whether a cahow had entered.

In the context of caring for wild birds, a baffler or baffle is anything that keeps a predator away from a nest box or feeder, whether it be a wobbling guard, a slick length of stovepipe, or an upside-down dome. In the case of burrow nesters like the cahow, the device must protect a ground-level entrance, so the only option for making one is to block the passage to the nesting site and hope that the bird you're protecting is smaller than the predator that's trying to get in.

Cahows' bodies are quite a bit shorter than longtails', but the diameters of the two birds are a very close call. To determine the largest opening the longtails could not get through, Thorsell had an aquarium staff member make an 18-inch-square box with a removable lid and a 4-inch hole on one side. Over the hole was a round piece of plywood with a series of eight more holes ranging from 2¼ to 3½ inches in diameter—like the dial on an old-fashioned telephone. Thorsell would capture longtails and put them in the box. Since they were "not really interested in getting out," he would then "grab them by the bill and pull them through" the various-sized holes.

Based on his experiments with the box, the first baffler Thorsell tried had a 2¾-inch hole. The longtails couldn't get past it, but when he put it in front of a burrow at night, neither could the cahows. "It became obvious a round hole wouldn't work," he says, "because the birds walked with their wings down." He began to devote the extra time afforded by living on a deserted island to experimenting with horizontal openings in an elliptical shape, pushing sand up against the baffler entrance to see how much of it was displaced when a bird came or went. He tried holes of a dozen or more sizes, finally settling on the idea that each must be custom-made for the cahows in that particular burrow.

Pough later said he had thought of trying bafflers because he hated to see the longtails getting killed. "We all knew that if you make the hole in a nest box the right size," he said, "you can keep the English sparrow out, and let the house wren in. I thought, Maybe it will work with this one—the longtail looked a little bit bigger." It was the first time such a device was used for seabirds, and without it the cahow would not have survived.

✦

Each baffler is a rudder-shaped slab of spruce or pitch pine, weather-grayed and pockmarked, with the name of the island and the burrow number it belongs to hand-scratched over a center cutout smaller than a mail slot. Propped up against nest entrances and held in place by buried rocks and wooden wedges, they're low-tech—rustic, even—yet they remain, fifty years later, perhaps the most important element of the cahow conservation program.

"Ninety percent of the cahow population is still on islands that are vulnerable to tropicbird colonization," Wingate says. "Without the bafflers, we'd risk losing 90 percent of the chicks to nest-site competition."

The devices are so crucial that the idea that something might go wrong with them still haunts Wingate. "I have a recurring dream," he says. "I've got cahows nesting in the house, in the bedroom or under the floorboards and things like that, but I've forgot to leave the door open. I suddenly wake up in horror that maybe a chick has starved."

Yet it would be years after Thorsell's 1954 trip before the bafflers began to make a difference.

Though Wingate had often accompanied Perkins and Shepard to the Castle Harbour islands during their stays in Bermuda, by the time Thorsell arrived, the younger man was at Cornell University in Ithaca, New York, studying zoology (there was no ornithology major). He returned home occasionally between 1953 and '57, but for the most part stayed abroad, bunking with classmates' families during shorter holidays and spending his summers on school-sponsored birding expeditions to Mexico and the Great Plains.

By the end of his junior year he was considering continuing to the doctoral level, and went so far as to apply for a Rhodes scholarship, but it was not granted him, perhaps because of the one consistent caveat in the otherwise glowing recommendations of his elders: Though quite athletic, he was literally not a team player. As Mowbray had tactfully written for Wingate's Cornell application, "His sporting activities have been less of the conventional types of organized games than the more vigorous sport of hill climbing, etc., in search of interesting or new wild life."

Wingate's heart doesn't seem to have been in going to Oxford anyway, or to Cornell, or to Louisiana State University, whose nascent birding program was also pursuing him. "I just sort of dropped the idea," he says. "On the one hand I had a sense of guilt about it because everyone was wagging their fingers at me and saying go and get your doctorate. I definitely had a sense I wasn't following the best advice. On the other hand, I couldn't forget Bermuda, couldn't forget the cahows. I had to come home. They probably would have been extinct by the 1970s if I hadn't."

Since Thorsell had spent all his time on the island experimenting with the proper size for a baffler, when he left in the spring of 1954 only one nest was protected. He returned the following year to make sure a gravid female "could get through the hole without popping the egg," but his original recommendation stood, that each device should be custom-made for the size of the cahow pair using it. "The path that the parents use should be determined," he wrote, "then an oversize (2½ x 6") baffle should be placed in the path at the burrow entrance and through several steps the correct sized smaller baffle should be installed." After Thorsell left, Mowbray continued, sporadically, to experiment with materials, using limestone instead of wood in some cases, and with portal sizes, probably trying to come up with more universal dimensions that would not necessitate constant tinkering.

Thorsell had made clear that the devices seemed "the best hope" for saving the cahow and recommended their installation take "the highest priority." "When I left for the final time," he recalls, "I said,

'Well, the tools are there, Mowbray can handle it.' I didn't realize it was in jeopardy."

Wingate returned to Bermuda after graduating in 1957 and found bafflers on only about half of the burrows that had by then been located. "That's the same thing I noted when I went back there," Thorsell says. "Only one of my baffles was installed. The rest were made by Louis and were the wrong sizes."

In the six years since the rediscovery, Mowbray's enthusiasm for the cahow project seems to have dimmed. "Louis was a fish guy," Thorsell says. "He wasn't bird-oriented; he was sport-fish-oriented. And he wasn't as energized to the value of endangered species as the Americans were." It was only out of a sense of obligation, Thorsell believes, and "to keep Mr. Frick happy," that Mowbray continued working with the cahows at all.

As early as 1948, three years before the breeding grounds were even discovered, Pough—described by Thorsell as "one who opened doors and pushed people in"—had been scouting around for someone who could work with the cahows full time should they be found. "[Do] you know of anyone in Bermuda sufficiently interested in the conservation of birds to undertake this?" he had written to Fred Hall. He knew Mowbray wasn't the man for the job, diplomatically telling Frick the following year, "I get the impression that, interested as Louis S. Mowbray may be, he is far too busy as Curator of the Government Aquarium and Museum to give the matter the time it would require."

Thorsell, who had lunch with Pough in New York a couple of times a year, remembers "he kept saying we're trying to get a warden on the payroll." Once his continued interest in the cahows came to the older men's attention, Wingate became the natural choice, and by the time he graduated from college, he says, "Louis was happy to hand it over to me."

He wasn't as happy, however, with Wingate. "After I came back from university," Wingate says, "I suddenly knew more about ornithology than he did. It was sort of an awkward transition where I went from being a boy who was no threat to his authority to being sort

of brash and self-confident." For the first few years, Wingate technically remained under Mowbray's oversight, working on grants from
Frick, the New York Zoological Society, and the Bermuda Aquarium.
But he had long since started to go it alone, kayaking out to the cahow islands when he was home and keeping detailed notes on the
birds. Now that he had official sanction, he took it as carte blanche,
sometimes turning up on radio, in newspapers, and at speaking en-
gagements without first discussing things with Mowbray. "I probably
offended him a couple of times by not respecting his seniority or not
crediting him," he concedes. "I remember giving interviews and not
mentioning Mowbray because that was in the past. I later learned that
was a faux pas. 'Thanks to Louis Mowbray, I've been able to carry on.'
That's all I needed to say. You don't know when you're young."

After a while, Mowbray, miffed but probably also relieved, more
or less faded into the background.

✦

Wingate's first task, he knew, was to get the baffler situation sorted
out. Only about half the nests were blocked, and even those were
not secure, with too-big entry holes or careless installation. Mowbray
"might have gotten out there every two or three weeks," Wingate says,
"which was hopeless for a bird in crisis. It didn't help at all." Wingate
decided the only way to really get to know the birds and what they
were up against was to plant himself on Inner Pear for six weeks.
Luckily, by now the island had shelter: a four-by-six-foot shack built
so that Thorsell could be marginally more comfortable in his second
year there. In March 1958, Wingate threw his sleeping bag, his Coleman lantern, a few field guides, and some other basic necessities into
a punt and rowed out to take up residence.

He spent many hours making bafflers out of rock, which was all
around him and easier to use than bringing wood to the island. He'd
cut a slab of limestone with a hatchet, then use chisels and files to chip
holes out of the center. "If you chose the hardest rock," he says, "you
could cut into it without breaking it." Like Thorsell, he kept trying
different hole sizes, blocking the entrance with twig fences in case he

missed a cahow entering or leaving. His results were nearly identical to the measurements of Thorsell's one perfect baffler—2¼-by-5 inches with a quarter-inch notch at the bottom for the bird's sternum—though at the time, owing to Mowbray's haphazard record-keeping, Wingate hadn't seen the paper detailing the 1954 experiments.

He also toured the other islands, rowing a half day to get to Long Rock and an entire day to reach Horn and Green. He did thorough biological surveys, mapped every longtail nest he came across, and poked into every crevice for more cahows, finding none. "That was also when I first explored Nonsuch thoroughly," he says. "I remember landing on it just for a bit of variety. I realized it was the only island that could support a big population of cahows. But I didn't yet see the bigger picture."

That year, Wingate was able to save four cahow chicks by baffling the burrows and destroying any established longtail pairs that arrived, having nested in the crevice the previous year—for he had learned that once a pair had taken up residence, "that was their damn home and nothing was going to stop them," not even a baffler. "Nest-seeking birds are not similarly motivated. If they saw one that was baffled when they were nest-prospecting, they would say, 'Oh, it's too small.'"

By April, when he packed up his camp on Inner Pear, adult cahow activity was beginning to wind down and the chicks were being left alone for longer and longer periods. But after he returned to the mainland, Wingate still continued to visit Castle Harbour as many nights as he could in a used 12-foot molded-wood hull he'd purchased with a grant from Frick. Watching his first generation of chicks preparing to leave the nest reinforced the deep emotional attachment he would have with the birds throughout his life. "'It's just Wingate,' he said softly, 'Go back to sleep,'" reads a description of him lifting the lid off a burrow at night in a 1968 *Sports Illustrated* story. "They sleep very soundly," he continues. "I don't impose myself on their life history. I try not to touch them. I just hover over them in case they need help, like a fairy godmother or a mother with a teenage daughter. I protect them from circumstantial fate. I have a feeling that they know it now."

A week or so before a young cahow—now fatter than an adult—is ready to fledge, it is abandoned by its parents, which return to sea to molt. Once the chick realizes this state of affairs, it emerges from the burrow to begin life on its own. On its first night out, it simply explores the world around it, unfolding its wings and flapping them a few times while facing away from the wind so that it doesn't accidentally become airborne. On each successive night it grows bolder and works its pectorals and biceps harder, eventually facing into the wind so it can feel the lift and know what it's like to fly without actually leaving the ground for more than a second or two. It gazes at the stars a lot, perhaps in part to help fix its position—its *exact* position; not just anywhere on the speck of land that is Bermuda, but specifically on a rock that, in the vast scale of the nearly featureless ocean, is infinitesimal, and even more specifically on the dark, narrow, overhanging fissure in that rock that it just walked out of.

When the chick is finally ready, it gets to the highest point it can find. If its nest is near a cliff, it goes to the largest rock with a view of the horizon and lifts off like a helicopter; if the burrow is beside a tree, it uses the claws on its webbed feet to scrabble up the leaning windward side, fluttering its wings for balance and a little extra push and poking the tree with its bill the way a cross-country skier uses poles on an incline. Not infrequently, Wingate was the highest point in the vicinity as he sat beside burrow entrances waiting for fledglings to emerge, and he wasn't surprised the first time one walked along his legs, up his arm, to his shoulder, and thence his head before bobbing its own head for a few minutes to gauge the horizon and then speeding off into the night sky. "By the time that happened, I was aware that as long as you didn't make any sudden moves, they didn't treat you as anything dangerous," he says. "They come out of the burrow and explore their environment, pecking at vegetation and anything different. Quite often they would come up and nibble at my clothing, working it over with a vibrating bill. That happened on nearly every watch, especially if they'd already been out exercising and I was a new item in their environment."

In the early days, he tried to witness every fledging. "I'd watch them take that tremendous leap from the snug, dark burrow where they're fed and never see the light of day to suddenly having to come and face the real world and plunge out into the blackness of the sea," Wingate says. "You can see the tension building up. They all have different temperaments. Some are very deliberate about it; they come out very matter-of-factly, like an aircraft pilot going through his checklist to make sure everything is working before takeoff. And others are very dithery. You can see they are worried, unsure of themselves, having a terrible time building up to that great plunge they've got to take. They dither and dither and dither, and go halfway back to the burrow after giving up for lack of sufficient courage. Then they get back to the burrow entrance and say, 'No, I'm sorry, I've got to do this after all. I can't spend another night in the burrow.' And they try again and then they go. Sometimes I felt like pushing them overboard. You sort of begin to anthropomorphize them and picture yourself in the same predicament."

Wingate has no problem with seeing what are usually considered human qualities in cahows or any other creatures. "I am a firm believer we are so close to animals," he says, citing Jane Goodall's chimpanzee research as paving the way for biologists to study the inner lives of their subjects without risking their careers. "Every time we think we have an edge over them in some respect, we discover that some animal, it could even be an insect, invented it or evolved it millions of years ago. The more we delve into animals, the more we realize that some of them, at least, have all the intelligence we do. The opposite of anthropomorphizing is far worse; I take it as tantamount to the attitude that the rest of nature is inferior to us. I don't buy that at all. I treat them on an entirely equal basis with humanity—neither above nor below humanity, but on an equal basis."

In the case of the first three chicks to fledge, Wingate actually missed the big moment because he didn't yet know its exact timing, but he sat vigil during the exercise periods. By the time the fourth chick was ready, he was getting better at reading their behavior, and he was determined not to slip up. He spent four nights in a row by the burrow, concealing himself under a blanket—he didn't yet know how truly blasé cahows could be about the presence of humans.

The fledgling needed to get out to sea soon or it would starve. "The cahow showed signs of increased restlessness even before dark,"

Wingate wrote in his diary. "Occasionally it teetered as though very weak," and it took long rests between exercise bouts. The bird dawdled so much that Wingate dozed off just before it finally left. When he woke and dashed to the cliff edge with his flashlight, he found that instead of flying the bird had plummeted thirty-five feet, straight into the water. Never having seen a cahow fledge before, he didn't know whether that was the usual procedure, but he suspected something was wrong.

"I clambered down the cliff side and jumped into the boat, pulled up the anchor, and motored around to the island's seaward side to follow it," he says. "The bird was swimming in circles, preening and drinking lots of water." When juvenile cahows are abandoned by their parents, they remain at the nest site for a week or two without water, breaking down the fat stores they've built up for hydration. But Wingate knew this chick had been without its parents for much too long, and was underweight and thirsty.

As a member of the order *Procellariiformes*, which also encompasses shearwaters, albatrosses, and several dozen other species of petrel, cahows have two short tubes, with nostrils at the end, on the tops of their bills (some *Procellariiformes* have only one large central tube). Scientists haven't quite figured out the function of the tubes, also known as naricorns, or of the enlarged nasal gland behind them. Included among the hypotheses are that the tubes may aid in the detection of air speed and currents or help the birds recognize one another or select a mate. It is likely the birds' sense of smell assists in their homing ability; when scientists plug the nostrils of storm petrels or sever their olfactory nerves, most of the birds are unable to return to their nests. And it seems clear the gland helps petrels find food through scent. But what is known for sure is that it acts as a mini-desalination plant by removing salt from "tubenose" birds' blood that they then sneeze or simply let drip away. So drinking seawater didn't put the fledgling in danger of further dehydration.

Wingate again dropped anchor, waiting to see what would happen next. When the bird eventually began to paddle toward the sea, Wingate found himself hitched on a reef. He had to detach the anchor chain to get away from the island, tying it to a float so he would find it on his return. He didn't want to frighten the bird by starting the engine, so he rowed, with the bird in the lead, out to the boiler reefs, past a shoal, and into the open ocean. Soon he was in mile-deep water nearly a league from land.

It became more and more difficult for the exhausted Wingate to keep an eye on the bird, which he feared was becoming waterlogged. He lost sight of it around three in the morning. "Finally there was an extra deep swell and he just vanished," he says in *Sports Illustrated*. "He may have taken off. He may have been swallowed by a shark. . . . It was probably a good thing he disappeared. Otherwise, I'd still be following him."

Wingate looked back to find he was so far out at sea that he could barely discern the lights of Bermuda. He started the motor and headed in, barely negotiating the treacherous boiler reef. He located his anchor chain, reattached it, and spent the rest of the night trying to sleep in the wet boat.

During the entire episode, it wasn't the possibility that the boat wouldn't start and he'd spend days adrift with no supplies that bothered him. "It was basically, I realized that I might be looking at the last hope for a species," he says. "Not just for an individual but a whole species. The life or death of that chick could have meant the difference between survival and extinction. That was my thought at the time, and it had tremendous meaning for me. They were so close to extinction that every chick counted. That could have been the tipping point."

CHAPTER FIVE

Building a New, Old World

WITH THE CAHOWS GONE for the season, Wingate spent the summer studying the migratory patterns of avian tourists and fretting over whether the cahows would make it after all. It was during this period he met the other great love of his life when a new face turned up at Aldie, the family home. "My parents, desperate for cash to pay off the house, took in boarders," he explains, "and there were two or three Cable and Wireless employees who stayed with us." Bermuda has a long history, continuing today, of importing foreign workers, particularly from the United Kingdom, to fill temporary positions. Jaime Morrison, a friend of one of the Wingates' boarders, had come from Woking, Surrey, a few years before and had married Wingate's sister Aileen; now Jaime's seventeen-year-old sister, Monica Ann, known as Anita, arrived to take a job as a legal secretary for a few years. "A lot of English girls did that," Wingate says. "They got away from the dreary climate, out to the tropics, with the intention of emigrating. And if they had family that was always a draw. So she was fresh out of secretarial school and wanted to experience the world."

Wingate fell in love at first sight, and it was a convenient, if clandestine, courtship, since the two were living in the same house. While Anita could "dress up to the hilt if we were going dancing or something like that," for their first date, he took her to collect giant land crabs in Hungry Bay, on Bermuda's south shore, for Childs Frick. "It was a good excuse to get her out at night," he says. To Anita, who Wingate says was "constantly plagued" by men asking her out her first few months in Bermuda, expeditions with Wingate seemed more interesting than going to a bar to sit around talking.

"I remember one time we went six miles out in my tiny blue boat," he says, "on a flat dead, glassy calm April day. I was doing research on shearwaters and other ocean birds at the time, so I went far enough out that Bermuda was a little sliver on the horizon. I stopped the engine and we sat for about five hours, looking at plankton and sargassum. We found a little loggerhead turtle, asleep, and put him in the boat until he woke up. We watched a black-tipped shark swim by. It was just a magical day."

He was smitten enough that he mentioned his adventuresome new girl in a letter to Pough, though the response probably wasn't what he'd been expecting. "I think it would be a great mistake for you not to get an advanced degree," Pough replied sternly. "It means several more years of hard work . . . living on a small income and putting aside any idea of getting married, but it will I am sure pay great dividends in the end. . . . Today's world is a scientific world, but you are really not [a scientist] today without a Ph.D. . . . I know of several young men who could have had brilliant careers who threw them away by marrying too young."

Wingate, as usual, was not to be deterred. He and Anita were wed on New Year's Eve 1959 in St. Mark's Anglican Church in Smith's Parish.

A photograph in the *Mid-Ocean News* shows a fresh-faced Wingate in a white dinner jacket and black bow tie leaning over his bride as she signs the wedding register with a bespectacled minister looking on. Anita is a wisp, her curly dark hair caught up under a Juliet cap and veil, and her eyes such a light green they appear almost translucent on the black-and-white page. Bagpipes played at the ceremony, the story reports, and the couple were driven in a shiny black convertible back to Aldie, where family and friends gathered in the lantern-lit garden to celebrate.

"Anita was a mere child when she first came out here," remembers Walwyn Hughes, who would become Wingate's boss in the mid-1960s. "She was only eighteen when they got married."

"They were a great couple," adds Hughes's wife, Betsey, sitting beside him in the family room of the couple's Hamilton Parish house. "She doted on him. She was his helpmate in every respect. Anybody who would go out to that island or wait for him to come home after some of his crazy jaunts out on those rocks, when you didn't even know whether he was going to make it back alive or not, would have to be in love."

In the first flush of romance, Anita would sometimes accompany Wingate out to Castle Harbour to monitor the cahows. "I'd set her to watch one bird while I watched another," he remembers. "I'd come back to ask her, 'What happened to your bird?' and she would invariably be in a deep sleep. Her bird would have gone out and come back in, and she never knew it. She wasn't geared for long, boring night watches."

Lacking the fanaticism required to sit for hours waiting for a second's glimpse of a dim, shadowy form that might never appear, Anita more often stayed at Aldie, where she and Wingate continued to live during their first few years of marriage. In the daytime, she worked at the law firm of Appleby, Spurling and Kempe, bringing in the couple's only real income, of about £60 a month—something like $1,300 in today's dollars. She spent many evenings rehearsing for roles or working backstage with the Bermuda Musical and Dramatic Society. Her independence was one of the qualities that attracted Wingate to her. "We both did our own thing, which was healthy," he says. "Spending all your time together is what kills a marriage."

Wingate continued to find plenty to occupy him in Castle Harbour. "Louis Mowbray was managing the grant I was working on when I came back from school," he says, "and one of the first things I did was approach him to say, 'Nonsuch really is the only hope for the cahow. Let's lobby to make it a nature reserve based on the bird's international reputation.'"

A half dozen or so derelict buildings stood on the island, which the government had bought from a private owner in the mid-1860s to use as a quarantine station for the passengers and crews of arriving ships who might be infected with yellow fever or smallpox. The compound, built in 1868, was never used much as a hospital, though; Nonsuch was too inaccessible and outbreaks, in any case, dwindled when it was hypothesized in the 1880s that yellow fever was spread not from person to person but rather by mosquitoes, which in Bermuda were "villainous," according to one visitor. "They started using screens on windows and nets on beds," Wingate says, "and keeping the garrisons away from the marshes." A program was also begun by the government to fill in the country's wetlands, often with garbage, and to pour oil on the surface of the remaining swamps to suffocate the mosquito larvae developing in them. It did help keep the mosquitoes from breeding, but also destroyed the water for birds and other wildlife. "I read one unbelievable recommendation by some official from the British imperial government to pour in the foul black waste oil from all the Royal Navy ships that came into Dockyard," Wingate says. "No one took it seriously, thank god." Eventually, the problem was solved by the introduction of the *Gambusia* minnow, or mosquito fish, which fastidiously controls the bugs.

The compound included a sick ward and a recovery ward, two detached kitchens, a warden's cottage, a small octagonal lookout later used as a chapel, and a lilliputian mortuary in which bodies once awaited burial. There was also a cemetery that Wingate had been told contained scores of unmarked graves. Rising above them were two headstones: a white marble marker bearing the name of Knut Anderson, a Swedish ship's surgeon who had died at age thirty-one, and a dark granite obelisk for the Laidlaw brothers, sailors who were called heroes for getting their ship to port and saving its passengers before their deaths of yellow fever in 1878. Though Wingate couldn't have known it at the time, a third headstone would soon be added.

In 1928, more than two decades after the hospital was abandoned in favor of a more modern one on Coney Island, across Castle Harbour, the government had spruced up the buildings on Nonsuch enough that William Beebe could put his laboratory there. After Beebe decamped to the mainland, Arthur St. George Tucker, who had been the island's caretaker and who had skippered the boat *Gladisfen*, from which Beebe and Barton launched their spherical contraption, was asked by the Bermudian government to take on the rehabilitation of two teenage boys who had been arrested but were deemed too young to send to prison. Tucker decided he liked the duty so much that he turned the place into a reform school.

By 1948, when the school relocated to Fort Cunningham on Paget Island, almost three hundred boys had passed through it, and most of them, according to Wingate, "became good citizens." Having learned such skills as cooking, animal husbandry, sail stitching, and engine repair from Tucker and his wife, Elsie, they went back to the mainland to become farmers, fishermen, and carpenters.

When the Tuckers left, a woman in her fifties moved into the warden's cottage, catching fish and farming vegetables, her primary company the dogs, goats, rabbits, and chickens she kept. Technically, her husband was the caretaker, but as a barber in Hamilton, he only had time to come out on weekends. Wingate called her the Witch of Nonsuch. "Not in the derogatory sense," he quickly adds, "but in the old-fashioned, medieval sense of being equivalent to a shaman. She knew all the old herbal recipes and things like that."

A John Bartram for modern times, the woman had grown up on Cooper's Island and didn't hold with newfangled ideas like automobiles and air-conditioning. But age was catching up with her. "She would always say, 'I've been offal sick,'" Wingate remembers. "*Offal*, that was the way she said it."

⊹

By the time Wingate returned from school, the unoccupied buildings had been written off by the government and were close to ruin, ransacked by vandals and stripped of their fixtures, and even the cottage was in disrepair. Literally all but one of the two-thousand-plus cedars on the island were dead, making it appear from the water like a giant floating wire hairbrush. The understory had been shaved to nothing by overgrazing and, without the cover of trees to protect it, swept away by gales. Even the migratory and land birds had disappeared, heightening the sense of lifelessness. But when Wingate looked at Nonsuch, he saw another world.

"Beebe's book was my inspiration to want to live there," he says. "I had read it avidly when I was a boy, and it was about the magic of living on Nonsuch. I never dreamed the opportunity would arise." But it made perfect sense; if he were on the island full-time he'd have a

constant view of the cahows' breeding grounds, making it much easier
to safeguard and study the birds.

But it wasn't merely for convenience or to fulfill his romantic no-
tions of island life. Wingate realized it was the only way he could
protect Castle Harbour when he landed on Nonsuch one day to find
its only living cedar gone.

The U.S. Navy had requested permission from the Bermudian
government to set up a temporary communication mast on the island. "Why it had to be there I don't know," Wingate says, clearly still
inflamed by the memory. "It had to do with antisubmarine warfare.
Anyway, the government sort of casually let them do it. They erected
this mast on the south neck of Nonsuch, and it appears this live cedar
was in the way of one of the four guy wires that held it up, so they
just cut it down without any qualms. And it was the only cedar that
had survived out of the two- or three-thousand-odd trees that were
growing on the island. It was really big and really healthy, and the
only reason they cut it down was they wanted to put a stay wire for
the mast where it was growing. It was just so wanton. I was sick to
my stomach."

Wingate hadn't yet come up with the idea of restoring Nonsuch to
its precolonial state, but he knew it would make a "fantastic" nature
reserve. "Saving the last cedar was terribly important to me," he says,
"and to have it cut down, that really hurt."

He and Mowbray were getting nowhere convincing the legislature
that Nonsuch needed a proper warden, though, until they caught the
attention of Sir Julian Gascoigne, then the governor of Bermuda—a
post that was equivalent to today's premier—and an ardent, monocle-
wearing conservationist. "A classic," in Wingate's words.

"The caretaker was out there with her dogs and goats and things,"
Wingate says, "and the one dog was always killing longtails. I arranged
a picnic to go out with Gascoigne to show him the potential of the
island. I beached my little boat, leaving in the bow a big, lovely picnic
basket Government House had provided." He gave the governor a
tour of Nonsuch, mentioning that domestic animals were incompat-
ible with the idea of a nature sanctuary. "When we got back, the dog
had ripped open the picnic basket and eaten the entire dinner. This

so effectively made the point with Gascoigne that it all happened very quickly afterwards."

All thirty-six members of Colonial Parliament voted in support of the plan. "The government basically said, 'You want to live out there?'" Wingate recalls. "'You're crazy, but go ahead.'" Wingate paid no rent but also received no salary, continuing to live on grants, mostly from Frick and the New York Zoological Society, but also, for the occasional side project, from the Smithsonian and the American Museum of Natural History.

In May 1961, Nonsuch got official protection. A few months later, restoration of the buildings began. The public works department lent Wingate the use of a few laborers to help him make the main house—the former recovery ward—livable, and together they replaced broken glass, patched cracked walls, scraped peeling limestone, cleaned woodwork, and painted. The men also converted a section of the porch to a contiguous kitchen, for which Wingate dug an entire cesspit by hand in one day. He and Anita moved out there in June 1962, along with their seventeen-month-old daughter, Janet. The following month, Anita would become pregnant with the couple's second child, Karen.

There was as yet no dock at the protected north beach, so everything the young family needed—furniture, tools, books, food, clothing, and diapers; blocks of ice, since there was no refrigerator; lanterns, since there was no electricity; eighty-pound propane cylinders to fuel the stove; five-gallon cans of gas for the generator that started the pressure system to pump rainwater from the cistern to the house—had to be dragged over the beach, past the bones of cedars, through the scrub, and to the compound, three hundred yards away and uphill every step. "Island living," Wingate says of the memory, "is tough, tough, tough."

A small herd of feral goats remained on the island, whether descendents of the animals belonging to Beebe, the training school, the Witch of Nonsuch, or someone else who'd stuck them out there to graze Wingate didn't know, but he knew they wouldn't be easy to catch.

He enlisted the help of Dewey Marquardt, a friend from the Department of Agriculture and Fisheries who was missing three toes on one foot from an accident he'd had while wildcatting for oil in New Mexico. A "genuine cowboy from the American West," as Wingate calls him, Marquardt had grown up in Wisconsin and had worked as a ranch hand, a driller, a logger, and a smoke jumper before he'd met Sara Gregg, a Bermudian visiting the States, and moved to the country to marry her.

"Dewey said, 'I can lasso them,'" Wingate recalls of the goats. "He got a few of them but the rest turned out to be quite too wild for him. I had a lot of experience with guns from my specimen-collecting trips during college, and I had some double-aught buck, four big pellets in a shotgun that could shatter the head of a cow, so it was pretty humane. I hated to do it—it was awful—but I shot the rest of the goats over the course of that first winter, till there was one female left who had two kids. I felt sorry for her. I let her wean the kids and we got someone out to catch them, but she was a real survivor. She had the ability to just vanish. I hunted her for days and days and days, but after we took her kids, I think her spirit waned. It was a bit sad. One time just as I was about to take a shot, she flung herself off the cliff. I thought, Gosh, she decided to commit suicide. But I looked over the cliff and there she was."

He eventually downed the nanny and hung her horned skull in the lab—one of the former kitchens—along with some other curiosities. It remains on Nonsuch today, packed in an unlidded Styrofoam cooler on top of a file cabinet in the cottage, just one of the many moldering belongings Wingate had to leave behind when he returned to the mainland in 2003.

Wingate's first task on taking over the caretaker's position was to do a biological survey of the island. During a trip home in the summer of 1955 he had met Walwyn Hughes, who at the time was the agriculture department's plant pathologist, and Hubert Jones, then a horticulturalist with the department. Because his studies at Cornell had taught him to look beyond birds into the surrounding ecology, Wingate began to learn more about the plants of Bermuda with the two, and also started paying closer attention to endemic lizards and native bats, sketching them in his diary, keeping detailed notes on sightings, and even trying to trap a few. He was already well-versed in the natural history of Bermuda, and his fossil hunting had turned up some important finds, including, in 1960, a nearly complete flightless rail called "new to science" by University of Florida paleontologist Pierce Brodkorb. Knowledge of all these subdisciplines allowed Wingate to recognize that many of Bermuda's introduced animals and plants—including the mainland's ubiquitous whistling frogs and the poinciana, frangipani, oleander, and other ornamentals imported by the government en masse to replace the scale-spoiled cedars—had never reached Nonsuch.

A plan began to coalesce in his mind. Why hadn't he seen it before? It wasn't just the cahow that deserved to be saved, but the country's entire natural heritage—the sedge grass and buttonwoods, the night herons and skinks, the hackberries and cicadas. Nonsuch was small and isolated enough that he could keep mammalian predators at bay, yet large and topographically diverse enough that it already harbored most of Bermuda's main habitats, from sandy beach to rocky coastline to upland forest. If only he could bring it all back, it would create for the cahows not just a good habitat, but the ideal habitat—the one they had evolved in, life-sustaining and irresistible.

He would never live to see it all come together, of course. "I was really thinking to do something for the future," he says, "just hoping that the next generation would still believe in it." If the conditions were just right and he could save enough birds now, there might one day be so many of them that they would spill over onto Nonsuch and go back to the way of life they had had before man had come and despoiled everything.

Yes, he would create a holistic habitat—a living museum. It was a challenge that would take not years but decades. "Not decades, even," he says. "It took four centuries to get to where it is now. I'm thinking at least a century to bring it back to where it was." He would have to do what he could with the time he had.

✦

The various elements required to re-create a vanished ecosystem, Wingate knew, would have to fit together like a jigsaw puzzle—one whose guiding box-top picture had been torn to bits, leaving only tantalizing scraps of a corner here, some edging there. But the island's surface was far from a blank slate on which to lay the pieces.

Though the goats had eaten much of the understory, a few hardy and fast-growing plant species had survived; and with no competition, they had been marching unchecked across the island for more than a decade. Most prominent among them were the coarse St. Augustine grass, the native-compatible sage bush *Lantana involucrata*, and the spider lilies Elsie Tucker had planted along the walkways. "The lilies were all over the place by that point," Wingate recalls, "tens of thousands of them, all the way to the cemetery. And they grow in clumps, so I had to cut them down with a machete and then dig out the bulbs with a mattock. It's probably what started my back problems. That, and pull-starting the old outboards." Wingate threw the bulbs into the ocean, and to his surprise they floated to the mainland and colonized beaches all over Bermuda.

The first year, he focused on setting out rat bait around the island and culling the invading flora himself, pulling up thousands of plants by hand. By 1963, he had made a deal with Arthur Tucker's successor, Tony Muirhead, wherein about forty young men from the Paget Island training school spent two weeks on Nonsuch each of the next three summers. For them it was a change of scene and a chance to learn about nature; for Wingate it was a much-needed free workforce. "They were very disciplined boys," he says. "I got a hell of a lot of work out of them. Single-handedly working through the winter months by myself had gone very slowly."

He was able to devote significant time to culling that first winter because, though he still checked on them daily, he felt he'd done as much for the cahows as he could for the time being. He was still puzzling, though, over how the population had been able to maintain itself with every nest being taken over by longtails every breeding season for so many years. Since the early days, he'd been using mirrors mounted on poles to see round the bends in cliff-side crevices, but in many cases the tunnels curved more than once. The islets had no soil to record the footprints of entering and exiting adults, and they were so close to sea level that they were constantly sprayed clean by waves, which erased any excreta or bits of feather that might have stuck in another habitat. A year after the initial expedition, which had turned up only seven pairs of the birds, on Inner and Outer Pear, he had gone out with Paul Shepard and found evidence, in the form of guano, that two burrows on Horn Rock were occupied; in the next year or two, he came across similar proof that two more crevices, on Green Island, were being used. Beyond that, nothing.

There must be more cahows somewhere, he reckoned, but if there were, the time he spent combing the harbor islets had given him no clues to their whereabouts.

He rarely saw birds flying over the islets, despite countless hours sitting vigil on calm, moonlit nights. Then, on an overnight trip to Inner Pear in the fall of 1958, he woke in the early-morning hours in the teeth of a sixty-knot gale to find cahows darting across the still-dark sky above him. The island, along with Long Rock and Outer Pear, had been included in the ninety-nine-year lease to the American military, so Wingate was by then well known to the base commanders. With a flashlight, he Morse-coded an SOS to the watchtower. Controllers shone a bright light back to confirm they had received the communication, and Wingate returned with the message that he was all right and would wait out the gale, not mentioning he had no food and little water left. He ended up being marooned for two more nights, but he was so excited he barely noticed his self-imposed discomfort. Cahows, he now knew, were most active on the stormiest nights, when the wind could carry them in effortlessly from their fishing grounds hundreds of miles away.

It was that insight that allowed him to find the remainder of the burrows on a night in February 1960, on which he would not otherwise have been out—he recalls it as being "wild" with high winds and rain. He was heading toward St. David's from Inner Pear when he passed Long Rock, which he'd searched thoroughly during his six-week residency in the harbor two years earlier, but this night he saw

birds over the island. When he returned the following day to investigate further, he identified signs of occupation in seven more burrows. He hadn't seen it before because he'd been there in March and
April—but February is one of the most active months, with subadults
returning for nights of aerial courtship and adults incubating their
eggs. "It's really just a matter of refining your searching skills," he says.
"When we found these birds in 1951, we really had no idea about their
lives, or about the timing of anything."

It had taken almost a decade, but he finally had an accurate notion of how many adult pairs there really were. "At that point there
were about twenty-one visited nest sites," he says, "but in terms of
established pairs, two adults and an egg, there were eighteen of those.
Prospecting birds might visit a site for a couple of years and not settle
there. In some cases they might lay the first year they become a pair,
but it's usually two or three years before they can produce a chick."

More important than giving him a head count, though, the burrows
on Long Rock seemed to be safe from tropicbirds, solving the riddle
of how the cahows had held on for so many years. Wingate baffled the
crevices anyway, and that year, for the first time, was able to record a
significant decline in chick mortality. Between 1958 and 1960, he had
seen only about two chicks a year survive to fledge, despite the bafflers;
but in 1961, with every nest protected, that number doubled, and from
then on no more chicks were lost to longtail predation. By 1962, the
year he moved to Nonsuch, an astonishing eight juveniles flew out to
sea. "At last I was rewarded with the privilege of seeing new cahows
created before my eyes," he wrote in *Canadian Audubon* magazine.

With breeding success increasing, he wanted to be sure any young
birds that might return to Bermuda had a place to nest. In 1954, Mowbray and Thorsell had come up with the idea of aiding in the bur-
row-building and had carved a few holes into the hardened sand on
the cliffs of Inner Pear. Their location and relative shallowness made
them in the end better suited for longtails, but the very first year they
were in place, a new cahow pair colonized one of them. "That was
when I realized that one of the limiting factors for population growth
was the lack of burrows," says Wingate. "We thought we were dealing

with the last few birds and that burrows weren't the limiting factor, but burrows of the right depth, size, and features were. The moment Mowbray dug more of them, there were birds out there ready to colonize them."

Longtails and cahows were not natural enemies—they had peacefully shared Bermuda for millennia before human beings had crowded them onto such thin slices of habitat that competition became inevitable. Seeing how quickly the new nests had been colonized told Wingate he needed to re-create the niche separation the two species had once enjoyed. It was during his six-week stay on Inner Pear that it dawned on him the position of the artificial nests was crucial. "It was such a beautiful breakthrough," he says. "It was so much safer and easier to build them on level ground, and I realized that's where the cahows would prefer to nest anyway. There just wasn't enough soil on top of the islets for them to dig where they wanted to." Using a mattock, Wingate would punch a hole into the island's surface—there's often sand underneath a thin limestone crust—and lengthen it to form a trench about six feet long. He'd then make a roof for the trench by molding concrete over wire mesh or wadded-up newspaper, creating a tunnel that mimicked the design of a natural cahow burrow's longtail-discouraging entrance. "The final touch was to create a viewing hole over the nest chamber with a removable concrete lid," he notes. Eventually he also began bringing grass over from the mainland and placing it in front of the burrows. "On the most barren islets like Green," he says, "the birds were unable to find enough vegetation to make satisfactory nests and were using hard items like stone or coarse bits of deadwood that were inadequate to protect the egg from breakage. It occurred to me that providing grass at the burrow entrances would not only solve this problem but also provide better insulation and warmth retention in the nests."

He dug one artificial burrow on each of the colonized islands, and also had a wooden one near the back door of the house on Nonsuch for young birds that wouldn't make it without intervention. He built it for a particular chick that had come out of its burrow on Horn Rock one night to exercise, but did so a little too vigorously and tumbled twenty-five feet down the cliff face. All night the chick struggled to return to its burrow, eventually reaching a height of ten or twelve feet before again plummeting seaward. "I thought, Well, it's only going to do that again," Wingate says. "It was very windy at the time and the burrow was right near the cliff." He waited till dawn, then went around the island in his boat to collect the chick. It spent the next day sleeping in a dresser drawer in his and Anita's bedroom while he made the box for it, with a hole on one side and a removable lid.

For the next few nights the chick emerged from the nest and exercised uncertainly, perhaps afraid of repeating its spectacular plunge. Finally Wingate got tired of waiting and picked the bird up. He held it aloft in one hand, which he slowly pumped up and down a few times before suddenly letting it drop. When the bird found itself hanging in midair, Wile E. Coyote style, it shot up a hundred feet and headed out to sea. "I was relieved to see it actually get clear of the island," Wingate says. "I would have had a hell of a time trying to find it in the thickets if it hadn't."

The longtail population had been decreasing on Bermuda since the 1950s, primarily due to feral dogs that roamed the island at the time and development that had destroyed nest sites, so Wingate also dug a few longtail burrows, including one on Nonsuch. One Easter he made a kite in the shape of a longtail—Bermudians commemorate Good Friday by flying kites, often homemade—and played it out along a shoreline hillside to see whether the birds would notice. "Nothing happened until it crashed over the cliff edge and began swinging back and forth against the cliff face," he wrote in the October 1978 monthly bulletin of the Department of Ag and Fish. "The effect on the longtails was immediate and dramatic. From far and wide they all converged on that point and began landing on the cliff beside the kite." Wingate later used this ploy to decoy longtails to nest in parts of the mainland they didn't usually colonize.

So the Castle Harbour bird populations were settled for the time being, and the Wingates, too, were getting more ensconced as Karen's March 1963 birth approached. "One night very close to the time," he remembers, "we had a big gale that marooned us for at least twenty-four hours if not more. I remember telling Anita, 'God, I hope that baby doesn't come tonight, because there's no way I can get you ashore.'" As soon as the weather moderated, the family departed for Aldie. Anita gave birth two days later. "When we came back, Karen was just a little bundle a few days old. And again there was a gale that struck when we were almost across the harbor. We couldn't get to the dock, so we had to wade ashore with her and Janet at the north beach." Ferrying a toddler and a tiny infant across the tumultuous sea in his "cockleshell" of a boat didn't seem to give Wingate pause.

"The incredible thing about youth is you have the attitude you're immortal," he says. "And on Nonsuch, the house is so big and the view is so beautiful that once you're on the island you might as well be in paradise, even in a gale. We were supremely self-confident that all would be well, as long as we could get back to the island. We loved it, loved the excitement. It was always in the back of my mind that if something went wrong the children could die, but we were always on our p's and q's, always anticipating and never taking chances."

Nothing could touch them in their magical land, but getting on and off the island was another matter. Traveling in his puny bow rider meant being drenched with salt spray, and when Anita was working, Wingate would have to make extra trips across to fetch her at given times. "It was a bit awkward," he says, "because we didn't have a phone, so it all had to be arranged beforehand. Oftentimes things would change and I'd go over in vain, battling over in a gale or something. And sometimes the weather was too bad to take her back, so I'd basically have to go over just to say, 'Sorry, I can't pick you up,' and she'd spend the night at Aldie."

It was equally frustrating for Anita. "Mummy'd get cross with him for being late," recalls Janet Wingate, now a textile artist living in the Czech Republic. "He's just one of those people who's never on time, and in those days there were no mobile phones. They'd agree to meet at the dock to go out to Nonsuch at x time, and he'd invariably be late. And the boats were always breaking down, because he was using them in such rough weather. It was a bit trying, I think."

There were several times the family was marooned for so long in bad weather that they almost ran out of food. "We were too ambitious," Wingate says of that year. "We thought we could live out there year-round, and we stuck it out, but it was grim. We were cut off for such long periods."

On their fourth wedding anniversary, two months before Karen's birth, the couple had planned to leave Janet at Aldie and go celebrate with friends on the mainland, but a gale hit so quickly that Wingate wasn't even able to get his boat beached in time. "It came on like a wall of wind," he remembers. "I couldn't risk getting in the boat to bring it around to the island's lee, where I could beach it. I just watched it smash to pieces on the cliff." Finally, three days after the storm hit, the seas had calmed enough that he was able to swim the quarter-mile to Cooper's Point. He walked into the restricted U.S. base until he encountered a patrol officer who gave him a lift to the Bio Station, where he kept a spare boat. He put in at St. George's for supplies and a phone call to his parents before returning to Nonsuch.

He was lucky that time. A few years earlier, knowing where the military dredges dumped their discarded treasures from the sea floor, he had taken a girlfriend to look for shells near the base. "Suddenly this marine came over with a gun, saying, 'You're not supposed to land here,'" he recalls. "We argued a little bit, gently, but agreed to leave. Then she turned to him and said, 'What would you have done if we'd refused to leave?' This marine had a southern accent and he said, 'Shoot ya.' I don't know if he had a smile on his face when he said it."

✦

By 1963, the Wingates had decided they needed to spend winters on the mainland. Anita got a part-time secretarial job at the Bio Station, and they rented one of the cottages used in the summers by visiting scientists. Wingate quickly made an impression on the community. "I was often greeted by our neighbor on her way to work," he wrote in an article on frigate-bird migration for a 2006 issue of the Bermuda Zoological Society newsletter. On the morning he saw his first frigate bird in Bermuda, he'd stepped outside just as the neighbor was passing by. "Good morning, David," she said. But Wingate, as usual, was distractedly scanning the sky. "Frigate!" he cried, rushing back into the house for his binoculars.

"It was the talk of the party that evening at the station," he says. "I could detect tension in the air, people glancing in my direction. Only when I realized what had happened and explained, with Anita's help—she was very bubbly and everyone loved her—did it become a big joke. All that day this person had brooded over it and complained about it. I had totally forgotten she was walking by in my excitement at seeing the bird."

He also created a stir in the birding world that year, when he took his second trip to the Caribbean in search of the black-capped petrel, a close relative to the cahow and a bird with a similar history, except that it disappeared around 1879, outside of a few sightings in the 1920s and '30s. By 1941, the introduction of the mongoose into Haiti—one of two main breeding islands, the other being Dominica—was believed to have spelled the end of the black-capped petrel, or at least of any significant colonies of the birds. Many scientists were convinced the rare sightings of previous decades had been of relict individuals.

But Wingate rationalized that if the cahow could hang on for 330 years with no one knowing about it, the similarly evasive black-capped petrel, too, might still survive—particularly in light of the stories of locals, who spoke of a ducklike nocturnal bird that visited Hispaniola in winter. All previous searches for the birds had been done in the daytime; Wingate's approach would be to get as close as he could to the sheer cliffs of La Selle Ridge in Haiti and of Trois Pitons and Morne Diablotin—a peak named after the "little devil" itself—in Dominica, the two most likely final breeding colonies, and try to zero in by listening for the bird's weird cries.

On his first trip, in the fall of 1961, he'd found no live birds. He and a Bermudian friend had trekked through the Dominican rain forest at the height of the wet season with no luck, and in Haiti, political fallout from the assassination of Dominican Republic dictator Rafael Trujillo that spring had prevented Wingate—his friend had returned to Bermuda—from ascending the mountain. He'd hired some porters and was merrily snapping pre-expedition photographs in Furcy, a town at the foot of La Selle Ridge, when the police approached and arrested him. They interrogated him for two full days and then, finally satisfied that he was not a spy, released him to catch the next flight out.

Before his arrest, he'd scoured Port-au-Prince with the help of an English-speaking cabdriver he'd employed full-time, and in two days had located four stuffed specimens, in places as diverse as a convent school and a waterfront bordello. "The madame was a plump lady," he recalls, "and her hobby was collecting birds. She had a huge bouncer who guarded the money box. I had to step up on the table over the money box to reach the specimen, and you could see the guy bristling. She offered me her best girl, but I turned that one down."

All of the specimens had been collected since 1951 by people who'd had no idea what they were, and all were in the city of Port-au-Prince. "These birds are attracted by bright lights," Wingate says, "but with a single light source they get confused. That's why moths spiral into lamps at night. They try to navigate by it but keep the light on their left, say, and end up in going in a circle. And fledglings are completely naïve."

On his second trip to Haiti, in the winter of 1963—after the cahows had laid their eggs but well before the critical hatching period—he found likely breeding spots by consulting a U.S. Army geodetic survey, then arranged through the British consul, who was a birder, to reconnoiter the mountains in a helicopter belonging to the U.S. marine base on the island. He paid an interpreter $10 a day, a fortune in Haiti at that time, and traveled through some desperately poor areas whose inhabitants had never seen a white man. Then, after a couple of unsuccessful night watches, he got three thousand feet up the cliff face and developed a splitting headache. "I had to collapse," he says. "But it turned out we were right where we wanted to be. We made camp there, and an hour later we heard the first petrel. When it came over the ridge it sounded like a jet plane at high speed. A half hour later, they started calling, almost precisely the same as the cahows."

Wingate identified nearly a dozen colonies on the trip, but was unable to reach any of them, as they were on sheer cliffs thousands of feet high. He was assured by the locals it was impossible to get to the nests and was initially concerned that his sightings would be disregarded for lack of a specimen, until the island's people told him of how they caught the birds for food. "It involves lighting a moderate fire on the cliff top above a colony on moonless nights when heavy fog shrouds the mountains," he later wrote in the *Auk*. "Birds flying near the fire in these conditions become disoriented and crash either directly into the fire or onto vegetation nearby." Wingate tried the method and obtained proof that he had found the birds, as well as, since one of them was too burned to use as a specimen, dinner for the night.

Finding nesting petrels in Haiti was a feather in Wingate's cap, so to speak, but being near so many of the birds together in one place only served to remind him of his primary goal. "Seeing the big colonies up in the mountains was very inspiring to me," he says. "It made me think, This is what I'm working towards. One day it'll be like this on Nonsuch."

He had by now culled enough invaders on the island that he was ready to begin introducing native and endemic flora. Except for a few dead trees he'd harvested for wood, he'd left the cedars' skeletons where they stood as a scaffold for new growth, sometimes clearing away one or two at a time over the next two decades as they were felled by wind or rot. As Bermuda's ecosystem had evolved over the past few hundred thousand years, cedars had become its foundation. "It's a pioneer species," Wingate explains. "In the precolonial forest, if you had a hurricane or forest fire and were starting off with a clean slate, the first thing that would happen is the birds would distribute the cedar berries, and they'd thrive because they'd have no competition." Cedars grow fast, usually reaching maturity within twenty-five years, and they are crucial as a windbreak, since, unlike most other trees, their roots penetrate deep into the limestone bedrock. Without the cedars, the rest of the native flora has little chance against the hurricanes, tropical storms, and even everyday high winds that are a fact of life in Bermuda.

Unfortunately, in the early '70s, the cedars still were not viable; Wingate knew it was pointless to do a mass-planting because he had been trying with thirty or forty ankle-high seedlings every year, and every year the scale got them and they died. So he began instead with endemic palmettos and native olivewoods—the only appropriate trees that were available, since the government nursery was filled with ornamentals. He'd bring over twenty or thirty at a time in gallon cans. An old photograph shows him standing in shorts and a white T-shirt in the stern of a twelve-foot pram with a miniature forest sprouting from its deck, the boat sitting low in the water from the weight.

He planted about a thousand trees that first year, digging the holes himself, ferrying each batch over from the mainland after carefully dipping the pots in a fast-acting pesticide and checking the plants for whistling frogs first, schlepping them up from the boat, and taking care to place them in a way he thought might mimic their natural positions in the ecosystem. And after the first winter gale hit, he stepped out of the house to find half of them flattened and apparently dead. It wasn't until the following spring that he learned the seedlings had simply been burned back by the salt spray. "Most of them ultimately survived," he says, "but it was a depressingly slow start. Every winter things would just be burned away, and every year it was a bitter setback, but the following spring it would resprout. I just simply realized it was going to take a lot longer at that point, and became resigned to the idea that I might never see significant results."

CHAPTER SIX

A Discouraging Decade

ANCIENT BIRDS, WITH THEIR fragile, hollow bones, did not fossilize particularly well, and seabirds, especially, left few traces of their existence, for the obvious reason that they spent little time ashore and the coastlines and islands where they once nested more often than not eroded away. But as far as anyone can tell, *Procellariiformes* is an order that goes back, more or less as it is today, 23 million to 34 million years, to the Oligocene epoch. It contains the families *Diomedeidae* (albatrosses), *Hydrobatidae* (storm petrels), *Pelecanoididae* (diving petrels), and *Procellariidae* (petrels and shearwaters), and exhibits the largest size range of any avian order, with wingspans from twelve inches, for the least storm petrel, to twelve feet, for the wandering albatross, which holds the record for the longest span of any living bird.

The volcanoes that eventually gave rise to Bermuda also date back to the Oligocene. It's not known exactly when the islands first made their appearance above the water's surface; the Walsingham formation is at least 800,000 years old, but periodically rising sea levels meant the flora and fauna that existed there then can't necessarily be found there today. Though present-day Bermuda has a total landmass of 21 square miles, the archipelago has at some point in its history been as large as 250 square miles—during the last glacial period, 12,000 to 110,000 years ago, sea levels were 400 feet lower than they are today—and as small as just a couple of hundred acres. The greatest inundation occurred about 400,000 years ago, and left only bits of higher-elevation landmass exposed.

"Sea levels were twenty meters, or about seventy feet, higher than at present," says Storrs Olson, curator emeritus of the vertebrate zoology department's division of birds at the Smithsonian Institution. "We know it didn't completely cover the island because we've got skink and land-snail fossils from that period, and both are still alive today." Wingate was the one who first came across these remains. He'd been systematically exploring caves all over the country when he stumbled onto a marine deposit—a fossilized beach—on a cliff at Government Quarry, along the southwestern edge of Castle Harbour.

He contacted Olson who, with Paul Hearty, then director of conservation at Bald Head Island Conservancy in North Carolina, examined the fossils and substantiated evidence of mollusks and other aquatic creatures beside several bird species that no longer breed in Bermuda, including a crane, a duck, a couple of flightless rails, and the short-tailed albatross, which is now limited to a few islands in the northern Pacific. Cahows, Olson says, were everywhere: "They're the commonest thing you find in any Bermudian fossil deposit."

Because petrels are such an old family and the marine environment hasn't changed, the birds "have had all that time to master—to perfect—the ability to fly over the ocean and exploit its food," says Wingate. "I'm constantly marveling at their amazing adaptations."

Juvenile cahows fly almost continuously for the first two to five years of their lives before returning to Bermuda to mate. They might stop to bob along on the water occasionally, particularly when they hit a calm, but they risk being eaten by sharks and other large fish when they do. No studies have yet been made of birds flying with electrodes attached to their heads, though scientists at the Max Planck Institute for Ornithology in Seewiesen, Germany, are working on it. They believe cahows and other *Procellariiformes* can fall into slow-wave sleep while flying, turning off one hemisphere of their brain and closing one eye at a time to do so. "Bihemispheric SWS may also be possible during flight when constant visual monitoring of the environment is unnecessary," writes the institute's Niels Rattenborg in the journal *Naturwissenschaften*. According to the paper, it is unlikely that deeper REM sleep occurs in flight, since it is accompanied by lowered muscle tone, but Rattenborg is unsure about the sleep patterns of nearly constant flyers like the cahow and, for example, the sooty tern—

coincidentally also called the wideawake bird, for its cry. "Perhaps they have a way to either get deeper sleep in flight or to do without it," he writes in an e-mail. "At this point anything is possible."

Most birds have highly developed pectoral muscles—they're what makes a chicken's breast the meatiest part—but it's likely that cahows have an additional adaptation that allows them to keep their wings outstretched almost endlessly. A 2005 study published in the *Journal of Morphology* looked at the musculoskeletal structure of black-footed and Laysan albatrosses, called "the elite of avian gliders" by authors Ron Meyers and Eric Stakebake, and very similar morphologically to cahows. The researchers concluded that each of an albatross's shoulders contains a tendinous sheet that extends through the entire pectoralis muscle to act as a brace that locks the wing in place. "This fascial 'strut,'" they write, "passively maintains horizontal wing orientation during gliding and soaring flight." They also found that many albatross muscles contain slow-twitch fibers, which are "specialized for sustained contraction with high fatigue resistance."

Since 2009, Jeremy Madeiros has been tagging some cahows with data loggers to learn more about their lives at sea. About a third of the birds seem to be homebodies, never straying more than a thousand miles from Bermuda, at least in a given year. But Madeiros has recorded others flying as much as five hundred miles a day over a range of millions of square miles. The minimum flight distance recorded over the course of a year is 36,000 miles and the maximum, 82,000. Averaged, that's the equivalent, over the bird's forty-year lifespan, of flying to the moon and back five times. "It's the same kind of distances the albatrosses are doing," Madeiros was quoted as saying in the *Royal Gazette*, "and these birds are a quarter of the size."

Cahows have low wing loading, which basically means they weigh very little—just over a half pound—and very large wings, with a span that can reach almost thirty-six inches, or twice the length of their bodies. "There are different strategies for being efficient in flight," says Bret Tobalske, director of the University of Montana Flight Lab, "but if you're going to be up in the air a lot, the best design is to have a long, thin wing, like *Procellariiformes* do. They force the bird to fly really fast. Broader wings suit a bird to fly more slowly." Land birds, he adds, tend to have broader wings in part because they must avoid more obstructions.

Extremely acrobatic fliers, cahows dip and rise among the waves and often frolic as close to the water as possible, taking full advantage of two aerodynamic principles that let them use the wind's power, rather than their own, to propel themselves forward.

The ground effect allows a bird to hover over the surface of a wave. "The air they're pushing down with their wings is smacking into the water's surface and bouncing back up at them," Tobalske says. "In terms of the amount of force the bird has to generate, it's cheaper to fly by ground effect because it reduces their drag."

Dynamic soaring is a little more complicated. "Petrels are just remarkably adept at sensing differences in pressure," he says. "You have a sense of when the wind is blowing on your skin, but they make their living at it." As wind moves across the huge open space of the ocean, it creates what's known as a boundary layer, in which the air moves slowest when it's closest to the water's surface and picks up speed the higher it goes. "By just tipping upward slightly into the boundary layer," Tobalske explains, "the bird continues to climb. It just keeps going up and up and up. Once it gains a bit of altitude it turns around, which rapidly blows it downwind, into the lee of a wave. It can then move sidestream very quickly and start all over again."

In the stormy weather cahows prefer, the boundary layer may be more permeable in some spots. "You have to be really finely tuned to find the best side of each wave—both ocean waves and airwaves," says Tobalske. "*Procellariiformes* are masters at dynamic soaring. They're incredibly sensitive to their environment. It's just mind-boggling to think of how to maneuver in this very turbulent air pattern and capitalize on it. It's basically like hopping from one wave of air to the next. If you hop at just the right time, you can bounce around on the updrafts. Petrels are phenomenal at what they do."

Over land, cahows are fluttery and almost batlike, since they lack the uplift from the swells. Staying near the water's surface also allows the birds to snatch the squid and small fish that get caught in upwellings; their curved beaks and serrated palates make it easier for them to hang onto the slippery creatures while soaring back upward. Madeiros's data loggers have shown some diving activity, but, unlike those of certain shearwaters, which can go down as far as a couple of hundred feet, cahow dives are shallow and infrequent. Researchers working with other gadfly petrel species have found that they tend to be surface gleaners, says Madeiros, waiting until night falls and bioluminescent prey appear within skimming distance.

Cahows' flight is most dazzling when they are courting, as the birds Chris Burville photographed were. Courtship flights begin, like they did that day, in the late afternoon as the birds cavort off Bermuda's shores while waiting for darkness to fall, but they continue through even the blackest skies. While it's clear that cahows must have extraordinary night vision, it is also probable they can track one another's display flights through sound and changes in air current. "We also think they must have echolocation ability," Wingate says. "Maybe that's part of the reason for their calls. In Haiti the black-capped petrels would be flying in the dense cloud fog of the mountaintops. It was like pea soup out there. You'd hear them fluttering over and wonder how they could see at all."

Cahows seem to have evolved to be nocturnal partly in response to the many diurnal birds that once populated Bermuda's shores, notably a *Buteo* hawk whose bones were plentiful enough in the Government Quarry deposit that it had to have bred on the island.

"Nocturnality gives birds an edge simply because it's harder for other birds to see them," Wingate says. "Being nocturnal was a huge benefit on islands with no mammals. Another possibility is that on seabird islands, where the number of birds is so vast, segregating by day and night might mean all the birds won't be crowding the airways at once, making it difficult to come and go." Cahows are relatively safe at sea despite daytime predators like skua and frigate birds because even a huge population of them would have been widely dispersed over hundreds of thousands of miles of ocean. "And they're so agile and fast that a skua would take one look at them and say, 'Oh, it's hopeless. I'd never catch that bird,'" Wingate says.

Adult cahows are also completely silent. Like an old married couple who barely exchange a word while polishing off their blue-plate specials, paired birds, it would seem, have said all they need to say. "Once they're together," according to Wingate, "it all happens inside the burrow. They have incredibly strong pair-bonds. With a newly established pair, every time you lift the lid off the nest you find them *in flagrante*. After they've been together for about ten years, you find them asleep. Their world and ours are so different when they're at sea, but the interesting part is on land their world and ours are, in some ways, closely paralleled." Coupled cahows are remarkably faithful to each other, usually staying together until the death of one partner compels the remaining bird to seek a new mate. "When a female fails to return," says Madeiros, "the male waits and waits the first year, then the next year he tries to attract a new mate."

It's hard, in the pitch dark of a night watch, to tell exactly how many subadults are in the air, but sometimes there are what to Wingate, who remembers when there were only seven known pairs of the birds, seem like "droves" of them zipping back and forth over the islets. Occasionally one shoots past the boat and disappears back into the darkness in a flash. Anchored just off Horn, say, Wingate can sit nearly immobile for thirty or forty minutes simply waiting, his binoculars fixed on the island as he compensates almost instinctively for the jumping motion of the waves. The vigil would seem lonely if not for the payoff: He's been able to make out as many as six birds flying together, calling to one another with three distinct cries—*aaaaweek, aaaaw-eek*; *ooooh-eek, ooooh-eek*; and the ecstatic *cueet, cueet, cueet* Wingate calls the puppy whine. "You know the sound when you step on a puppy's tail?"

Other times he feels lucky to see a single pair. "We still don't know all the parameters that make a good courting night," he says.

Courtship season begins in November, when established adult pairs return to Bermuda to mate. It's unclear exactly how they find their way back to their little speck of land in the vast, featureless ocean, but many factors may come into play. Since cahows leave Bermuda at night, it's unlikely that visual clues to the terrain are terribly important; the birds do seem to fix their position by the stars during the exercise period before fledging, but this wouldn't fully explain their incredible homing ability, especially considering their preference for cloudy nights. It has been known for more than a century that many bird species—including, most famously, homing pigeons—navigate using the earth's magnetic fields, but the question has always been how. Recent research suggests some birds may actually be able to "see" these fields, processing them with the same area of the brain that handles vision, while other studies have shown that certain species have iron-rich magnetite crystals in their beaks that act as built-in compasses. It has also been proposed that some birds imprint on the low-frequency sound waves of the Earth that are particular to their home locations, and that *Procellariiformes* in particular might use their highly refined sense of smell to identify geochemical cues in the water—a process that may be made easier for cahows by Bermuda's location at the western edge of the Sargasso Sea. It is likely that these factors work together, along with an element of learning from one's elders.

"Subadults need the stimulation of seeing adult birds come and go before they'll fly into the harbor," Wingate says. "The way seabirds operate, they usually respond if there are already birds nesting on an island; that means it's safe for them, too. If there are no other birds, they avoid the island. It's called social facilitation." About seven in ten returning juveniles find their lifelong home within yards of the burrow they fledged from; the remaining 30 percent are seduced away by mates from nearby islets.

The initial courtship phase lasts until early December, when subadults follow the adults as they return to sea during their prelaying exodus; having mated, pairs fly off for six weeks as the egg develops. It's not known whether they stay together during the exodus, and Wingate and Madeiros have differing opinions on the question.

While Madeiros believes it's rare for cahows, whether paired or not, to encounter one another in the open water, Wingate points out that on his frequent deep-sea expeditions with the Bermuda Institute of Ocean Sciences—formerly the Biological Station—he most often sees birds flying in pairs. "Two is more common than any other number," he says. "I've seen it in longtails, terns, shearwaters. But we're not sure about cahows because they haven't been tagged as pairs yet."

Either way, the offshore wooing resumes when the juveniles trail the adults back to Bermuda shortly after the established females prepare to lay in January, and continues through the incubation period and the parents' visits to feed the growing chick.

In its first year back in Bermuda, a subadult might not even land. It's the male that finds a burrow—or, in the past, built one—before trying to attract a female and lure her in, and nest prospecting is a more arduous task than one might think. Because he's philopatric, or loyal to his birth site, a young male will often return to the burrow from which he fledged only to find himself kicked to the curb when he realizes his parents still live there. He might then attempt another burrow and get shooed away from it by someone else's parents. Even when he locates a promising site, he'll sometimes visit for a year or two first; then, says Madeiros, "it's up to the female. If he manages to attract her to come to ground, she'll go and inspect the nest, and if she likes what she finds, they'll do more aerial courtship before settling in."

It can take anywhere from a year to "almost indefinite," Madeiros says, for the male to find a mate. "Some seem to go through a whole pile of different women, and never settle down for more than a year with any one," he says. "Maybe it's because they have disgusting table manners or something, I don't know." In nature, the male will find a burrow location and perhaps what Madeiros calls "a starter burrow," but won't necessarily have dug the female's dream home by the time she moves in. "Even in these artificial burrows," Madeiros says, "if it's not deep enough to satisfy both of them, they'll find a seam of soil between the concrete and the bedrock, and dig underneath it and make a mess of what you've built for them. They seem to have an innate urge to dig."

Persuading an interested female to alight might be the biggest challenge an eager male will face. "Even the adult birds coming in to feed a chick will fly over time after time, buzzing the island until they pluck up the courage to land," Wingate says. "They might do ten or fifteen miles just in the process of homing in on the burrow."

It's a tricky and dangerous operation, especially on a barren island with no soil, and no matter how many times they've done it, the birds always look like they're crash-landing. With each pass, they fly slower and slower, until on their final try they suddenly flutter to a stop, fold their wings, and drop down. The first time must be the hardest for a bird that has spent the past forty-eight months with nothing but air and water beneath it. "You can stretch out your arms and flap them up and down," Tobalske says, "but imagine how much more challenging that would be if you were holding two long poles. That's what the petrel is stuck with. Their wings are perfectly designed for gliding, but not for the slow, flapping flight they need to land."

When a male finally does close the deal with a willing mate, he'll often find himself sitting on an inviable egg for the first season before a chick finally hatches. "Just inexperience, I guess," Wingate says.

✦

Since cahow mating takes place in the darkened nest chamber, it's hard to say exactly what goes on before the act itself, but the "mutual satisfaction or affection" Murphy and Mowbray discussed in their 1951 paper suggests that courtship rituals—the bird version of foreplay—cement a pair's relationship before they get down to business. Albatrosses take *Procellariiformes* mating dances to their most entertaining extreme, strutting about in unison, bobbing their heads at each other, coyly looking away, and "fencing" with their bills for long stretches. Some of this kind of bonding behavior is seen in the synchronized chasing flights of subadult cahows and in the preening, cuddling, billing, and circling Murphy and Mowbray witnessed inside the burrow.

In general, the weight of bird species' eggs corresponds with the length of time the eggs take to hatch, except in the case of *Procellariiformes*, which have longer incubation periods than their egg size would suggest they should, perhaps in part because they evolved in the absence of predators. Cahow eggs take almost two months to develop—about the same as an emu's and nearly four times as long as the similar-sized pigeon's. Because of this long incubation period, the chicks are "semi-precocial," or relatively mature, when they hatch; their eyes are open, they have thick gray down, and they can walk, but they cannot find their own food, as a fully precocial bird like a duckling can. Most ground nesters are precocial or semi-precocial, having evolved that way so that hatchlings would have some chance of escaping predators; Wingate speculates that for cahows, intraspecific competition may have played a role. "The chicks would have needed to ward off other cahows that tried to invade the burrow," he says. "That would happen a lot in a big population where there's a shortage of burrows and always someone looking for a new one. When you thrust your hand in the nest, a cahow baby will peck at you. There's an element of surprise when something pecks at you in a dark burrow."

Each pair of the birds lays only one egg a season, in part because laying is such an enormous drain on the female. Imagine if women gave birth to thirty- or forty-pound babies—by the time the female cahow lays, the egg is a quarter of her body weight. "She lays it," Wingate says, "and the very next night the male comes in and takes over the first eight- to twelve-day incubation stint so she can go off to sea and recover. They're very well-synchronized." He learned this by color-marking a pair of birds with paint in the early 1960s and monitoring their comings and goings for fifty-one nights in a row.

After about fifty-three days, half of the eggs hatch, and the cost of feeding the chicks—they eat as much as a quarter of their body weight every three or four days—is also high; Madeiros's data loggers have tracked cahows traveling as much as ten thousand miles before they return with a single meal for their hatchlings. "They are foraging all the way up to the edge of the pack ice in the St. Lawrence," he is quoted as saying in the *Royal Gazette*. "That's why we think the food for the chicks when they first hatch is krill, from places with very cold water temperatures. It is a speciality for them, right after they hatch, and then they switch to squid and fish."

Until the baby fledges, males and females take one- to two-week turns incubating the egg, and afterward, they continue to alternate feeding trips, following storms to Canada for krill and to the Azores for spawning shrimp.

By the early 1960s, Wingate was seeing an average fledge rate of 44 percent—triple what it had been in the early 1950s. In 1961 he felt especially hopeful; it was the first breeding season after he'd discovered all eighteen nests, and a record twelve chicks left the islands. The success rate remained stagnant for a few years, with seventeen or eighteen pairs producing seven or eight chicks, but he expected the population would grow rather quickly once it got beyond this plateau, even taking into account the fledglings that would be lost in their first year or so of life—a number he now knows to have been 60 percent or more.

In 1966, exactly four years after the first batch of chicks he'd saved from longtails had hatched, he was thrilled to see that there were now twenty-one pairs of birds, all of which had produced eggs. But when hatching time came, only six of the chicks pipped, giving Wingate a mere 28.6 percent survival rate. "It was really puzzling," he says, "and I remember feeling very discouraged. I couldn't understand what was happening. The more birds I got, the fewer chicks I seemed to have." He considered the possibilities that established pairs were becoming too old to bear healthy offspring and that inbreeding due to the population bottleneck of the past few decades meant fewer chicks were fit enough to survive. He worried they might have reached, literally, the end of the line. That fear became even more acute when he figured out what was actually causing the chick mortality—and realized it was completely out of his hands.

Dichlorodiphenyltrichloroethane, or DDT, is a white crystalline powder that is practically odorless and all but insoluble in water. It was first synthesized, from chlorine, alcohol, and sulfuric acid, by a German chemistry student in 1874. No practical use for it was found until 1939, when the Swiss chemist Paul Hermann Müller, testing a variety of substances in search of one that would kill clothes moths, discovered it was lethal to insects and long-lasting; so long-lasting, in fact, that even after he'd cleaned the container he used for his experiments, the bugs he put inside continued to die. Cheap, easily mass-produced, and not apparently dangerous to humans or domestic animals, the chemical was adopted almost immediately and with unreserved enthusiasm by Europe and the United States, initially to protect allied troops against insect-borne malaria and typhus.

After the war, DDT was sprayed over crops and dusted on livestock by the agriculture industry and showered on pets, floorboards, and furniture by homeowners to control household pests. You could cover your children's rooms in wallpaper impregnated with the stuff, and cotton and jute flour sacks were coated in it before being used to store food. In one 1946 magazine ad for a brand called Knox-Out, a smiling dog, apple, housewife, cow, potato, and chicken form a chorus line and belt out "DDT is good for me-e-e!"; another ad from around the same time shows cockroaches with the faces of Hitler, Mussolini, and Stalin being slammed by a cannon blast of the stuff. Kill a bedbug—defeat fascism!

DDT did a fabulous job of arresting morbidity from insect-borne pathogens, basically eradicating malaria from North America and Europe and decreasing cases of the disease from 75 million to about 50,000 in India and from almost 3 million to double-digit numbers in Sri Lanka. But many insects, including mosquitoes, quickly developed resistance to DDT, and it wasn't long before questions were being raised about the chemical's safety. The beginning of the end of DDT's reign is often said to have been the release of conservationist Rachel Carson's best-selling *Silent Spring*, which detailed the insecticide's devastating effects on nature, particularly birds, and introduced the citizens of the United States to environmentalism. Carson pitched the story to *Reader's Digest* in 1945, but it wasn't until 1962 that her book was released.

Among the studies to reveal the curse of the "miracle chemical" were those done on the Michigan State University campus and in surrounding East Lansing beginning in the late 1950s. They showed that high levels of the compound were building up in earthworms in the vicinity of trees that were being sprayed to control the beetles that carried Dutch elm disease. The earthworms were then eaten by robins, which were dying in significant numbers. The Michigan research was followed by many other papers, including one in 1967 by D.A. Ratcliffe of the British Nature Conservancy that documented thinning eggshells and increased chick mortality in birds of prey since 1950.

It's now known that the problem wasn't so much DDT itself, but metabolites of the insecticide called DDD and particularly DDE, which persist in the environment and accumulate in the insects and animals eaten by carnivorous birds. These metabolites cause calcium deficiencies, leading to thinner eggs, and disrupt the birds' hormones. Not all birds are susceptible to these effects; chickens, for example, appear better able to withstand the compound than the many species of raptor, waterfowl, and passerine to which it is quite toxic. In humans, DDT has now been implicated in breast and other cancers, Parkinson's disease, decreased fertility, and premature births. Despite this, there are those who call for its return.

In a way it seemed like a long shot, since the compound had never been used on a large scale in Bermuda and, in any case, cahows fed so far out at sea. But Wingate's observations of what was happening in cahows were so consistent with reports coming from the States about populations of eagles, falcons, hawks, and other birds that in 1965 he sent two unhatched eggs and three dead chicks to New York to be analyzed by biologist Charles Wurster of the state university at Stony Brook.

Wurster was among those gathering ammunition for the first legal salvo against the use of DDT. Along with Dennis Puleston, a British-born environmentalist and professional adventurer; Victor Yannacone, a brash but innovative New York lawyer whose motto was "Sue the bastards"; and several others, Wurster would become a founder, in 1967, of the Environmental Defense Fund, which started in a small room above the Stony Brook post office.

Wurster found DDT residues in every sample Wingate had sent. In a 1968 paper in the journal *Science*, the two note that the mere presence of the chemical is not enough to prove it was at fault in the cahow's breeding problems, but point out that "other potential causes of the observed decline for the Bermuda petrel appear unlikely." The birds were watched so carefully by Wingate that human disturbance was impossible, and he and Wurster ruled out inbreeding, since no deformed chicks were being born, the gene pool was growing, and pairs that had recently begun laying inviable eggs had bred successfully in the past.

The finding broke new ground in that it showed DDT buildup in a thoroughly pelagic bird species, which meant the insecticide was widely enough disseminated that it had made its way into marine organisms—in this case, the phytoplankton, zooplankton, small fish, and squid that form the cahow food chain—as well as terrestrial ones.

The EDF used its stockpile of international studies, including the cahow paper, to win a lawsuit to end the spraying of DDT in Suffolk County, New York, then moved on to statewide battles before going national. The organization succeeded in getting the U.S. Environmental Protection Agency to ban the substance on June 14, 1972.

But for Wingate in the 1960s, eventual victory seemed unlikely. "The fundamental difficulty was up till then I felt I had total control over the fate of the cahow on its breeding grounds and assumed it was safe at sea," he says. "But now it was out of my hands. It gave me an overwhelming sense of helplessness. The birds were dying, and there wasn't a damn thing I could do about it."

✦

Demoralized, Wingate did the only thing he could to keep from giving up hope. He turned his attention toward reforestation. "I put the cahow project on automatic and tried not to think about it too much," he says. "I was always looking for something that would work, something positive. If the cahow wasn't positive, then let's see if we can make a go with palmetto planting. It was a way of coping, really, to always look for the positive things and try to promote them without neglecting the things that weren't going so well."

One thing that was going just fine, thank you, was Wingate's career. "Governor Launches a 'Living Museum,'" reads a two-part story that started May 17, 1966, on the front page of the *Royal Gazette*.

The articles include five photographs of various island officials and members of the press listening raptly as Wingate, dressed formally in Bermuda shorts, knee socks, and a plaid jacket, holds forth on the island's progress to date and his hopes for its future. The governor, John Roland Robinson, Lord Martonmere, is quoted as calling the living museum a "splendid project" that would one day become an important tourist attraction. Wingate must have blanched at the thought of hoards of "dickey birders," as he calls those who look only for trophies to be checked off lists, descending on his beloved island, but he stood by diplomatically as the governor planted a ceremonial yellowwood and even got down on his hands and knees to look inside the wooden cahow box meant to simulate a burrow at the back of Wingate's house.

Wingate had been living on a shoestring woven together by grants, Anita's job, the rent-free housing at Nonsuch and Aldie, and his occasional stints on the parks department's payroll under Hubert Jones, who by now had been promoted to parks administrator. Jones made room in his budget for small expenses for Wingate like tools for planting and piping to irrigate the seedlings on Nonsuch. But Wingate's position with parks wasn't very secure, so when the Bahamas National Trust invited him to become its director, he was tempted. If he moved to the Bahamas, he thought, he'd be working with millions of seabirds, not just a handful; it was a British colony, so his and his family's lifestyle would remain about the same, and, in an archipelago 255 times the size of Bermuda, he would be able to expand his influence enormously. "But I was so fixated on Bermuda and the cahows," he says, "I didn't want to leave." He also didn't want anything to do with an office job, but he used the offer as leverage with the Bermudian government. It was just the thing Gordon Groves, then director of Agriculture and Fisheries, needed to spur the legislature into creating a position for Wingate. As Bermuda's first conservation officer, he would finally have a salary and a budget for his project. The budget was less than the dogcatcher's, but never mind, it was a job.

"I guess I was the one who looked after him," recalls Walwyn Hughes, then the department's assistant director. "We gradually built up the new section around David. There were a few industrial staff at his disposal, and he got help from the parks department from time to time, but it was pretty much a sole enterprise, a lone experience."

Hughes pauses. "He always was an individual," he says. "He's a free spirit, no doubt."

From the start, Hughes knew Wingate wouldn't be an archetypal civil servant. "I can tell you that I had to cocoon him from—" Hughes begins, trying to be delicate. "There were many in the department who felt that his hours of work and work ethic and so forth were not those of a civil servant, which they weren't, of course, but in his own way he was putting in plenty of time and effort." Often, in fact, Wingate put in eighteen-hour days. His official duties included site visits to proposed developments, producing educational materials, and giving lectures to conservation and school groups. He was in charge of the few government reserves around the mainland and was also heavily involved in the management of protected lands owned by the Bermuda Audubon Society and the National Trust, since they provided habitat for many of the endangered species that were part of his mandate. After work, if he wasn't giving a talk somewhere or running up to Somerset to rescue an injured bluebird, he'd go back to Nonsuch and start work on the living museum or with the cahows, both of which he had always considered side projects, because he had started them before he became conservation officer. Still, Hughes adds, "in public service, people expect you to be in the office, where they can see you and talk to you. That wasn't the case with David. You had to trust that he was getting on with his job, which in my view, he was." But his unconventional methods earned Wingate plenty of sniping.

Hubert Jones remembers that monthly staff meetings always seemed to begin without him. "David was always late," he says, "and he would come in panting because he was always rushing to get there, and he'd interrupt the meeting to say what he was doing. It was so habitual we knew it was an act." But, in fact, it seems to have simply been Wingate's natural state.

"He is to this day late for everything," says Wendy Blyth, who was Anita's best friend. "It was recognized he'd be late. Even when he was supposed to be attending certain official things, he'd be late."

"He abhorred bureaucracy," says David Saul, to whom Wingate ultimately answered when Saul was finance minister in the early 1990s. "'Come in and do a report? How could I possibly do that? The weather is too good, or the cahows have landed.' And I don't think anybody ever went to get him. I demanded a tighter control on the unguided missile every year I met with Walwyn for the budget. Well, you might as well have told the tide not to come in."

Saul and Wingate began working together again in 2004 on a conservation program called Buy Back Bermuda. "Even now," Saul says, "he struggles to work in a committee atmosphere, struggles to play team. Because nothing in his background would have ever prepared him to reach a consensus, argue a point, fight for a promotion. The man had the ultimate job; he did not need to be promoted to anything. Basically he was set adrift on Nonsuch to do what he thought proper. And everything—everything that's planted there, everything that lives out there, every sign that was installed—everything was entirely up to him. He was left alone to do the job that was his dream job, that he loved. And in the end he succeeded brilliantly."

Perhaps, but in the thick of it, Wingate didn't always see how he'd ever succeed at all. The first year he did a mass planting, his daughter Janet, who was three or four at the time, went around pulling up every seedling he put in the ground. "She had a very strong character," Wingate says. "And children are always pushing the limits of what they can get away with from their parents. The more I tried to persuade her that this was the worst possible thing she could be doing to me, the more she would do it. It just got beyond the point of ridiculous. It lasted the whole summer."

By the mid-1960s he had culled most of the aggressive invading flora on Nonsuch to virtually nothing. But he'd seen the palmettos and olivewoods burned back year after year by salt spray, and realized they were never going to thrive without the kind of windbreak the cedars had once provided. He'd have liked to use buttonwoods, but government horticulturalists were not yet propagating native species, so none were available. Wingate reluctantly conceded he'd need to plant a nonnative substitute to protect the struggling seedlings. He decided to go with fast-growing tamarisks and casuarinas around the island's periphery, with the intention of phasing them out gradually—by girdling, not chopping—as the other plants took hold. The tamarisks worked out all right, since they're fairly compatible with the native forest, but it wasn't long before he wished he'd never seen a casuarina.

"I fell for the it's-too-good-to-be-true line," he says of the trees, which had been chosen by the government as the primary cedar-replacement for the mainland, where, unlike on Nonsuch, the dead cedars had been clear-cut and burned, removing valuable habitat for birds and insects and destroying a huge amount of excellent timber in the process. "It was like burning gold," Wingate says of the practice, which was stopped before all the wood went to waste.

The dense foliage, rigid skeletons, and shorter-toward-the-coast-line growth pattern of cedars force the wind to ride up over their tops. By contrast, casuarinas, imported from Australia and also known as whispering pines, have open foliage that air blows right through. They can grow as much as three times as high as Bermuda cedars, in environments that would prostrate the endemics. By the mid-1970s, Wingate's casuarinas were getting too tall to continue protecting the inland forest, but he knew that if he cut them down he'd be back to square one. So he started pruning them to keep them short and bushy, using the dead cedar forest—as low as two feet nearest the coast-line—as a height guideline. "Once I started topping the casuarinas," he says, "they started emulating the cedars beautifully and performing the same function, but it became very time-consuming and very, very labor-intensive." There were about six hundred casuarinas on Nonsuch, and Wingate topped them in batches, usually staying at the job for about a week at a time. He'd stand in the crotch of the tree ten or twelve feet from the ground, using one hand to steady himself and the other to cut branches with his bow saw in the hot summer sun. More than once a branch fell on him when he misjudged the wind, and after his retirement he actually toppled from a tree into the brush below. But it worked, and at the time he had no alternative.

When Hurricane Emily hit Bermuda in 1987, the mainland got an object lesson in why the native trees had been there in the first place.

"The casuarinas came down like ninepins," Wingate says. "We had 70 percent blowdown in some cases, where the casuarinas had become a monoculture." Since then, the government and private landowners have begun phasing the trees out, but it hasn't proved easy. "Unfortunately they've started self-seeding in the coastal zone," he says, "in places where you'd think they'd be most marginal—barren rocks and roadcuts and things like that. And when they reach their full height the wind can act as a lever and they break chunks of the cliff off. It's an absolute disaster."

Perhaps Wingate's chief complaint about the Nonsuch project after his retirement—one that he used to mention time and again, so badly did it frustrate him—was that the casuarinas weren't being topped regularly, though in recent years that has changed. "Keeping those trees as similar as possible to the cedars until they're all phased out is so important," he says. "The fundamental lesson I learned out there is that everything's commensal and interrelated. You have to respect all aspects of the program equally and restore them all together. In the process you find out that some things are more important than you thought."

꙳

As late as 1970, despite nearly ten years of work, Nonsuch still looked like a barren wasteland. The eight thousand or so seedlings Wingate had planted were anywhere from knee- to chest-high, and the defoliated cedars he'd left as habitat and a hobbled form of windbreak still dominated the landscape. It wasn't surprising, looking at the place, that politicians were grumbling about the funds being spent there. "What is he culling and replanting native flora for when he ought to be planting pretty things like the poinciana to make a nice garden for the tourists?" one official asked during a walk around the island, according to a 1985 story in *Oceans* magazine. And a member of the board of agriculture, according to Wingate, "said he couldn't understand why government was wasting money on such a pie in the sky project." But Wingate kept plodding ahead.

There were a few things he wanted on Nonsuch that were causing him no end of headaches. One was the palmettos. He'd planted about seven hundred of them, only to discover, a decade later, that almost 20 percent of the seedlings he'd carted over from the mainland and methodically placed around the island were actually Puerto Rican hat palm. "The seeds in the government nursery hadn't been properly vetted," he says. "They had a palm collection in the botanical garden with about sixty species in it, and the seed they were propagating had been collected from there instead of from someplace where you knew they'd all be endemic, like Paget Marsh." The last remnant of valley peat-marsh forest, Paget Marsh still contained relict populations of native and endemic plants, since occasional flooding and the acidity of the peat had prevented invasives from overtaking them. "So the seeds got mixed up, and the two trees are so similar that no one noticed until they started to flower."

For Wingate, the purist, close enough wouldn't do. He ripped out all the hat palms and started again. "Cutting them down was rather painful and depressing," he says. "I was horrified to destroy my babies that I'd nursed along for ten years."

By the time he finished the culling, though, he had a different take on the calamity. "It taught me that I shouldn't worry about letting trees die," he says. "It's a process that, in nature, would have created a gap to be filled by the next succession of trees." And it gave him an opportunity to plant another local legend.

The yellowwood, like the cahow, had been believed extinct in Bermuda since the first settlers had logged it out of existence. The trees' wood was strong, fine-grained, conspicuously yellow, and hitherto unknown in England, making it perfect for the cabinets and inlaid floors of the rich. The lumber was shipped over by the ton, and logging so quickly took its toll that a 1632 proclamation prohibited the cutting, selling, or exporting of yellowwood (or cedar) without special permission.

When Governor John Henry Lefroy, the great chronicler of the history of Bermuda, came along in the 1870s, it was believed that only one yellowwood—later known as "Lefroy's tree," since legend had it the governor had carved his initials in its side—had been left standing. Sixty years later, when the Castle Harbour Hotel was built at Tucker's Town, Gus Baker, the resort's horticulturalist, located Lefroy's tree, along with sixteen others, in Paynter's Vale, a lonely hillside at the eastern end of Harrington Sound. When he later became Hubert Jones's mentor, Baker showed the trees to Jones, who introduced Wingate to the little stand. Wingate and Jones culled the invasives that were overtaking the yellowwoods, and the trees, which are incapable of self-seeding today because of competition from so many invasives, were propagated. Wingate credits Jones and Jones, Wingate for the seedlings that soon took root in the government nursery.

In 1970, a member of parliament suggested giving Bermudians some of the yellowwoods to plant in their yards to commemorate the 350th anniversary of parliament in Bermuda. About three hundred people took the seedlings, "but the tree is so slow-growing and vulnerable to bark damage from mowers and Weedwackers," says Wingate, "that ten years later, when I put out an appeal, I could find only three people who still had their trees. Once the yellowwood gets to young-adult size, about eighteen feet, it goes from being very vulnerable to being very rugged and surviving. But it's extremely rare because it's so difficult to grow under modern circumstances. It's the ultimate botanical challenge, even on Nonsuch." Only about three of the dozens of yellowwoods he has planted there have grown well. In the 1968 *Sports Illustrated* story, he is quoted as saying he'd like to be buried under one: "It's a great honor to be contributing to the growth of the yellowwood."

At the time, he was contributing to the growth of the yellowwoods, along with the casuarinas and other seedlings, by dousing them with castor pomace, a fertilizer made from the residue left after the oil is extracted from castor beans. Castor pomace is about 5 percent nitrogen, 1 or 2 percent potash, and another 1 or 2 percent phosphoric acid. "When you put that stuff around the trees they would grow like mad," Wingate says. He got into the habit, after seeing how well it worked, of ordering about a hundred fifty-pound bags a year, until he began to notice an explosion in the land-crab population.

The purple and red Bermuda land crab is about four inches across and has a pair of pincers that can deliver a painful nip if you get too close. The crabs, which are natives, breed in the ocean but spend most of their adult life in inland burrows that hasten erosion and are damned inconvenient for anyone walking around on the grass. For years the animals had been considered a pest on Bermuda's golf courses, where poison would be set for them; they'd always been on Nonsuch but had been kept in check to an extent by the island's limited resources until the high-protein pomace started showing up. "I'd see the crabs clustering around the trees after I put it out," Wingate says, "particularly after a rain. It would clump together and they'd pick it up with their pincers. That's how I realized what the problem was. It was a free banquet."

"There were probably millions of crabs on Nonsuch when I was a kid," says Hubert Jones's son Chris, who summered on the island with his family in the 1960s and '70s. "At night, they'd be all over the ground, which was like Swiss cheese from their burrows. They'd get in your hair from the palmetto trees and latch onto your flip-flops."

"It was always funny to put a crab in someone's wetsuit," recalls Alan Marquardt, another longtime visitor.

The crabs proved more than an annoyance when Wingate decided to try to increase his plant collection with endemic Bermuda sedge, which he calls the botanical equivalent to the cahow. It doesn't proliferate on the mainland because rats eat its seeds before they can grow. "There were only fifty specimens of sedge left in the country," he says, "in Paget Marsh. I took a half dozen, and the land crabs ate them all. I was traumatized by it because I'd risked taking the rarest endemic plant in Bermuda from its last reserve, and the gamble failed."

But not everything looked so bleak. By the early 1970s it had become clear that a few cedars had persisted on the mainland. "They stood out like green thumbs," says Wingate. "On a whole hillside of dead trees you'd see one that was just as healthy as it had ever been." Natural selection had conferred marginal scale resistance to about 4 percent of the original cedar forest—trees that had gone through a period of severe defoliation but eventually bounced back—and strong resistance to another 1 percent, which had remained totally healthy throughout the infestation.

"If a genome contains a trait for resistance to a pest," Wingate says, "as long as the population isn't exposed to that pest, the gene isn't needed and may be randomly eliminated. In this case, when the scale arrived, fortunately the genes for resistance hadn't been completely eliminated."

By about 1970, the government nursery had started growing cedars from the seeds of the resistant trees. It would take a couple of years for them to germinate and reach a size that could be transplanted, so in the meantime Wingate prepared Nonsuch by culling any baby cedars he found growing on cliff sides, where starlings would drop the trees' seeds. "It seemed self-defeating to be pulling out cedars when I wanted to get them on the island," he says of the four or five dozen trees he removed, "but I thought if I could keep the scale off Nonsuch a while longer, I could give my seedlings a good head start."

Hopeful but wary, he planted six hundred cedars in 1972. For three years they grew, reaching a height of eight to ten feet before scale carried over on the wind settled onto their waiting leaves. In the end, a third survived—about what he expected, and two hundred more cedars than had been living on Nonsuch in thirty years.

✦

He also began faunal introductions around this time, first of an endemic white-eyed vireo, *V. griseus bermudianus,* known here as chick-of-the-village. A warblerlike gray, yellow, and white bird with striking white irises, the Bermudian subspecies was once, along with the catbird, a dominant land bird on Nonsuch, but its numbers diminished as its cedar habitat began dying out, and the few that remained were killed when Hurricane Arlene hit the barren island in 1963.

"I had expected the vireos to recolonize from the mainland once the forest began to get re-established," Wingate says. He'd seen a few of the birds on Nonsuch in the 1960s, but since they never started breeding, he eventually realized these were migrating transients from

North America. "The local race has greatly reduced flying ability," he says, noting that the trend toward flightlessness is typical in bird species on mammal-free oceanic islands. "They turned out to be so sedentary that they wouldn't cross Castle Harbour, so I figured if I wanted them on Nonsuch I'd have to bring them myself."

Though the island's tree canopy was still quite low, its thickets were dense enough that Wingate felt confident the vireos would be safe. He set out fine-meshed "mist nets" on the mainland and captured four pairs of the birds for his initial introduction. They began nesting immediately, and even reverted to the fearlessness early settlers had found in them. "They won't let you catch them," he says, "but they will approach within feet of you. They're very cheeky. I remember one day I saw a pair of chicks following along behind their parents through the foliage, foraging. One of the chicks came within reaching distance and I very slowly put out my hand and stroked its breast with my finger. To me that was a momentous occasion."

Turtles aren't mentioned as often as birds in the early accounts of Bermuda, perhaps because they didn't make as much of a ruckus. But "On the Geology of the Bermudas," a pamphlet written in the 1830s by a Richard Nelson of the Royal Engineers, recounts that skeletons of sea turtles found buried on the beach measured an astonishing nine feet long and seven feet across. When the settlers arrived and began harvesting them, there were at least three and possibly as many as four species of marine turtles breeding here: the green turtle, hawksbill, leatherback, and loggerhead. Their story is a familiar one.

"The Tortoyse is reasonable toothsome (some say) wholsome meate," writes Strachey. "I am sure our Company liked the meate of them verie well, and one Tortoyse would goe further amongst them, then three Hogs. One Turtle (for so we called them) feasted well a dozen Messes, appointing sixe to every Messe." Their eggs, too, were harvested "five hundred at a time in the opening of a shee turtle."

As for the cahows, the yellowwoods, and the cedars, in 1620, legislation was passed to protect the turtles, but again, it didn't help. It appears the last species to stop breeding there was the green turtle, which managed to hang on in dwindling numbers until the 1930s.

Wingate wondered if he could get breeding turtles to return. He wrote to Archie Carr, the founder of the Caribbean Conservation Corporation and then the leading authority on sea turtles. For several years, Carr, with the help of the U.S. Navy, had been shipping turtle hatchlings around the Caribbean from a rookery in Tortuguero, Costa Rica, hoping they would imprint on their new surroundings and return to breed.

Since the project didn't fall under his government purview, Wingate needed to find private funding. He approached Clay Frick, who sat on the board of the CCC. Frick not only lent financial support, but he and his daughter Jane also became enthusiastic participants in the endeavor. In 1966, Carr sent a shipment of hatchlings to Bermuda, but bad weather interfered with their release and many ended up being reared at the aquarium. "It was pretty much a flop, that first year," says Wingate. By the following year, Carr had come to the conclusion that to properly imprint on a place, the turtles probably had to hatch there. "If you move them all over the world they're just going to get confused," Wingate says. "They won't know where to go back to."

Jane and Clay Frick went to Costa Rica to shepherd back an experimental shipment of eighty-six eggs, which Wingate and they buried on the south beach of Nonsuch and at Frick's place on Castle Point. A couple of months later, fifty-six of the eggs hatched.

In the next decade, 23,000 eggs were brought to Bermuda; 69 percent of them hatched. But in 1971, it was discovered by a French researcher named Claude Pieau that the sex of a turtle depends upon the temperature of the sand in which it incubated. The news took some time to reach Wingate, but when he learned of it, around the mid-'70s, he began checking temperatures on the hatchery beaches and was stricken to discover they were all too cold to produce females. "The original population must have been adapted to hatch at lower temperatures," he says. "It underscores the importance of saving subspecies, in case a replacement species doesn't have the same adaptations. But even today, in the center of a big clutch there's a lot more metabolic heat, so you can probably always expect a few females."

"Those turtles should begin maturing around 2012," author Storm

Cunningham wrote of the project a decade ago, in his book *The Resto-ration Economy*. "Wingate lives for the day he sees one return to nest."

"I hadn't given up hope at that point," Wingate says, "but I think by now we pretty certainly can. I suppose there's still a minute chance that a green turtle could return to breed, but it would be hard to find a mate. And we haven't seen any evidence of randy male turtles knocking about. My hopes have been receding since the 1990s for any chance of it."

But he's glad they tried. In 1968, Wingate, in private talks, con-vinced the island's four remaining turtle fishermen to voluntarily stop trapping the animals on the condition that the government compen-sate them for their nets, which Clay Frick later used to capture turtles for tagging. Wingate, the Fricks, and Leonard Ireland, a biologist from SUNY Buffalo who had come down to help, learned a lot from a pure research standpoint during their work with the turtles, but more important, the project raised awareness of the creatures in Bermuda. Its legacy is extensive ongoing study by both Bermudian and visiting scientists. And today, if you're out in a boat in Bermuda, you're almost sure to see a turtle or two popping up for breath; the island's shallow reef platform and large sea-grass beds make it an ideal nursery for young turtles to graze in before returning to the Caribbean to breed.

✦

Wingate didn't have such good luck with the endemic Bermuda ci-cada. Like their North American relatives, Bermuda cicadas were ex-tremely long-lived and grew quite large—up to two inches—but what A.E. Verrill described as their "peculiar musical note" was quite dis-tinct. Over the years, it earned them the names singer, scissors grinder, and—from the early settlers, who thought, writes Butler, that the bugs sounded like "the whirle of a spindle"—good housewife, though only courting males made the noise.

"Cicadas were a big, very noticeable part of Bermuda's culture as a harbinger of summer," Wingate says. "You used to hear the first ones around the fifth of June. The sound of the singers was deafening in the cedar groves. You could hardly hear yourself think; their loud buzzing used to drive people mad."

In their larval stage, the bugs fed on live cedar roots; the death of the cedars, in combination with the arrival of kiskadees in 1957, made them rare on the mainland by the early 1960s. But they were still plentiful on Nonsuch, in part because it turned out their larvae could also feed on the roots of tamarisks, which Wingate had planted along the northern bluff, and in part because he shot any kiskadees that appeared on the island. But ultimately, keeping the cicadas going was a battle he couldn't win. "By the '90s you might hear one in early August, which used to be the peak of the season," he says, but even as early as the late 1960s he knew their days were numbered.

In some ways, the '60s were disheartening for Wingate, with his floral introductions meeting with one disaster after another, land crabs taking over Nonsuch, and DDT keeping the cahow population from growing. But he tried to keep perspective. "In the short term," he says, "everything is going wrong at the same time and you think, God, this is the end. I had to keep saying to myself, 'Let's see how things work out next year.' In the long term, you realize you're slowly making progress."

CHAPTER SEVEN

Coming of Age

DESPITE THE SETBACKS, LIFE on Nonsuch remained charmed. In 1965, the House of Assembly approved £1,000 for the renovation of the cottage "to alleviate the isolation of the family of the warden," according to a memo from the director of public works. In a *Mid-Ocean News* story that year headlined "Loneliness of Living on Nonsuch Island," Anita is quoted as saying she is "not the sort who likes to live with a lot of people around me"; but she admits it would be nice to have someone with whom to share babysitting, grocery shopping, and day-to-day life.

"We didn't want to become rock-happy island lovers," Wingate says, "and didn't want the children to grow up without friends around them."

They invited Wingate's colleagues Hubert Jones and Dewey Marquardt and their families to begin spending their summer holidays on the island. The Joneses—including Rosalind, who at seven that first year was three years older than Janet Wingate; Heather, six; and Christopher, four—moved into the cottage for four weeks in July. When the Joneses went back to the mainland at the end of the month, they helped the Marquardts bring in their belongings for August. Dewey and Sara; Alan, a few months older than Janet; and Barry, a year older than Karen, came the first year, and Carla Marquardt was born the following year. Anita's best friend, Wendy Blyth, and her two children—Katherine, a year older than Janet, and Peter, two years younger—stayed in the main house periodically throughout every summer. And, with Wingate's renown growing through newspaper and magazine stories, there was a steady stream of visiting birders and scientists to help him with his various projects. "All sorts of eccentric people," remembers Karen Wingate. "What was the name of that weird chap? A bearded, funny little fellow. Drank like a fish."

The Wingates and their visitors, including the children, knew even as they lived it that their time on Nonsuch was something to be treasured. "I used to look forward to it with a passion," says Barry Marquardt, who now lives in Sussex, England, in a house he calls Nonsuch. "It was like Robinson Crusoe, being out there on the island all by ourselves. It's a boy's dream."

"We were like a small little society on an extended adventure," Carla adds.

Until they reached school age, the kids ran around naked from sunup until dusk. "I guess it was Janet," recalls Charlie Zuill. "When she went to school, they had a hard time convincing her she needed to keep her clothes on." When the children were toddlers, their mothers would take them down to the north beach, which was calmer than the south beach and had some shade, to play in the sand while the women read. When they got a bit older, they became water rats, swimming, sailing, cliff diving, snorkeling, and fishing the days away. "I suppose the adults were watching us," Karen says, "but we weren't aware of it at the time."

The wreck that had been scuttled for William Beebe was particularly alluring, filled as it was with "mysterious, twisted shapes covered with yellow-green sea algae," as Janet Wingate writes in *Nonsuch Summer*, a young-adult book about her childhood. They liked to swim underwater through the barge lengthwise at low tide, when air pockets under the deck made it safer. They had to worm their way through small rusted holes in the hull, keeping away from the sea urchins that lined the sides and the moray eel's den toward the center.

When dinnertime approached, Anita would often send the children to catch something for her to cook. Mostly they fished off the wreck for snappers, with the rule, says Jim Lightbourn, that "if you caught it you had to eat it." Lightbourn, a marine contractor, and his family began spending the first couple of weeks in September on Nonsuch around 1970. He would sometimes stop on his way out to the island to snorkel for spiny lobsters, which hide in reef crevices and are caught by looping a noose around their tails. "I made a box to keep them in the wreck," he says, "and when I got six or eight, Anita and the girls would come down to the cottage and we'd have a lobster feast."

Shark hunts were also popular. Occasionally they'd go out with poles—Janet once landed a four-foot puppy shark in the little Whaler, which caused "pure pandemonium," according to Alan Marquardt, until it died—but mostly they did it the lazy way. They'd set the lines in the evening, baiting them with bream and squirrelfish caught at the barge and stringing them across the rusted metal ribs of a wreck that protruded from the water between Nonsuch and Cooper's Island. Then they'd go out in the morning to take the sharks off, hooking sharpnoses and grays three, four, or, rarely, as much as six feet long. Everyone would have shark steaks for a day or two, and Jones would make his special-recipe shark hash.

During storms and in the evenings, the children would gather on the porch or by the fire inside the house or cottage to play cards or board games, sing around the piano, or bake cookies with their mothers. Much of the adults' socializing took place on the porch of the main house, where Dewey Marquardt would sit for hours with a hot toddy listening in on the airport's control tower on his short-wave radio. "Those were gorgeous days," says Delaey Robinson, a St. George's resident who stayed in the main house for a few summers as a college student and did his thesis on the skinks. "We really enjoyed ourselves immensely. Perhaps my dearest memories of Nonsuch are of gatherings on the porch overlooking the Atlantic. We took our meals there and enjoyed long conversations there, day and night, sun and moon. We loved it." Wingate's porch-front telescope provided lessons in the stars and also gave everyone advance notice when a boat was approaching the island, which, as often as not, earned the interlopers a slap on the wrist for attempting to land in a protected area.

To the kids, at least, Wingate was a larger than life figure. "A force unto himself," Carla Marquardt says; Chris Jones describes him as "a bit Hemingwayesque. Not that I knew of Hemingway at the time."

The Joneses had a thirteen-foot Whaler with a 20-horsepower outboard; as conservation officer, Wingate now had a 17-foot Whaler with a 90-horse motor. "David always had bigger boats, bigger engines, and he was a bigger guy of course," Chris Jones says. "You'd see him coming from a distance with binoculars around his neck and the hat and glasses, always rushing around, always leaping in and out of his boat or clambering on and off of rocky cliffs and islets." Whenever he appeared, Jones continues, it seemed he had an announcement to make—a tree had fallen, a longtail was in trouble, the generator was out of fuel, or there was some new development in conservation.

Wingate's boating skills were legendary. "Getting onto and off of those cahow islands in the winter," says Robinson, "particularly Green Island, my god, nobody else would even try to land on that. You're bound to break something, like the engine, for instance, if not a leg. The waves could easily dash the prop on the rocks, but he'd drop anchor a little way off and motor astern just enough to leap at the most treacherous place." An old photograph shows just how precarious this feat could be: Wingate's jumping out of the boat as though he were on a trampoline, way up in the air holding the stern line, with the jagged rocks below him and the Whaler already being carried far off by the swell.

He would get frustrated with boat motors, water pumps, and any other devices with moving parts. "He'd be cussing the engine left and right," Robinson says. "I've never seen him get angry at a person, but he loses it with mechanical things."

Wingate couldn't spend as much time with the kids as the other fathers, who were on holiday at Nonsuch while he continued working, though they all have colorful memories of him. In the mid-'60s he had an old Morris Minor station wagon with the top cut off brought out to the island from the Bio Station to make getting things up from the dock easier. "One of the dead cedars had fallen across the path," says Carla Marquardt. "The jeep just fit underneath the tree. We'd get in that thing and bump down the pathway in the middle of the island, ducking just in time as we flew under it."

Some of those who were children on Nonsuch are convinced to this day there is a ghost on the island, and Wingate didn't discourage the tales. "I remember we'd always haul ass past the graveyard because of the ghost," Carla says. Her brother Barry swears when he was alone on the island he would hear a noise like "someone driving a heavy wooden stake into the ground with a mallet. *Thump, thump, thump*. It was always during the heat of the day."

Wingate, a great storyteller, would get the kids all wound up about the ghost and then jump out from the bushes at night with a sheet over his head. Then there was the time he shot a teacher. Indirectly.

"David had chickens and a rooster in back of the house," Chris recalls, "and the rooster got loose and of course was crowing all the time. I had my friend Mark out there, and the Audubon summer camp was there too, with a teacher who looked like the tennis player Jimmy Connors. David was running around after the rooster with a shotgun, and Mark and I were trying to follow the action. You never knew where David was, you'd just hear the shotgun. At one point he was at the west end of the house, and the campers were down by the chapel, and he fired down the path at the rooster."

"They were perfectly aware I was hunting with a gun," says Wingate. "Just as I got my nice clean shot as the rooster was crossing a pathway, someone stepped out from a building."

Some of the buckshot bounced off the hard-baked earth, and a couple of pellets lodged in the teacher's behind. "My mother was a nurse," Chris says, "so she took them out."

Ricochets aside, Wingate was a crack shot. He'd had an air gun since his early teens, and had refined his skills on his collecting trips in college and during his compulsory military service right after, which in Bermuda is not a full-time job but is instead similar to the U.S. Army Reserves. "The military's not really my thing," he says, unsurprisingly. "Once every two weeks you have to go and do the drills and dress up in this silly uniform, and I was always the worst-dressed person anyway. My uniform was always wrinkled and my boots weren't polished." While in the military he got special permission to leave camp nightly to monitor the cahows, though he stretched his hours away a bit to make time to visit Anita, too.

He always seemed to be shooting at kiskadees, anole lizards, and any other invaders that managed to get on the island. "You could hear the pellets landing all around you," says Alan Marquardt. And of course he continued collecting bird specimens until 1973, when guns were banned following the assassination of Bermuda's governor. After two or three years, the government returned Wingate's guns, but by then he was no longer interested in collecting for its own sake.

"I was the last of the career birders to bridge the transition from bird collecting to bird watching," Wingate writes in an unpublished history of birding in Bermuda. "I candidly confess that I was caught up in the collecting mania, too, because there was no one around to verify some of the incredible new records that I was getting and [when I was young] real ornithologists advised me that it was important to collect what I was seeing as proof." In 1968, when he was leaving for the black-capped petrel expedition in Haiti, he got to the airport and realized he'd forgotten his gun. "So I sent my sister Katharine gassing back in the car to Aldie to pick it up for me," he recalls. "She comes running into the airport, waving a gun, yelling, 'Here it is! Here it is!' And nobody blinked. Can you imagine?"

Walwyn Hughes's wife, Betsey, remembers well the trauma Wingate's collecting once caused her. "When we were first married," she says, "I looked out the window one day and saw this beautiful bird, very small. I had never seen it before. I said, 'My gosh, Walwyn, come see it.' Walwyn said, 'We'd better get David Wingate. This is something quite extraordinary.' Up comes David, and the next thing I hear is a gunshot. He killed the bird!" Walwyn Hughes laughs at the memory. "Now, I ask you," continues Betsey, "if you were in that position. I said to Walwyn, 'I will never, ever again tell you about a bird to show to David Wingate.'"

"That's the sort of single-mindedness of David," Walwyn says.

✦

If Wingate was Indiana Jones, Anita was Laura Petrie. Many in his circle were initially surprised by the match. "When we were nineteen, twenty," says Jim Lightbourn, "I wouldn't have said that he'd have much success with women. He was a shy fella that way. He wasn't that guy out after girls. He had birds on his mind."

"The first thing you would think was they were not made for each other," says Wendy Blyth. "She was very vivacious, very outgoing, very amusing, and just sort of, very beautiful. I don't mean that in a negative way to David, but she was extremely attractive."

"She was petite," remembers David Saul, "and she had jet-black hair and beautiful eyes. She was a very cultured English lady. Now, just take her and put her out on that island with this—nut."

But Anita thrived in Bermuda. By the time the girls were toddlers, she had a good job as secretary to the director of the National Trust, was starring in plays at the Bermuda Musical & Dramatic Society, and was vice president of the Paget Ladies' Lawn Tennis Association. In marked contrast to her husband, she had quite a glamorous image. "Her clothes are always smart and in the height of fashion," Janet writes in *Nonsuch Summer*, and indeed, in the newspaper story about the living museum, Anita looks very Jackie Kennedy, trailing behind Wingate and the governor in a sleeveless white sheath dress, white flats, and white-framed cat-eye shades.

"Karen and I love to watch her get ready for a party," Janet continues. "She is a very young Mum, and full of bounce. She comes bursting into rooms singing . . . and kicks her legs in the air—more like a girl than a mother." To a person, everyone who knew Anita in those days uses the words *vivacious* or *bubbly*, or both, to describe her.

Despite her normally chic appearance, she spent most of her days on Nonsuch in a bikini, dressing only for weekend shopping trips to St. George's. And she didn't seem to mind the inconveniences of island life. For the most part, she did without electricity; an underwater cable installed for the training school in the 1930s had been severed when the airport was built, and since the island had been more or less abandoned, the Bermuda government never asked the Americans to replace it. The small backyard generator would be on for an hour or two each evening, but illumination was generally by candle or Coleman lantern. "You squirt a little methylated spirits into the dish and light it with a match," Wingate explains of the labor-intensive process. "That preheats the thing so that when it comes on the gas starts to flow under pressure, and you get this really bright flame through the element."

The generator was also periodically needed to get the indoor plumbing flowing, since, as in all Bermudian homes, it used the rainwater that rippled down the limestone roofs and was collected in cisterns. "Whenever the tank ran down and the water wouldn't come out of the taps, I had to turn on the poor little generator," Wingate says. One of the cool freshwater cisterns, decommissioned for drinking water, was used as the family swimming pool, but real baths were taken in a metal tub in the yard that heated the water by solar power.

Refrigeration was similarly challenging. "Hubert used to go to St. George's and come back with a big block of ice to heave up the steps," says Ann Jones. "That's when we all got cold drinks, which was very nice." By the mid-'60s Wingate had snagged a couple of used propane fridges when a summer camp on Hamilton Harbour's Ports Island finally got an underwater electric cable and had no more need for them. "I can't remember how we got along without a fridge for the first couple of years," he says, "but my dear wife went along with it, and it must have been absolute hell."

She also went along with the many creatures, alive and dead, invited and not, that were always taking up space in her house. The least unusual among them was Biscuit, a yellow lab Wingate had brought home that, despite the no-dog rule on Nonsuch, was allowed to accompany the family there because he was so well trained. "He accepted the skinks and the baby longtails I fostered as other pets in the family," Wingate says. "He used to get jealous because we'd feed the skinks, and of course labradors are very greedy. He knew he wasn't supposed to eat the food we put out for the skinks. You could see the strain on him, but he wouldn't touch it." Biscuit expertly retrieved the kiskadees Wingate shot so he could analyze their stomach contents, and accompanied Wingate around the harbor when the sun wasn't too hot. When the family went back and forth to Nonsuch in the boat, "Biscuit would love to stand right up on the bow with his paws on its lip," Wingate says. "If I went just the right speed, I could get his floppy ears on a plane and they would stay horizontal. One day I made a sudden stop to see what he would do. He did a perfect headstand on the bow. I sped up again so he wouldn't fall overboard, but a perfect headstand." For the most part, the dog took Wingate's renegade boating with aplomb, though he did look "a trifle alarmed," according to Wingate's diary, the time his best friend almost capsized him in a storm.

Not so well loved were the cockroaches that overran the island. They were the big kind that in the United States are called water-bugs or palmetto bugs. "It wasn't uncommon for them to come up on the dinner table and surround your plate," says Wingate. "Sometimes you'd have two or three waiting for a bite to eat." The legs of the kitchen table and the food cupboards were placed in little pots of water to keep the ants away, and jumping wolf spiders the size of tarantulas hovered in the corners of the ceiling. "You could hear them crunching on the cockroaches at night," Wingate recalls. Land crabs, too, got in and scuttled across the wood floors after dark, terrorizing visitors.

Of course, he actively encouraged the skinks. "One time we counted fifty-seven skinks on the porch," he recalls. The porch was the source of easy meals—so easy, the scavenging lizards began to feel comfortable enough there that they'd bite diners' toes to remind them to drop a scrap. "We fed the skinks tuna fish," Wingate says. "They'd be dancing on the porch to keep their feet cool on the hot concrete. There would be sparrows eating as well, and the skinks would push right between the sparrows' legs to get a little bit of cheese or tuna."

When whales beached on the mainland, Wingate had them towed out to the island. "They left one on the south beach to rot," remembers Barry Marquardt. "I can tell you that was one smell. But it was quite interesting because you could go down there first thing in the morning and the crabs were just all over it—ghost crabs and land crabs. And the birds were always picking at it. It was kind of cool to watch it disappear." That skeleton ended up in the Bermuda Aquarium; the vertebrae from another whale, left in the water to be cleaned by the fish, still sit like surrealist ottomans on the floor of the chapel.

Sara Marquardt, always a bird lover, would bring an orange-winged Amazon parrot named Happy to Nonsuch with her every year. "He'd be up in a tree watching people come down the path," Carla says, "and he'd wolf whistle. Come tea and Dubonnet time, he'd come in to the porch and have a little shot of sherry."

Barry amends the story. "Happy whistled at my mother," he says, "but dive-bombed my father. He hated my father. He'd pick things up off the table and drop them on his head."

A masked booby spent a few days in the bathroom while Wingate built a pen for it on Nonsuch's south point, and whenever the kids saw a baby longtail bobbing on the harbor's surface, unable to fly for one reason or another, he would rush out to rescue it, fostering as many as three at a time until their feathers recovered. He called every one of them Willy.

Anita gamely decorated the house with finds the kids turned up on the beach: shells, fan corals, glass fishing floats that had made their way over on the currents, an African carving of an antelope, minus one horn. "That went on the mantelpiece," Wingate says. "God knows where it is now." Wingate made a mobile of two bird skeletons, a cahow on top and a longtail beneath, that hung in the living room. He wanted to add a shearwater but the opportunity never arose.

Even at Aldie, there was a virtual zoo of Wingate's devising. "You'd go to take a bath and there'd be a snapping turtle in the tub," says Karen, who once picked up a dishtowel and accidentally killed three tiny bluebirds concealed in its folds. "You could never take a bath or shower without taking the turtle out first. It was a bit frustrating for teenage girls. People would bring him animals that were hurt, and they would end up in the aquarium eventually. I remember there was a python one time that someone had imported illegally. It spent the night in a bag in our house. And there were always birds in the freezer. Mum would go to get something and get scratched by a pair of talons poking out of a plastic bag."

According to a newspaper story with the strapline "Hazards of a Nonsuch Island Housewife," Anita drew the line at dead rats in the fridge. But otherwise, she seems to have borne it all stoically—one might even say enthusiastically—in the name of love. "Everything they did out there, they did together," says Walwyn Hughes. "Not everybody would be happy with that sort of life. It's not exactly the Four Seasons out there."

Still, summers, according to Wendy Blyth, were "like a blissful family dream, out on an island enjoying the children enjoying themselves."

✦

But the little society was jolted awake from its dream one sweltering August day in 1973. Wingate was ashore, putting in an appearance at his office in Camden House, a grand plantation-style building erected in the early eighteenth century. Now the premier's official residence, Camden sits on the lush grounds of the thirty-six-acre botanical gardens, on the downward slope of Point Finger Road just behind the King Edward VII Memorial Hospital. Wingate had been installed there in 1966 when he became conservation officer; until it was decided the rooms were too small, the location had been slated for a new natural history museum, which he was to curate. He did his taxidermy there and also turned up occasionally to catch up on paperwork.

On Nonsuch, it was what Alan Marquardt calls "quiet time." The Wingate girls were up at the main house reading on the porch, and the Marquardt kids were in the cottage with their comic books. "It was the hottest time of day," Alan says, "but we weren't allowed in the water because we'd just eaten lunch." Anita, as usual in her bikini, was doing some housework. She had hung the laundry out to dry and gone on to put a longtail box into an old oil barrel the family used to burn the island's waste. Then she did something she had probably done a million times before: squirted a bit of methylated spirits into the barrel and lit a match. "But what she didn't know," Wingate says, "was that the trash was smoldering underneath. The spirits must have gassed off."

"There was a big *whoosh*," Alan says, "and we heard her scream. My dad grabbed a bucket and we ran up toward the main house. You could smell her hair. She was screaming my dad's name. 'Dewey, help me! Help me, Dewey!'" Barry's memory of that moment is nearly identical: the *whoomph* of the explosion, the smell of burning flesh, Anita's "chilling" scream.

By the time the Marquardts reached her, Anita was on the ground, wrapped in a damp sheet she had grabbed off the line to smother the flames. "My father or mother opened the sheet," Barry recalls, "and her skin was just peeling off everywhere. It was one of those images you can never forget."

A phone line had been installed on the island via an underwater cable to the military base a few years before, and Sara Marquardt used it to call for an ambulance to meet them at Tucker's Town. "I was kneeling beside her holding her hand," recalls Karen Wingate, "and she was saying, 'Call the hospital and ask what painkillers they can give me.' I remember very clearly Sara Marquardt saying, 'Yes, we've called. The ambulance is on its way,' and she said, 'No, what can you give me for the pain?'"

The boys raced ahead to blow up an inflatable raft for the bottom of the boat while Dewey and Sara helped Anita down to the dock. Carla recalls her saying she had walked onto the island and would walk off, though she fainted at least once on the way. Barry has no memory of being left on Nonsuch to look after his sister and Janet and Karen, by now in tears and terrified, while Alan went with the adults in the boat. "I remember it being rough that day," Alan says, "and there was salt spray, and she had all these open wounds and was just wrapped in this sheet, and the saltwater was soaking right through it. She was coming in and out of consciousness, and my mum and dad were doing their best to comfort her. We had to go slow to keep the salt spray down, but we still beat the ambulance to the dock."

Wingate had had a late lunch that day in the hospital cafeteria, a short walk through the botanical gardens from his office. Around the time he was placing his order, Anita, with second-degree burns over nearly 70 percent of her body, was being rushed into the emergency room at the other end of the hospital. As he sipped his tea and bit into his ham and cheese sandwich, she was being dosed with Demerol and penicillin, fitted with an IV drip, and made as comfortable as possible in a private room at the end of the surgical ward in the hospital's east wing.

Unaware of what was happening just yards away, Wingate strolled back through the oleander and poinciana to Camden and went to see Hubert Jones, whose office was down the hall, when he was greeted with the news. Dewey Marquardt had called, but when he couldn't reach Wingate, he'd spoken to Jones instead. "Dewey said it was very serious," Jones recalls. "I remember him saying she actually walked up the steps at the dock to the ambulance, and he was surprised she could do that, with all of her skin burned."

Jones and Wingate hurried back up Point Finger Road on their motorbikes and found Anita's room. Jones didn't stay, but he remembers her saying to him, "Oh, Hubert, I look so terrible." Wingate was distraught but outwardly stoic. The hospital staff told him everything would be fine, so after a few hours he returned to Nonsuch to be with the girls. "Many people were calling," he says. "I had sort of a set spiel to say, 'Well, the doctors assured me that even though it's a terribly painful experience for her, she should be okay.' I think the big concern at that point was whether she was going to be horribly scarred, because she had such beautiful skin and such a perfect body."

The following day a surgeon, Dr. Paul Brian Counsell, removed the damaged tissue, and took over from the Wingates' family doctor, J. H. Woolf, as the primary physician on the case. Afterward, Anita was sedated but stabilized. "She was reasonably cheery and talkative when I went to see her," Wingate says, and because her face was untouched by the flames, she looked to him like her old self. That evening, her fluid drip "failed to function," according to a later story in the *Royal Gazette*, "and because it was difficult to get re-started, it was taken out, and it was decided to try her on full fluid orally."

For three days, she remained upbeat, though Wingate often had to convince her to take a drink. "She was heavily doped," the *Gazette* quoted him as saying at the time, "and wouldn't drink unless there was someone to persuade her to do so. She certainly could not reach the drinks brought in on her dinner tray. She could barely move her arms."

On Saturday, her fourth day in the hospital—the same day a two-paragraph story in the *Gazette* reported "Mrs. Wingate satisfactory"—Wingate noticed she was becoming restless and depressed. His mother suggested he hire a private nurse to be with her round the clock. "He was given the impression [by the hospital] that there was no great seriousness about the case," the paper later reported. "He was not advised that a private nurse was either advisable, desirable, or possible, and only after his parents pursued it was he told it was possible." Hospital staff continued to assure him Anita would be well enough to take the trip to Maine the couple had planned for later that month, and arrangements were made for the nurse to start on Monday.

On Sunday, Counsell went golfing without checking on Anita first because, the *Gazette* reported, "he was not unduly concerned about the patient." Wingate went in to the hospital around 3 P.M.—the start of visiting hours—and was appalled by his wife's appearance. "Her eyes were completely sunken and rolled up in her head," he is quoted as saying, "her skin was yellow, and she was barely able to communicate with me." He rushed out to find a nurse. "I said, 'You have to do something, that girl's dying in there,'" he says. "They couldn't have looked at her for at least six hours."

Wingate frantically tried to reach Counsell and Woolf all afternoon, but both were out. The nurses finally got hold of Counsell around 5 P.M., and he recommended they put an IV into Anita's neck, since the veins in her arms had collapsed. "But the artery had collapsed, too," Wingate says. "They were stabbing away at her neck for about a half hour, and they couldn't do it. The nurse was in great distress at that point." Just as Counsell arrived, around 5:30, the *Gazette* reports, "the patient started to vomit and almost immediately stopped breathing."

The nurses had asked Wingate and his mother, whom he'd also called, to leave the room. From the waiting room, he says, "I could see scatter action happening—oxygen tanks rushing by, doctors and nurses rushing by, and I knew it was bad. I don't know whether it was an intern or the doctor—it may have been Woolf—who came in and said, 'Sorry, we've lost her.' It was just so quick, such a shock, that I couldn't face going back in to see her. The Anita I knew was gone. I only wanted to remember her alive."

Wendy Blyth had been out of the country at the time of the accident, but when she returned a few days later, she went out to now-quiet Nonsuch to look after the girls. "What was really dramatic," she recalls, "such a stunning experience I can't even tell you, was when David phoned and told me she had died, but said I was not to say anything to the children." Blyth, barely able to keep it together, went to the cottage to tell Sara and Dewey Marquardt. "They saw from my face that the worst had happened," she says. "I had just gone completely white. It was one of the most impossible things in my life, but I carried on till David came back."

When Wingate returned, he took the girls for a walk along the south beach to give them the unexpected news. He remembers the conversation as "terribly emotional," but he tried to put on a brave face. Until the next morning. "I always used to get up earlier than Anita and make a cup of tea and take it in to her," he says. "I did this for the girls, and I just broke down."

"When he told them and they came back up to the house," says Blyth, "I really wanted to put my arms around him. He needed that. But I couldn't. There was nothing I could do."

Even today, almost no one who knew Anita can talk about the time without tearing up. Like Wingate, his daughter Karen remembers everyday moments as the hardest. "She sewed," she says, her eyes misting, "and she taught me how to sew. One day after she died there was a pile of sewing, and I suddenly realized, 'What will happen without her? Who is going to repair my nightie? Things needed repairing.'"

✦

Funeral services were held ten days after the accident, on August 16, in St. Mark's Church, where a little over decade earlier the young couple had pledged that nothing but death would part them. "Her funeral was hugely attended," Wingate says. "I remember crowds standing outside the church. I was just overwhelmed by the outpouring of support. It took me totally by surprise, but of course it was very comforting."

There was a viewing at the funeral home, but Wingate didn't attend. "My philosophy is once you're dead, you know, the body is just a body," he says. "And if you've lost it then the challenge is to remember the spirit, remember the person, and I thought I was always good at that. I enjoyed talking about her, reliving happy experiences with her. It made me feel better and made the children feel better. You'd often get a good laugh, and it was easing. That was all we had to cling to."

Anita was buried in St. Mark's cemetery, and Bermuda law required that she remain there for a year and a day after her death. During that year, Wingate lobbied to have her brought out to Nonsuch. "I liked the idea of having her buried there," he says. "I had always told her that's where I wanted to be buried, assuming it would be the other way round." He got permission to have the casket removed from St. Mark's and reinterred in the old cemetery, in a ceremony attended only by family and friends. He dug the grave himself.

"It was weird," says Alan Marquardt. "We used to play games in the graveyard. It had that spooky feeling to it. I guess it was surreal that we were actually going to put someone tangible to us in there." Carla Marquardt says the children were "more respectful" of the little enclosure after Anita's burial.

Wingate didn't want to sue, but a lawyer named John Ellison was at the time president of both the National Trust, where Anita worked, and the drama society, to which she was so devoted. "He volunteered to take the case almost against my will," Wingate says. "He said he owed it to me and to Anita because it was about time the hospital was called to order for the kind of neglect that had been allowed to happen. I didn't want to blame the doctors, because they face crises every day and they're human. It may be partly due to neglect, but you need your breaks." But Ellison argued the case would be important in exposing the hospital's weaknesses for future burn patients. "In fact there was a very bad burn case not long after," Wingate says. "A brilliant architect. He was much more badly burned than Anita, in a boat explosion, and as a result of what had happened with her case, they immediately rushed him out to a burn unit in Boston. He made a full recovery. So I realized then that the court case had done a service to the community." Wingate accepted only a small settlement, enough to put the girls through college.

The legal proceedings may have been short, but it was decades before Wingate fully came to terms with Anita's death. "What's the expression?" he says. "I didn't have closure."

He marked her grave with a sapling yellowwood but, like the tree planted by Lord Martonmere in 1966, it died after a year or so. Eventually he got a little better at keeping the trees alive, and there are three of them on Nonsuch today. "I still feel the yellowwoods were planted in her memory," he says. "Winning that challenge, eventually succeeding with them, that was for Anita."

In 1975, when he had workmen with heavy machinery come to the island to dig a freshwater pond, he carefully chose a craggy boulder from Walsingham and had it loaded onto the barge. "It's a very hard, ancient limestone full of calcite and flowstone," he says, "very beautiful. It looks like an outcrop of Walsingham pinnacle rock. I wanted something natural." But it would be another quarter-century before he could come up with the words to memorialize his wife. "In loving memory of Monica Ann 'Anita' Wingate, 1941–1973," reads a plaque added to the headstone in 2003. "Beloved wife of David B. Wingate and mother of Janet and Karen. Taken swiftly in the prime of life. Like a shooting star she lit up the lives of all who knew her."

CHAPTER EIGHT

A Habitat Takes Shape

NONSUCH WAS NEVER QUITE the same again, and neither was Wingate.

"He became less playful and fun," says Karen Wingate. "Before that, he would come and join us at the beach, porpoising through the water. He just became a more serious person. His spark of youthful lightheartedness seemed to go." According to his sister Aileen, Wingate's hair turned prematurely gray.

"I suddenly had more responsibility," he says, "so I couldn't afford to be carefree. But also, before the accident I was totally naïve. It was a very bitter experience for me, and it made me cynical, I'd say. For a long time I felt like I was sort of floating in an unreal situation." His marriage to Anita had been "extraordinarily happy," he maintains. "And I'm not just putting gold trimming on it because I'm remembering someone at her prime. I admit I wasn't strong enough to get through the grief without going a bit crazy."

The birds were his salvation. In the two or three weeks remaining on the island until the girls started school again, he threw himself into a survey of longtail nests he'd begun before the accident. "People said I should take a break after Anita's death," he says, "but I instinctively felt the one solid thing I had to hold onto besides the children was Nonsuch, so I just stayed with it. I really absorbed myself into it and carried on, if anything more intensely than before. I didn't know what else to do with myself. Nonsuch was the only thing that kept me going."

When school began, Delaey Robinson went with the Wingates from Nonsuch to Aldie. "David was in quite a tizzy," Robinson says. "He couldn't even boil water, I don't think. Well, he could make tea, but that's about it. So I lived with them at Aldie for a time to make sure the girls went to school fed and clothed and so on."

It was only a matter of a few months, though, before Robinson was replaced—gradually, at first—by Elizabeth Roche, an acquaintance of Anita's from BMDS, who initially began coming to the house in October to fit the girls for costumes for the Christmas pantomime.

"David was a good catch," says Robinson, "and there was a bit of competition for him, I think." In a society as small and closed as Bermuda's, there is always talk, but even the girls realized it was too soon for Wingate to start a new relationship. "Elizabeth is a fabulous person," Karen says. "We get on really well now, but she wasn't my mother."

Wingate, though, felt lost dealing with the children. "There are things that a man can't help girls with," he says. And domestically, he was hopeless—not only with the cooking but also, says Karen, with "shopping, cleaning, buying clothes for us children, anything. He felt he needed Elizabeth for these things, but it was a rebound."

Even before he and Elizabeth wed, in January 1975, he knew it was a mistake, but, says Wendy Blyth, "It's very hard for David to say no to any woman who's interested in him." Wingate essentially concedes this fact. "When I realized Elizabeth and I were not a love match, I got cold feet," he says, "but by then she was so ingrained in the family that it became very awkward to break it off."

A little more than a year after their wedding, his third daughter—Rosalind, called PB, for Putter Bug, by Wingate—came along. He was determined to stay in the marriage as long as he could, but eventually, of course, it became too difficult. "One day I left a note for Elizabeth and simply walked out," he says. "PB was about twelve, I think, so I hoped she would understand, but I had horrendous guilt about it at the time. It turned out she understood better than anybody." In 1992 he married a third time, to Helge Trapnell, an Austrian expat he loved but eventually realized he couldn't live with. When Wingate retired in 2000, she moved to Nonpareil, a house they had bought in St. David's, while he stayed in the Nonsuch cottage for three years before going to live with Penny Hill. But "Penny is very ordered," he says. "She likes life to be predictable, and I can't stand routines. She can't adjust to my chaotic life."

Adjusting to her life, it goes without saying, is out of the question. In the summer of 2011, he took a cottage on his own in Southampton Parish.

Wendy Blyth believes that if Anita hadn't died she and Wingate would be happy together to this day. "They had a bond that was completely different from any other bond he's had," she says, mentioning, too, that Wingate, because of what Walwyn Hughes called his single-mindedness, can sometimes come across as less than completely attuned to the feelings of others. "David is never going to be helpful to any woman," Blyth says. "He just doesn't know how to do it. He's so incredible in every area of his professional life, so good at dealing with so many things. Women are just his failure, really."

"You don't have to be Sigmund Freud to say it was all predictable," adds David Saul. "Anita's death was so out of the blue and such a blow to him. His passion for the birds and for Nonsuch, I think, saved his sanity."

When the cahows returned that first fall, it was bittersweet for Wingate. "I identified so closely with the cahows because I grew up and would grow old with the same pairs," he says. "I knew them as individuals after ten years or so. One pair got established the same year I got married, and they started having chicks around the same time my own children were born, so I particularly identified with them. When they returned to the island in 1973, they were still going strong, and I had a twinge of envy and thought, Well, you outdid me on that one."

A few years later, Wingate checked the pair's burrow and found one of the birds dead inside it. "I put it down to old age," he says. "It had come home to die; it hadn't completed molting. So again I identified with them. The following year the remaining cahow returned with a new partner, so we remarried around the same time, too."

✦

One of the reasons Wingate had chosen Nonsuch as the site for his living museum was that it naturally contained most of Bermuda's main habitats: the sheltered north beach and southern surf beach and their dunes; the rocky shoreline, with its cliffy longtail habitat and low-lying tidal pools; the coastal hillsides, which are exposed to wet, salty wind directly off the ocean and are dominated by sea oxeye, buttonwoods, and, ideally, cedars; and inland valley, where trees can grow as high as fifty feet and the forest floor can develop a layer of dead wood and leaf litter perfect for cahow burrowing.

But two major components were missing. From the beginning, Wingate had dreamed of creating a space for fresh- and saltwater ponds, but he'd had trouble gathering the necessary funds and also working out the logistical difficulties; the dock on Nonsuch's northwest side was so far below the top of the island it could only be reached by stairs, and there was as yet no dock on the north side, which meant the heavy machinery required for digging the ponds would somehow have to be landed on the beach.

The latter problem was solved when it came to Wingate's attention that at its west end annex, the American navy had a landing barge—the kind with a drawbridge-style ramp in the bow, made famous in newsreel clips of the invasion of Normandy. The boat was still functional but wasn't being used, so he was given permission to borrow it to roll the trucks and bulldozers onto the south beach.

The other obstacle was removed by lucky happenstance. Queen Elizabeth and Prince Philip were coming to Bermuda for the ceremonial opening of the maritime museum in the restored Commissioner's House at Dockyard. The prince had been speaking in favor of conservation since the early 1960s, so the committee that planned his schedule decided one of his activities during the three-day trip should be a visit to Nonsuch. The government budgeted thousands of dollars to spruce the place up. Wingate had the buildings painted and installed a little educational display in the chapel, but the bulk of the money—along with a grant from the New York Zoological Society—went to making his ponds. It was the biggest expense he'd ever had apart from building maintenance, which, because of the difficulty of getting out to the island and the living museum's relatively low priority to the government throughout the 1960s, had been done only every third or fourth year.

In planning his planting over the past decade or so, Wingate had anticipated there might one day be a need for heavy equipment near the buildings, so he'd left a ten-foot-wide path coming up from the beach. He'd also precisely planned the siting of the ponds and what was to become of all the soil and sand that was excavated. "You can't dump it into the sea," he says, "and you can't ship it ashore; that would cost an astronomical amount. So I had to work out how much fill I'd have and calculate where it would be most useful." At 80 by 180 feet and as much as 5 feet deep, the freshwater pond contained about 1,500 cubic yards of soil—about what could be held by thirty-three extra-large dumpsters. The saltwater, or dune, pond, which was done in two stages, would eventually bring the total to three times that amount.

He first had the bulldozer operators dig out the freshwater pond, a heart-shaped basin in the center of Nonsuch with an earthen dam near its southwest end where the land began sloping downward. Because Bermuda's sandstone base is so porous, there are no ponds in the country more than a foot or so above sea level; the lighter freshwater that falls during rainy periods seeps down into the ground and sits atop the heavier saltwater coming up from underneath, and when there's no precipitation, the low-lying ponds often become brackish. But Wingate wanted his pond in the forest, twenty or so feet above the sea, so he had to create what's known as a "hanging," or separate, water table. To do this, he lined the basin with a flexible polymer that at the time was state-of-the-art: PVC. "Nowadays it would be considered a no-no," he says, "but at the time they were using it for lining irrigation canals and things like that." While he and an army of volunteers lay down the lining, using shovels to add six inches of soil over its top, the contractor began digging the saltwater pond.

He had it situated in the low-lying area behind the south-beach dune, with a starting size of about a hundred by a hundred feet. "I hoped I would be able to enlarge it some day," he says, "but this was a trial run because I didn't know whether it would survive hurricanes." Because it kept filling up with seawater seepage as it was being excavated, the dune pond had to be dug with a backhoe. The entire project, including moving the fill, took about six weeks. "For the scale of the job and the weather contingencies," he says, "I thought it went very quickly. We had to do it fast because I was paying through the teeth for the equipment."

Since there were no rains due anytime soon, he filled the freshwater basin with water from the island's cisterns, which needed to be cleaned anyway, and used the rubble that had been dug out to fill a slip that had been used by Arthur Tucker whenever the reform school's boat needed to be hauled out for maintenance or a hurricane. "It was quite a big slipway and a major quarry cut on the island," Wingate says. "It was like a big scar in the living museum, so I wanted to soften it by filling." He linked the filled area to Nonsuch's pathway system, making a gradually sloping road through the slip to the shoreline. A few years later, he and Jim Lightbourn built a concrete dock on that side of the island. "It made the island more manageable for unloading plants and propane tanks, and also for heavy equipment," he says. "The bay is very shallow, so you can only bring a barge in at high tide. But at least you don't need to land machinery on the beach anymore."

Over the next few months, with the help of Steven DeSilva, a "very keen" apprentice—Wingate hired several through the Department of Agriculture, Fisheries and Parks beginning in the early '80s—he planted. Black and red mangroves were the dominant flora in the saltwater pond, and cattails and bulrushes in the fresh. Wingate threw buckets of water and mud from similar habitats on the mainland into both ponds for the larvae and bacteria they contained, and stocked both with the endemic killifish *Fundulus bermudae*, which can live in either environment. "They're not that well suited for freshwater," he says, "or for the slightly brackish water we have in Bermuda. But I wanted to prove whether they would have lived in it in precolonial times, before we introduced the top minnow *Gambusia holbrooki*. Today you don't find killifish in freshwater because the top minnow, which is a live bearer, outcompetes it by eating the killifish eggs. They can live together in saltwater because the killifish is better adapted to that habitat." The killifish did well enough in the freshwater pond until minnows inexplicably began appearing a few years later. "The only way I can imagine the *Gambusia* having got there," he says, "is that a few fry stuck to the feathers of a duck that just made a short flight from the saltwater to the freshwater pond. I'll never really know. It's absolutely amazing how organisms can emigrate."

Within a year, both ponds were thriving ecosystems. But eventually the freshwater basin's PVC liner began to deteriorate. "It turned out the stuff not only gives off serious pollutants," Wingate says, "but also slowly volatilizes. It became so brittle that the tree roots began to crack and penetrate it. It started to leak in 1991 and the pond was drying up, so we had to redo it." By the time the pond began evaporating, he again had a reason to bring heavy machinery to the island: The former hospital's east ward had become dangerously decrepit. It had been damaged by an unnamed hurricane in 1948 and then had had its roof blown off in 1963's Hurricane Arlene. Over the years Wingate had been slowly picking away at the building, and one summer had another apprentice spend a month dismantling it block by block, neatly stacking the stone in the mid-island quarry from which it had been taken. "It made really good skink habitat at the time," says Wingate. "And today you would never know it's there, it's so well hidden in the vegetation."

But what remained of the building could not be removed by hand, and since the trucks and front loaders had to be brought over anyway, Wingate took the opportunity not only to replace the fresh pond's liner—this time with chemically inert, durable, high-density polyethylene—but also to enlarge the dune pond to double its size. "It had been so successful I decided it would be all right in a hurricane," he says. He used the fill from the enlarged pond and the building's foundation to extend the level terrace southward in front of the buildings. "In a hundred years," he says, "that terrace and the embankment beyond it could be the cahows' main natural burrowing place."

At the time the ponds were built, though, a quarter century after the rediscovery of the cahows, the number of pairs had increased by only seven, to twenty-five. The count had been hovering around that figure since 1968, when it had jumped from twenty-one pairs to twenty-four as chicks that had fledged in the early '60s started return-ing. In the winter of '68, there was a setback when two pairs were lost. "Every five or six years," Wingate says, "rats would get out onto one island or another. But this time a Norway rat got onto Outer Pear and killed all four adults and also the shearwaters that were nesting there." The difference between a brown, or Norway, rat and a black rat, Wingate says, is that black rats will generally take only eggs that have already failed and have no adults guarding them, or young chicks that are not yet able to defend themselves. "I've seen rats running on the islands during night watches and had no problem," he says. "But that's because they were black rats. Norway rats will attack adult cahows, and they're absolutely deadly."

After Wingate retired, in 2009, a black rat got onto Long Rock when the chicks were still small. A strong gale was blowing and it was several days before Madeiros was able to reach the island. By the time he discovered the rodent, it had killed five chicks. "Two were left," he says. "I had to block the surviving nests up and take a chance the parents wouldn't return. I set the whole island with bait boxes and within two days killed the rat. When I dissected it, it was full of baby cahows." Despite the mishap, Madeiros had a record number of fledglings that year.

Often the first evidence of a rat invasion was a gnawed prickly pear or two, and whatever fruit remained on the island would buy Wingate time to get some traps baited before the rats would go af-ter the cahows, having run out of less animated food sources. He'd set the traps inside a carton with a small hole so that cahows and other birds wouldn't get their necks snapped. Luckily, he says, "skinks can't be killed by warfarin because they have a different blood form."

With no other birds left to draw them there, the cahows never recolonized Outer Pear. But the following year two more pairs estab-lished on the other islands, making up the number lost, and success-ful fledglings nearly doubled, from seven to thirteen. "I was thrilled,"

Wingate says. He thought momentum had taken over, but for six frustrating years, the pair count remained around the same: twenty-four, twenty-four, twenty-five, twenty-five, twenty-five, twenty-six. The number of fledglings also barely budged, shooting up a little further, to sixteen, in 1972, but then returning to the low double digits for the next four years. "The population increase was agonizingly slow," he says.

✦

The ponds were still being built when Prince Philip arrived in mid-February, just in time to see a nesting bird or two. "I was wondering what he would think of a bulldozer churning up a nature reserve," Wingate recalls, but luckily everything else was in decent shape. Twenty-eight more cedars had been planted; the palmettos and olivewoods were up to twelve feet tall, and the hackberries were growing so well their excess seedlings had to be culled to protect the white stopper and Jamaica dogwood flourishing beneath them.

The prince met Wingate at Nonsuch. "He had all kinds of marine police security with boats who were supposed to surround and follow me," Wingate says. "I explained to them that landing on the cahow islands required a specially equipped boat of a specific size, and that they couldn't take him in a police boat. They were very, very reluctant to let him come with me." When permission was finally granted, the prince hopped into the Whaler and immediately began pulling up the anchor. "So I said, 'Well, he's a marine chap, let's do it.'" Wingate roared out of the bay and around the corner toward Horn Rock. "Suddenly there was no sign of the police boats," he says. "I guess they weren't as fast."

Eventually they caught up, and as Wingate was dropping the anchor—a precision operation, given that the anchor chain, once taut, needs to hold the stern within a foot or so of the landing rock to allow for dry disembarkation—Prince Philip climbed over the gunwale and into a tidal pool. "He was trying to be helpful," Wingate says, "but he got his feet wet. But I think he really relished the idea of getting

away from his security and just messing around in a boat for a change."
The two climbed up an eight-foot cliff to get to the top of the island,
where Wingate lifted the lid off a burrow. The prince asked several
questions before they began making their way back to the ledge where
the boat was tethered.

"Coming back down is always harder than getting up," Wingate
says, "but he had no hesitation. The police were sort of standing off
doing their nut, because they had no way of getting ashore to help him
down. He was so delighted, I could see, to get away from all that and
just be himself." Afterward, the grave-looking security men trailed after the pair as they walked around Nonsuch, the prince, photographs
show, dressed casually and Wingate uncharacteristically tidy in his
Bermuda shorts and blazer.

He had been apprised of the etiquette involved in tramping around
with royalty the day before in preparation for a ceremony at Government House in which the Queen bestowed orders of chivalry on
four Bermudians and awarded eight others with medals and badges of
honor. Wingate received an MBE, or Member of the Most Excellent
Order of the British Empire, for his work with the cahows (he would
later receive an OBE as well). "The awards are issued every year," he
says. "The only difference was this time the Queen came to Bermuda
to hand them out. Usually Bermudians fly over to get them at Buck-
ingham Palace. You don't have to, but it's probably impolite not to."

✦

Wingate considered the ponds a prerequisite for another major reintroduction he'd been intending to make for some time, one that had
become more urgent since the land crabs had begun tearing up soil
all over the island in the late 1960s. Diego Ramirez, in 1603, and *Sea
Venture* survivors Sylvanus Jourdain and William Strachey had all
written about black, white, and gray herons, in "great store and plenty,"
according to Jourdain. Because the birds nest in trees, they were better
able than the cahows to survive the pigs that were introduced in the
1500s, but they could not outlast human predation.

It is unclear when the herons finally stopped breeding in Bermuda, but in 1621 Governor Butler issued a proclamation "for the preservation of wilde foule, and in particular for the white hearnes, for their breedinge time draweinge nere, it was [not] doubted that, by the increase of newe commers, and especially boyes, a great waste might be practised upon them by the takeing awaye of their egges and spoyleinge of their nests."

Various species of heron were sighted for many years after that, usually during the migration season; nesting was rare. In 1846, a great blue heron nest was found in the mangrove trees at Hungry Bay, and in 1934, William Beebe came upon an empty nest he believed, because of the eggshells strewn about it and later sightings of the bird, to belong to green-backed herons.

The most recent nester appears to have been the yellow-crowned night heron (*Nyctanassa violacea*), which John Bartram recorded having found in breeding plumage in both Castle Harbour and Walsingham Bay in the early 1860s, and which Bio Station director Hilary Moore saw at Walsingham around 1940. The birds were present throughout the year, Moore wrote, at Long Bird Island, so named by early settlers for its extensive heronry. Unfortunately, in 1941, the American military leveled the 62-acre island, along with Jones, Round, Little Round, Long Cay, and Sandy islands, to make room for a runway.

Wingate knew yellow-crowned night herons, which feed primarily on crustaceans, had been abundant in the country before human colonization because subfossil bones had been found in the Walsingham formation at three separate sites, one of which contained a fully articulated skeleton. "The comparisons of this skeleton with present day *N. violacea* indicate that it represents a distinctive endemic form characterized by a stockier build, shorter tarsus, and a broader, heavier bill," Wingate wrote in a 1982 paper published in *Colonial Waterbirds*. He believes the Bermudian birds had evolved from North American yellow-crowned night herons, which range from New England to Florida along the east coast and as far west as the Mississippi. The adaptations noted in the fossils are all common in endemic oceanic bird species, and indeed, he continues, "are exactly the characteristics described for the Socorro Island race N. *violacea gravirostris*, which feeds primarily on land crabs."

Wingate was acutely aware that reintroducing the herons might not work, given the high density of the human population and the fact that the migrant birds did not seem inclined to stay. But he thought he had a shot. Since the species had disappeared, two Protection of Birds acts had been passed, in 1949 and 1975, and, except to a very few, select people, including Wingate, as conservation officer, firearms had been banned since 1973.

So with funding from a government anxious to prevent golfing tourists from breaking their ankles in land-crab holes, he brought forty-six nestlings from the Alafia Banks rookery in Tampa Bay, Florida, to Nonsuch between 1976 and 1978. To distinguish them from the migrants, he used DayGlo tags to band the comical-looking babies—whose scraggly, Johnny Rotten–style pinfeathers make their expressions of embittered contempt seem entirely appropriate—and housed them in the roofless east ward.

Just to make sure they would develop a taste for land crabs, he started sending his daughters and their friends out at night to kill or capture the creatures. "We'd go out with broomsticks and flashlights," recalls Chris Jones, "and get a hundred with no problem at all every night." The kids would toss the crabs into an old marble bathtub from the hospital that sat on the lawn behind the chapel, and Wingate would feed them dog food until they were needed. In the mornings, he would come out, stab them in the head, pry their carapaces off, remove their pincers, cut them in half, and bring a plate of them in to the herons, which, he wrote, "rushed in and clustered around the food dish in a crouching stance with widened gapes, rocking from side to side and uttering a 'chee chee chee' sound like a rattling of marbles."

As the herons began to fledge, they would fly away for short periods, continuing to return for suppertime until at last they were procuring meals on their own. It was the first time anyone had ever tried to translocate and hand-rear yellow-crowned night herons, and the survival rate was close to 100 percent. By 1980, Wingate had confirmed successful nesting in the forty-acre Walsingham Nature Reserve, just across Castle Harbour from Nonsuch, and five years later found a nest on Nonsuch itself. "My elation could hardly be contained," he wrote in a 1988 overview of the living museum project. "They continued to feed almost entirely on land crabs, reducing the Nonsuch population to manageable levels again and doing such an effective job on the golf courses on Bermuda's mainland that the managers were soon able to stop the use of poison baits for crab control." This, in turn, benefitted the wetlands in which runoff from the golf courses had begun to accumulate.

The heron introduction had a second bonus. During his previous attempt to reintroduce Bermuda sedge to Nonsuch, the land crabs had eaten all the plants. But once the crab population came under control, he tried a second planting, in the early '90s, that was a raging success. "The sedge plants not only survived," he says, "but seedlings started to germinate all around them. Who could have predicted the growth of the sedge on Nonsuch could have been dependent on a heron that eats crabs?"

Like most of the other species that have been imported to Bermuda over the years, however, the herons have also had detrimental consequences. "Ninety-eight or ninety-five percent of what David's done has been wonderful," says Jamie Bacon, the principal investigator for the conservation department's Amphibian Project. "But then there's maybe a couple of things that haven't been quite as wonderful, and the herons are one of them."

"When you introduce something," says Bermudian undersea explorer Teddy Tucker, "if it doesn't have exactly what it had when it was here originally, it'll eat whatever's most handy. A lot of times that makes other things extinct." Tucker, who lives on the waterfront in Bermuda's west end, says the birds have "adapted very well to living with humans. We've got a couple [in our backyard] that are almost domesticated. They'll eat the fish you're cleaning, hot dogs, meat fat, cat food, anything they can swallow. To tell you the truth, they're a perfect bloody nuisance."

The herons are killing two species that were introduced but that people have grown quite fond of over the years: the cockroach-eating cane toad and the cute, melodious whistling frog. They also prey on the hatchlings of diamondback terrapins, which number only about a hundred in the country and have a hard enough time getting by, since they breed only in golf course sand traps. A selective heron-culling program with an authorized shooter began last year at the Mid Ocean Club's golf course in Tucker's Town, "to give the terrapins some respite," says Bacon. "No one wants to do it, but it's a necessary evil."

The herons have also been known to nab the occasional skink, though Wingate maintains kiskadees are a much more important factor in the species' decline. When he analyzed the stomach contents of the flycatchers he shot on Nonsuch, every one had a skink hatchling or two in its gizzard. "Adults survived, but there was no replacement of hatchlings," he says, "so the population skewed toward aging adults. If heron predation were the main cause, you would see a decline across the board, because herons go for adults and babies. The sheer abundance of the kiskadee is a telling factor. They're like ten or twenty times as abundant in Bermuda as in their home range. The skink is headed for extinction, I believe, entirely because of the kiskadees." He admits, however, that the herons may "just be that added bit that tips the scale a little more."

The heron population has grown larger than Wingate had anticipated, perhaps, he speculates, because recent habitat changes due to increased hurricane activity have created more impenetrable thickets in which they can nest. Between 1953 and 1970, when the forest was still rebuilding from the cedar scale, only two major hurricanes hit the island; in the '70s, when trees were still relatively low, there were three storms—an unnamed one in 1970, and Alice and Faye in 1973 and '75, respectively.

During the reign of the low-stature cedar monoculture, Wingate says, "You could walk anywhere in the forest of Bermuda." When the cedars died, the new forest that replaced them—mainly casuarina, fiddlewood, allspice, and Brazilian pepper—was also open under the canopy, because the dead cedars provided rigid support for these trees.

The problem was much of the dead cedar that hadn't been cleared by the government had been harvested for timber, mostly by black marketers, and the new trees replacing it were not hurricane resistant. "The imported trees were tall-growing and easily uprooted, and basically they just shattered and the forest was flattened. It essentially became horizontal."

In the late 1980s, the hurricane cycle picked up again, bringing Emily, Dean, Felix, and Gert, so that by the time Fabian came along in 2003, Wingate says, "if you didn't have a chainsaw, you couldn't walk through the woods. The herons took advantage of that because they could nest without being harassed by children and so forth. That's one factor in the heron becoming more common than I expected it to be."

But he stands by his choice to bring the herons back, pointing out that the birds are not new to the island; they are regular winter migrants and often oversummer there as well. The real problem, he maintains, is an ecosystem out of whack.

As he found with the sedge, the tangled synergies among species can never be anticipated. "Everything in nature is interconnected," he says. "You cannot do anything without influencing everything else and readjusting the whole web of life. My policy was to only reintroduce things that were known to have been here before. But there are so many other factors now that may affect the ascent or decline of any species—other invasive species, pesticide use, population growth, automobiles. It's a complex fabric of cause and effect. Bermuda is so completely messed up right now, like Hawaii and most other oceanic islands, that there's only so much you can do and only in so many places. That's why satellite islands like Nonsuch are so important."

⁜

A second reintroduction took place just a few years after the herons, whatever some may think of them, arrived to stay. *Cittarium pica*, commonly known as the West Indian topshell, is a large black-and-white whelk, or sea snail, that has historically been an economically important food source throughout the Caribbean. It ranged as far north as Bermuda until, yes, human habitation. Topshell subfossils have been found by the thousands underneath shipwrecks, embedded in dunes, and littering cave floors around the country.

Early reports of topshell abundance include Henry May's 1594 account that the shells were burned with limestone and mixed with turtle oil to make caulk for the ship's seams, and John Smith's tale of a settler who hid in the woods during the 1615 famine and "lived onely on Wilkes and land Crabs, fat and lusty many moneths." It is unclear exactly when and why topshells disappeared from Bermuda. There is some speculation that disease or a temperature change may have got them, though A. E. Verrill recounts finding broken shells in the kitchen middens used at the Castle Island garrison during the War of 1812. The creature "has been so long extinct in the Bermudas," he writes, "that nothing is now known of its former presence in the living state."

He mentions at least one attempt, in 1901, to reintroduce the species from the Bahamas by releasing specimens into Hamilton Harbour, but, as with later tries in the 1960s and '70s, it was unsuccessful. The harbor, says Wingate, "has a low-energy coastline, whereas the topshell survives best in a high-energy coastline." More intense wave action keeps a broader band of rocky coast moist, allowing the snails to climb higher for the algae they eat while keeping away from their main nonhuman predator, the octopus.

Teddy Tucker is a demigod in Bermuda for his encyclopedic knowledge of the sea and for his own fascinating story, which includes his 1955 find of a 22-karat gold pendant reliquary with cabochon emeralds at the wreck of the *San Pedro*, a Spanish galleon that ran afoul of Bermuda's reefs in 1594. Believed to have been made in Colombia for a high-ranking church official, the Tucker Cross, as the bauble quickly became known, is even today considered by many to be the most valuable single piece ever taken from a shipwreck. After dangling on the dashboard of Tucker's boat for a while, it was hung on display in a glass-fronted safe at the Bermuda Aquarium until it was moved to the island's west end for the 1975 opening of the maritime museum, where Tucker was to present it to the Queen.

"Where's the real cross?" said Tucker, who had been waiting at the museum for the cross's delivery, the moment he touched the object. "That's not even funny," somebody answered. But Tucker wasn't kidding. The cross was missing, and a plastic replica had been put in its place.

"When the cross hung in the aquarium," says David Saul, "every day the safe was opened and closed, and if you went six steps around the corner there was a board that the key hung on." No one knows when the switch was made, or by whom, but it is assumed that a wealthy international collector arranged for the object's removal. An investigation by the Bermuda police, the FBI, Scotland Yard, and Interpol turned up nothing.

"So the next thing is," David Saul remembers, "I'm treasury secretary. And one day, clickety-clack, telex. My secretary brings it in and says, 'Have a look at that one.' It was to the minister of finance, David Gibbons. 'Dear Minister: I have the Tucker Cross. You and the people of Bermuda might like to have the real one back. . . . It is yours for $200,000. Signed, the Phantom.' So I said to my secretary, while you're standing there take this note. 'Dear Phantom: Thank you very much for your message. We are happy to know that the Tucker Cross is in safe hands. Thank you for the fake. No one can tell the difference. We have no worries about insurance. Indeed, we don't even care if this one is stolen too. Take good care of our property. Signed, the Minister of Finance.' The minister came in not long after, laughed at it, and signed it. And that was the end of it."

"Where do you look?" says Tucker, on whom the character of Romer Treece in Peter Benchley's *The Deep* is based. "They didn't even have a starting point."

Tucker moved on. "I used to travel back and forth all over the place," he says. In 1982 he took his boat to the Turks and Caicos. "I had a lifeboat on deck, so I gathered up a couple of sacks of topshells and put them in the dinghy, where they could be hosed down regularly. They were here in Bermuda once," he adds. "Why not put them back?" He'd discussed the idea in advance with the director of the aquarium, who sent a boat to Tucker's house to fetch the snails on his return.

After being quarantined at the aquarium, the whelks were released in various places around the island. Wingate asked for a batch for Nonsuch.

"When I heard that Teddy had brought them here," he says, "I said to Fisheries, 'Well, that was one of my next projects, to get permission to reintroduce the topshell. And if they're already here, we might as well release them on Nonsuch.' So they agreed to do it." Employees of the Fisheries Department actually handled the animals, Wingate points out, "so I wasn't involved at all except that I suggested using them to restock Nonsuch." He then followed their progress in a series of articles for the department's monthly bulletin.

Most of the snails were of breeding age, or close to it, when they arrived, but finding proof of reproduction would be difficult, since, like most mollusks, topshell larvae go through a planktonic "veliger" stage, during which they drift along with the currents, which allows new colonies to develop. The first evidence Wingate found of successful breeding came in the summer of 1985, when a half-dozen dime-sized babies were located in the north and east sides of Nonsuch; a 1989 survey found a total of 281 specimens, as far away as Devonshire Parish's south shore.

That same year, because the illegal harvesting of the snails for food had already begun, topshells were added to the government's list of protected species. By 2000 they had spread all along Bermuda's south shore, but, according to a 2006 paper Wingate wrote for the newsletter of the International Union for Conservation of Nature, there had also been "a marked reduction of harvestable age (medium to large) shells in areas where they had previously become abundant, most notably on coastal parklands where people have unrestricted access to the foreshore." Most of the confirmed harvesting, he points out, was for fish bait, but in at least one instance the whelks were actually being served as a gourmet dish at a local restaurant. Today, anyone caught taking a topshell faces a $5,000 fine, and though they are still being exploited illegally, the population has grown enough that it can sustain the poaching. Wingate hopes the snails' discarded shells might one day help to bring back native hermit crabs, which at last count numbered in the hundreds.

Things were really beginning to come together on Nonsuch. Herons and topshells were coming back, and there was even new hope for the cedars. In 1977, Barry Phillips, a horticulturalist from the Royal Botanic Gardens in Kew, arrived in Bermuda to work under Walwyn Hughes. Since Hughes had taken over as head of Ag and Fish in 1975, he and Hubert Jones, with input from Wingate, had been moving the government nursery away from ornamentals and back toward native and endemic plants. During the job interview, Hughes asked Phillips if he thought he could bring the cedars back. "I said I'd give it a damn good shot," Phillips recalls. "Nothing's impossible."

He began propagating from seeds and had some success but, he says, "we had no control over whether the resulting trees would have immunity to the scale insect." Though he knew that cloning from healthy trees would result in better percentages, his cloned trees weren't doing as well as he'd hoped they would until a Kew colleague suggested he try using the tips of juvenile trees rather than cuttings from mature specimens. "Once we took on that method," Phillips recalls, "we sort of went to town. It was a real breakthrough." Over the next decade, the government nursery went from having a few hundred viable saplings to about fifteen thousand.

Wingate planted some of the new batch on Nonsuch. There wasn't much space left on the island, since the olivewoods, palmettos, and hackberries were doing so well; as a pioneer species, the cedar couldn't grow up through a preestablished canopy. But in anticipation of another cedar planting some day, he had left empty the 140 or so spaces created when he'd removed the hat palm a few years before, and there was also a field he'd never planted because, he says, "In Bermuda there's such a strong cultural mindset of keeping arable land open in case you need it that even on Nonsuch, I had done it almost unthinkingly. It was just the paradigm of the time." When he dug out the dune pond, he increased the field's soil depth with the excavated material, making it the perfect environment for a small forest of about two dozen cedars. The rest he fitted in wherever there was a gap. Almost all of the trees survived—though at the time no one knew quite why.

It gradually became clear, as the cedars planted on Nonsuch by Wingate and around the mainland by Phillips and his team matured, that the trees did not all look alike, as they had before the scale insect had hit. "There were quite striking forms of cedar on the landscape that we'd been calling Bermuda cedar," says Wingate, "but it was becoming increasingly obvious that they weren't. There were at least three forms, maybe four."

In 2008 Wingate collaborated with Robert Adams, a biology professor at Baylor University in Waco, Texas, to do a DNA analysis. They found that most of the cloned trees were actually hybrids. The original *Juniperus bermudiana* had bred with *Juniperus silicicola*, or southern red cedar, a coastal variety found in the southeastern United States. Silicicola, which has finer needles, denser foliage, and a bushier appearance, with branches that grow lower on the trunk, is known as Darrell's cedar in Bermuda because it was first brought to the country in the 1940s by a J. D. C. Darrell, who obtained it from the Royal Palms Nursery in Lutz, Florida.

A few genuine Bermuda cedars did survive the scale, either because they had retained the genes that conferred immunity or because they'd hung on until biological controls started to take effect. Most of the ladybugs that were brought over to feed on the *C. minima* scale in the late 1940s and early '50s were eaten by anoles, but the two or three species best suited to Bermuda's environment survived, along with several species of tiny, scale-parasitizing wasps that were imported around the same time. "The wasps and ladybirds were terribly important because they are what enabled the old trees to stop dying just before there was a total wipeout," Wingate says. "They've slowly recovered, particularly in healthy growing situations like cemeteries that are free of competition."

A small percentage of the trees in the country today are pure Darrell's cedar, too. But "the average Bermudian is just going to be happy to see cedars reappearing in the landscape," says Barry Phillips. "They're not going to say, 'Oh, it's not real Bermuda cedar.'"

Wingate is one of those who is not too concerned about the details of the gene pool. Rather than writing a joint conclusion to their paper, which appeared in the journal *Phytologia* in August 2008, Wingate and Adams each wrote a separate addendum. "Adams thought it was bad that the trees had hybridized," Wingate recalls. "He has a concept of fixed species, and once they're contaminated, they're finished." Wingate took a more Darwinian approach. "From my point of view," he continues, "it's a way of saving the species. This is evolution in action, actually. It's something that could have happened naturally, you see—the birds could have brought the seeds of the silicicola."

The silicicola is less salt-spray resistant and more prone to uprooting and branch breakage during hurricanes. "But in the process of evolution," Wingate says, "what will happen is that with each generation, those trees will be excluded, so that eventually you will have a new Bermuda cedar which incorporates the hurricane resistance of the original trees with the scale resistance of the Darrell's cedar." Another example, he says, of the adaptability of nature.

CHAPTER NINE

Leaving the Nest

BARRY PHILLIPS'S SECOND MANDATE as horticultural officer was to start an apprenticeship program for young Bermudians who were interested in careers with the Department of Agriculture, Fisheries and Parks. Interns would rotate to different sections every six months in the hope they would find a field that suited them and stay in Bermuda once they'd received the training. One day a young man who worked in his family's grocery store came in to see Phillips at the suggestion of Elizabeth Wingate, a regular customer at the market. "She told me that Barry Phillips was trying to resurrect the Bermuda cedar," Jeremy Madeiros remembers. "I said to him, 'I can grow Bermuda cedar faster than anybody else on the island, I guarantee that.' I'd been growing them for years, using chicken manure."

Skeptical, Phillips went over to the Madeiros property and, sure enough, he says, he was "quite impressed by the size of the trees." Madeiros quickly got the job and, because he was interested in the work Wingate was doing with restoring native plants, did an early rotation at Nonsuch. He and Wingate clicked so well that both requested, and got, a second chance to work together during Madeiros's two apprenticeship years. "I started as a plant guy," Madeiros says, "but working with David made me wonder, 'Well, why are these particular plants here?' Birds were the main source. So the year that I spent with him gave me a more holistic view and helped me expand my horizons."

Wingate, meanwhile, continued to face challenges with the cahows. By 1986, he had forty nesting pairs and sixteen fledglings, both numbers about double his count at the beginning of the project almost a quarter century earlier. On February 4, 1987, all seemed to be going well—established pairs were laying and juveniles courting overhead—

when a completely unexpected threat arrived. "I was traumatized to find the predated remains of a cahow at the (B) complex today," he writes in his diary of a group of nests on Inner Pear. "This consisted of some grey underdown stuck in white excrement patches, scattered cahow body feathers and two intact wings laying about 10' apart & stripped of meat." As he stood there puzzling over what could have done the cahow in, a snowy owl announced itself, flying close by and landing on the cliffs east of Cooper's Island.

It was the same owl he'd excitedly recorded a couple of weeks before under the headline "Owl at last!" He and his friend Eric Amos, a fellow birder, had been checking the other end of the island one day when they'd seen the bird on the Dockyard jetty. It was the first snowy owl Wingate had ever seen. At the time, he had speculated that the owl, which was about twice the size of a crow, was living in Hamilton Harbour but had been driven to Dockyard over the weekend by boating noise. "It will be extremely interesting to find out where the owl feeds and to follow its progress throughout the winter!" he writes. A later addendum reads: "Famous last words."

On the day he discovered the killing, he called the owl's appearance "the most significant event of the cahow program since the 1960s." He spent the night cruising the harbor islands until he was satisfied the bird had left. The danger seemed over for a time, but three weeks later, on Green Island, he found two more cahows dead under similarly violent circumstances. "Alas," he writes, "as I returned towards south end of island I came upon the sight I dreaded most. Not one, but 3 wings of cahow plus a severed cahow head, indicating a minimum of 2 cahow kills. . . . I absolutely must get that owl soon!"

He began carrying his sixteen-gauge shotgun with him everywhere and stalking the bird whenever he saw it, only to have it fly away before he could get close enough. Within the next few days he found another cahow head and soon after, the remains of a fifth bird. The crisis was intensifying as the owl was becoming habituated to its new prey. Wingate appealed for public help in locating the bird, and, for the next month, spent nearly every day tracking it and every night standing watch in Castle Harbour before going home to lose sleep worrying about it. Finally, on March 5, as he was heading back toward Nonsuch in the boat, he saw the owl sitting on the island's north cliff beside the demonstration cahow burrow. After grabbing a .22 he'd borrowed from a local policeman, he crept through the casuarinas opposite the outcropping. The owl disappeared, but Wingate persisted, knowing it must be nearby. "Then came my lucky break," he writes. From the corner of his eye he noticed a streak of white along the rock less than twenty-five feet away.

Somehow, the owl—distracted by some tropicbirds flying in front of the cliff—didn't hear Wingate approach. Unfortunately Wingate soon realized he was carrying the wrong weapon; the .22 was sighted for thirty to fifty yards and might miss at such close range. He risked going back to the house for his twelve-gauge, and when he returned, the bird was still there, "fatally attracted by the tropicbirds," he writes. "I cocked the gun & stepped forward until the entire head and shoulders were in view, then fired. The blast pushed the owl right off the cliff & it fell 60' into the water. It was over."

Well, not quite. Wingate spoke to the Bermuda press about the event, and even let the newspapers take photos of the owl and cahow remains. "It's All Over for the Arctic Owl as One Shot Blows Its Head Off" read the headline in the *Royal Gazette,* which had been following the saga. Letters to the editor came down strongly on the side of the owl, and an article titled "Feathers Ruffled over Owl's Demise" reported that "nearly all people asked about the killing thought another, more humane method could have been used to deal with the owl." Even the London papers picked up the story, vilifying Wingate. His friend Eddie Wright, who is licensed to cull pest birds and helped Wingate in his hunt for the owl, recalls the whole episode as "very stressful and traumatic" for him.

But Wingate never doubted he had done the right thing. The owl was well beyond the southern limit of its range and probably could not have made the trip back home in any case. A tranquilizer dart, even if it could have reached the bird on a faraway perch, probably would have killed it on impact, and by the time Wingate could have trapped the owl, all the juvenile cahows might have been dead.

Though snowy owls are classified by the IUCN as having a conservation status of "least concern," they are protected, and they're not often seen in the United Kingdom. "From a British perspective," says Wingate, "they thought any conservation officer who would shoot an owl because it was killing birds, which they're supposed to do, has got to be sick in the head. But the story was taken out of context, because it was killing one of the rarest seabirds in the world. If that had happened twenty years earlier, it could have spelled the end of the cahows."

The upside, if there was one, was that all the chicks fledged that year, indicating no adults had been lost; it appeared the owl had caught only prebreeding birds that would have been spending time outside the burrows at night. Still, the incident did cost the cahows a year's population growth. "Basically what the owl did," Wingate says, "is knock out a whole cohort of birds that might have made up additional pairs the following year."

✦

Another threat, which he thought he had vanquished in the '60s, reappeared not long after the snowy owl episode.

From the start, Wingate and the American military, stationed just a quarter mile from Nonsuch on Cooper's Island, had viewed each other warily. The Cold War was in full force during the bulk of Wingate's time as conservation officer, and, with Bermuda considered of major importance in protecting North Atlantic sea routes, the base was a key antisubmarine-warfare hub authorized to deploy nuclear weapons.

If war had broken out between the United States and Russia, Bermuda would have been not only a launching pad but also a primary target. "That was the Damocles sword that hung over the project the whole time," Wingate says. "I was conscious that the whole project could be incinerated at any moment."

Obviously, security on the base was tight.

Despite permits and standing agreements with each new commander to approach the base in the service of the cahows, beginning as early as the late 1950s Wingate was repeatedly detained by troops who hadn't gotten the message or were simply exercising their authority. "They had three tiers of security and the coordination between them wasn't that good," he recalls. "You'd get your permission and go out there, and you'd get to a certain point and then another lot would arrest you. And then you'd get a little farther, and another lot would arrest you."

There was the time Wingate was bird-watching, by permit, on the base with Eric Amos. "The marines on guard out there saw us using binoculars," he remembers. "They said, 'You're supposed to be checking roads.' I said, 'Clearly you misheard. We're out checking *birds*.' The marine suddenly went icy cold and said, 'Get off my post.' The gun came off his shoulder at that point, so Eric and I looked at each other and said, 'He's letting us go, let's just go.'"

Another time, during Madeiros's apprenticeship, he and his assistant, Jaha Mallory, a large, decidedly unmilitary-looking Rastafarian expat worker from Trinidad, were doing a topshell survey along the shoreline where they could barely be seen. Madeiros was on the tarmac at the edge of the perimeter road, and Mallory was down on the rocks at the tide line, detaching the snails and bringing them to Madeiros in batches for weighing and measuring. "The first hint of trouble was when I saw security vehicles with lights flashing converging from several locations," Madeiros recalls. "I thought, Uh-oh, this doesn't look good. Next thing, there were several marines grabbing me and throwing me on the ground, with M-16s pointed at my back fully loaded and cocked." Madeiros, his face pressed against the asphalt, was trying to explain when he noticed Mallory starting up the seawall. "All I saw was the top of his head," Madeiros says, laughing. "His eyes appeared and he did a double-take. The poor guy hid in the rocks for like an hour, afraid that if he showed up they'd just shoot him first and ask questions later."

Less than ten days later, Madeiros and Mallory were back at the airport, this time with Wingate, who was in the boat just offshore, scouting out topshell locations for them. "The same thing happened, basically," Madeiros says. "Security vans start screaming in our direction, and the next thing we know all these burly marines start coming out and ordering us on the ground. David's like, 'Bloody hell, do I have to do this?' And a marine says, 'Sir, if you do not come out of the boat I will shoot your boat.' Once he's down, David says, 'I'm too old for this shit,' and I start giggling. The marine stomps on my back and says, 'This is no laughing matter.'" Eventually, after placing a call to the base, the guards let them go.

"Turns out they were just testing the sentries to see if they were alert and would catch us," Madeiros says. "The marine commander wasn't particularly happy we were doing the survey but had been ordered to cooperate."

The following week, the paper ran a story about one of the marines shooting himself in the foot by accident. "I remember joking with Eric about it and saying, 'Christ, we didn't know how close we were to being shot if they're that clumsy,'" says Wingate.

With their automatic weapons and signs reading USE OF DEADLY FORCE AUTHORIZED, the military never had a problem getting Wingate to back down. It wasn't as easy the other way around.

The first time David tackled Goliath was in the mid-1960s. NASA had been leasing space from the naval air station since the beginning of the Apollo program, and in 1965 the organization began constructing an AN/FPQ-6 radar system, one of many around the globe, to help track manned space flights. The main tower was on Cooper's Point, less than two-tenths of a mile from Outer Pear; its construction attracted Norway rats, including the one that swam onto the island and killed all the cahows and shearwaters.

But potentially worse were the survey reference targets needed to monitor the tower to make sure it didn't begin to settle into its foundation. Planned for Inner and Outer Pear and at least one spot on the point, these were thin masts supported by guy wires that on both islets would have spanned the entire upland. "It would have been utterly catastrophic for the birds," Wingate says. "They come whipping in over the island at night, and they wouldn't have seen the wires. They all would have broken their wings."

Luckily, at the time, Wingate's wife Anita played tennis with the NASA director's wife, and the two couples were friendly. "So rather than go through the bureaucracy and proper government channels," he says, "I sorted it out on a person to person basis, which made it a lot easier to get things done." He persuaded the director, Fred Healey, to use solid eight-inch piping painted white in place of wire stays. The birds could see the pipes, and there was never a problem, except on the day the mast was to be installed.

As Wingate was mooring his boat at Inner Pear, the workmen were hauling a heavy piece of piping from the boat up the hillside. He was worrying that they were trampling the delicate coastal plants, but when he got to the top of the cliff he found a much scarier scene: The foreman was preparing to pour cement into a natural pit in the ground to save himself the digging. What the foreman didn't know was that the depression contained two cahow burrows.

"The bird was so rare and on such tiny fragments of land," Wingate says, "that something as small as putting a mast on an island could have been fatal to the entire island's population. It illustrated how important it was to be there on these occasions and to be alert to the kinds of things that could go wrong."

The floodlights shining on the NASA installation—"more as an advertisement for the NASA program than for any practical purpose," Wingate would later write in a 2009 recovery plan—were also a problem. The lights illuminated Inner Pear, and though they didn't affect established pairs, they did inhibit courting birds. Several years after the lights were erected, Wingate noticed that new pair formation on Inner and Outer Pear had basically come to a halt. The birds were slowly moving toward Horn and Green. Ironically, these more distant western islands off Nonsuch had the fewest birds on them at the time and were actually less vulnerable to hurricane overwash than the eastern islands, so in the end the birds were actually safer. But Wingate still lobbied to have the lights turned off, and won.

He also fought proposals to extend the airport's runway and to install a navigational light on one of the islets. "It was all part of making the base commanders aware," he says. "Every time there was a change of base commander, we got a face-to-face meeting with them and explained the whole story of the cahow and the sensitivity of it and the global conservation concerns. It would have been very embarrassing for the military if the whole conservation world had come down on them because they caused the cahow's extinction because of some lights that could have been put somewhere else." He suspects these plans were dropped for other reasons, but says, "At least I put in my two bits to stop them."

The lighting issue reappeared periodically, though. TACAMO is military-speak for "take charge and move out," and the planes associated with that phrase were first deployed in 1964 as part of a system of "survivable" communications links for use in case of a nuclear war. When the bombs started to fall, the president and his cabinet and top military advisors would still be able to direct operations through the TACAMO planes stationed around North America. Until then, the aircraft were kept on constant alert, often flying for hours at a time to ensure the Soviets could never take out all vital military communications in one attack.

In 1974, the Navy TACAMO squadron VQ-4 began stationing crews and aircraft in Bermuda. There was always one and were often two alert planes on the ground on the north side of Runway 30, along the airfield's eastern edge. In 1975, the planes were moved to the opposite side of the runway, along Castle Harbour, and lighting carts were set up to provide security. The lights were usually turned toward the runway, but at least one serviceman made sure they were facing the harbor during his watches. "I always thought it was stupid to have the aircraft illuminated by the lights, making them great big well-illuminated targets," Scott Hartzler, at the time a lance corporal assigned to perimeter security, writes in an e-mail. "I always turned them outward to better observe anyone approaching the area."

Since they were inconsistently facing the harbor, Wingate was never able to pin down exactly what effect these lights had on the cahows, if any, so he never complained about them. But by 1987, the marines had tired of using mobile lights and decided they needed a more permanent solution. The commanding officer of the squadron at the time apparently agreed with Hartzler and had a bank of permanent floodlights installed facing into the harbor.

"These lights were so goddamn bright that they lit up Nonsuch like a full moon," Wingate says. They also hit Horn Rock, where the cahow population had been soaring since the birds had left the eastern islands to escape the NASA lights. Because the new lights were obviously installed precisely to illuminate the harbor, Wingate didn't even try to fight them. "It wasn't an incidental thing," he says, "so I knew it would be hopeless, especially once the Gulf War started." During the five years the lights remained on, no new cahow pairs formed over Horn Rock, and the mating population in general underwent a lengthy stagnation, with the exception of a small bump in 1989. It wasn't until 1992, when the lights were turned off—the TACAMOs made their final flight out of Bermuda in 1991—that the number of breeding pairs resumed its slow ascent.

A final near-crisis occurred in 1988, when military commanders decided they needed to move their baseball diamond to Cooper's Point to make room for more housing near the heart of the base. Wingate was initially on hand to monitor the construction but was dismayed to find that the site chosen happened to contain the last remnant of undisturbed native woodland on Cooper's Island and that, in anticipation of its clearing, someone had already cut down two young cedars growing on it. He contacted Stuart Hayward, a parliamentarian who'd been elected on an environmentalist platform, and a meeting was soon called between the U.S. consul general, the Bermudian environment minister, and the military's top brass. The virgin forest wasn't Wingate's only concern, of course. The stadium lights would have blinded the birds coming in to Castle Harbour; a few years before, he had succeeded in getting two lights hooded at the existing baseball diamond because they glared out into the harbor, and this ball field would have been far worse. "I believe the [Naval Air Station] and the U.S. Government," Hayward said at the time in the *Royal Gazette*, "would find it impossible to justify threatening the survival of the cahow for the sake of night baseball." The navy eventually shelved the plan, saying it would have cost too much anyway, according to the *Gazette's* final story on the matter, which began with the words, "The cahows have won."

Wingate was "hugely relieved" when, forty-five years ahead of schedule, the United States suddenly pulled out of Bermuda, not long after a 1992 report by Sam Donaldson found that with the end of the Cold War, the base was no longer needed but was being kept open as a holiday camp for top military officers at the expense of U.S. taxpayers. As if the closing weren't exciting enough, NASA handed Cooper's Island back to the Bermuda government in 2001 because of cuts in space-program spending and the advent of new technology that made the tracking station obsolete.

But the problems created on the base didn't disappear quite as easily as the troops and civilian employees. Ruth's Bay, a small beach inlet just south of the St. David's lighthouse, had been obliterated by being used for decades as a garbage dump. "The trash would pile up," Wingate says, "and they'd burn it and bulldoze it into the sea." Because it was in a "hidden corner" of Bermuda where there was little recreational boating, few people noticed the plume of ashes and metals that rode out daily with the tide. "There was a great rusty stain in the water that was permanent in that area," he says. "God knows what chemicals were in there." The Bermuda government couldn't say much, since until the Tynes Bay incinerator was built in 1994, it had been using Pembroke Marsh in much the same way.

Still, the U.S. military agreed to clean up the area before officially closing the base. The marine engineers—"who were always putting up lights or bulldozing this or destroying that," Wingate says—were replaced by workers from a New Jersey contracting firm who removed asbestos, PCBs, underground storage tanks, and solid wastes. They also lined the landfill ramp leading down to the water at Ruth's Bay with geotextile matting and then covered the trash dumped there with boulders from Government Quarry. Though that rock is the heaviest in Bermuda, it is still relatively light compared with, say, granite or basalt, and no sooner was the project finished than Hurricane Felix came along and washed away everything that had been done. "The seas got into the core of the dump and scattered garbage all over the airport and Clearwater Beach," says Wingate. "It was a god-awful mess." The military sent another contractor to come back and try again, using igneous boulders imported from Canada. "It was a patch-over job," he adds, "but to do it properly and return all that garbage to the United States probably would have cost millions."

Four of the head contractors were environmentalists—"on our side, for once," Wingate says—and willing to go above and beyond their mandate. Since at least the early '80s, Wingate had been beating the drum about making Cooper's Point a nature reserve after the U.S. lease was up, so he took the opportunity to get the project started. He worked with the men on clearing and planting four or five acres behind Clearwater Beach, on the west side of the point, converting the exercise trails to nature trails and stocking the forest with native and endemic plants. "I thought if we did that the Bermuda government could hardly go back on something that was already created," he says. The little park became the nucleus for the Cooper's Island Nature Reserve, a 12-acre area opened in 2010. "Forty years earlier than I expected," Wingate says. "It all seems too good to be true."

✦

Plus ça change, plus c'est la même chose, the French journalist Jean-Baptiste Alphonse Karr famously wrote in 1849. Wingate's life in the 1980s and '90s was the reverse: The more things remained the same, the more they were slowly changing. Nonsuch's precolonial forest was doing better than he'd ever imagined it would be by then, readying itself for the day the cahows would nest inside it; all that remained was to continue tending to the island, endlessly culling invasives and removing predators. Once the bafflers had been worked out and a few artificial burrows were being built every year, "I'd done everything I could do to help the cahows," Wingate says. "Now it was just a question of waiting for them to increase."

He continued his nest-by-nest monitoring, giving individual birds special attention whenever they needed it. In 1995, for example, an unusually small longtail got through a baffler and, for the first time in more than thirty years, a cahow chick was attacked because of nest-site competition. The baby was big enough to fight back until the longtail withdrew, but its lower mandible was broken nearly in half in the skirmish. Wingate discovered this just as a gale was coming on; he removed the chick from the nest and took it to Nonsuch for repairs, worried that he wouldn't get it back in time for its next feeding visit from a parent. He and his apprentice, Steve DeSilva, patched it up with Krazy Glue and a toothpick. Wingate used a pin to hold the tiny splint to the beak so he wouldn't glue his finger to the bird. After two tries—the second in driving rain and high winds just outside the burrow, since the first splint didn't survive the journey back from Nonsuch—the contraption held, and fifty-six days later, the chick, able to preen despite its slightly misshapen bill, became the first that season to fledge.

Wingate considered situations like this a routine part of cahow maintenance. The birds' population was climbing steadily, with the number of nesting pairs increasing from twenty-eight in 1980 to forty-three in 1990. By 2000, the year he officially retired, there were three times as many breeding birds and three times as many fledglings as there had been when he'd started in 1962. Wingate should have been happy—and he was, with the project. But personally, the new millennium would mark the beginning of the most miserable period in his life with the exception of the time following Anita's accident. "Oh! Forced retirement is hell!" he would write in his diary, years after the dread day had arrived.

His difficulties really began the year before he retired, when disruptive restoration work on the Nonsuch buildings commenced. The main house, with its sixteen-foot high ceilings, had been badly damaged in 1987's Hurricane Emily and its roof repaired rather than replaced. "I'd tried to patch it," Wingate says, "but it was getting dangerous. One day about four feet of plaster fell and just missed hitting my dog Max. I think it was Hurricane Gert that finally triggered the rebuilding, because it caused even more roof damage. It was getting to the point where the slightest hurricane"—nowhere but in Bermuda would you hear such a phrase—"would knock the ceilings down. I suppose in the end they thought it wouldn't look too good if I was killed by falling plaster."

The government allotted a huge pile of money for the repairs. In addition to replacing the old slate roof with SKB—an incredibly strong and wind-resistant fiberboard-cement-coated Styrofoam developed by a Bermudian for just this purpose—workmen fixed the ceilings, replaced the windows and electrical wiring in the main house, gutted the kitchen, refurbished the chapel, and upgraded the solar panels Wingate had started installing in the late '80s. Most of Wingate and Helge's belongings had to be moved into the laboratory during the repairs; she stayed at Nonpareil and he spent nights there too, commuting to Nonsuch once or twice a day to ferry workmen back and forth and sleeping occasionally in the west wing of the house, which remained livable during construction.

Around the same time, the government was also undergoing a restructuring after the Progressive Labour Party upended the status quo by defeating the United Bermuda Party, which had been in power for three decades. When Wingate had started as conservation officer, he'd been given free reign to do what he thought needed to be done, protected by Walwyn Hughes and his successors from having to worry too much about formalities. But over the years, bureaucracy had grown to almost Kafkaesque proportions, and the change of administrations didn't help.

In the 1960s, the department of agriculture had been joined and quickly overshadowed by Parks—which oversaw the conservation officer—and by the 1970s the two had formed a triad with Fisheries under the Ministry of Environment banner. After the PLP's 1998 victory, the three departments were split up and Conservation Services also became a separate, independent entity. When that happened, Parks, which managed all of the large beaches and parklands, got 152 laborers, and the conservation officer, whose nature reserves took up about a quarter of the parklands' acreage, got four. Fisheries was renamed Environmental Protection, which inevitably put it at constant budgetary loggerheads with conservation. While all this was taking place, says Wingate, "There was an immediate loss of com-

munication. It was very confusing because they were always juggling
ministries as well, so you'd be dealing with a different minister every
few months."

The shakeup didn't bode well for a man who had never been especially subtle in his questioning of authority.

At the end of July 2000—two and a half months before Jeremy
Madeiros was due to take over as terrestrial conservation officer—
the work crews were finishing up the Nonsuch house renovation and
Wingate was making plans to return to his little island full-time, when
he went to visit Candy Foggo, the new director of Parks. "Incredibly,"
he wrote in his diary,

> Candy tried to imply that I am expected to vacate the main house
> when I retire because the caretakership of Nonsuch is in the job
> description of the Conservation officer & automatically goes to
> him. If I am allowed to stay on Nonsuch at all, it would be in the
> cottage, where I would have to pay rent!! . . . I made it quite clear
> that if this was forced on me I might as well die.

Well, of course, one might think. What else would he expect? But
it had never really occurred to Wingate that he would be asked to
leave Nonsuch.

Because he had always considered the living museum and the cahow restoration a sideline—begun, he points out, "long before government had even thought of conservation"—he was shocked by the
news that he would have to give it up. "I still perceived it as my special
research project," he says, "and I hoped, now that I was relieved of my
official responsibilities, to be able to devote myself to it full-time. I
was looking forward to retirement, thinking, Wow, now I can really
focus on Nonsuch."

He had been imagining he would retire as a professor emeritus
of sorts, "where I'd be allowed to continue volunteering my time and
doing my research," he says, "and hand over the administrative side of
it to my successor, the way it is in the sciences. But certain people in
government believed I was just supposed to walk away and never look
back. I felt like the project was being stolen from me."

Jack Ward, who in 2002 became the first director of Conservation Services, agrees the fundamental problem was a difference in outlook. "David never prepared himself to retire," Ward says. "He never considered that in a structured, government role, when you retire, you need to step behind. I guess it's the contradiction between someone who's a passionate, committed individual pursuing his life's vocation, and actually being an employee in a government job. David was never good at that." Expecting to stay on with the cahows and live on Nonsuch, Ward maintains, was unrealistic. "You can't cherry-pick the best parts of your successor's job and not let him have any of that," he says.

Wingate says he had spoken with Bill Cook, Foggo's predecessor, about staying on, and Cook had agreed to try to arrange it. But nothing was in writing and Cook, who became very ill around this time and eventually moved back to the States, had never communicated the arrangement to Foggo—who, in any case, would have been free to ignore Cook's recommendations. "I don't know about Bill Cook," says Foggo at her office in Hamilton, where she is now a government labor-relations officer. "I can't speak to that. All I know is that the directive was given that the conservation officer was going in the main house." Madeiros says it was just government policy: If you weren't in the job, you didn't get the house. That was that.

But for Wingate, it wasn't so simple. Over the years, he had moved around quite a bit on the mainland, staying at Aldie or in his sister's cottage; at Elm Lodge, a house he'd inherited while he was married to Elizabeth and that she got in the divorce settlement; or at Nonpareil or various rentals. He had always regarded Nonsuch as his primary home. "Imagine how you'd feel," he says, "if you suddenly got a letter from government saying, 'We're putting another family in your house and you have to be out in a month.' It was not just walking away from a project, it was walking away from your lifetime home, with all of the memories and all of the personal touches that go along with that. It was very traumatic."

According to Barry Phillips, "Everybody thought it was the unwritten law that David would live there when he retired. He'd be given the use of the house for all those years of unbelievable effort and his unbelievable dedication to the well-being of Bermuda. He should have been made the lord provost of Bermuda or the next bloody governor for all he did."

Wingate knew it would only be a matter of time before age and his knee problems—caused by years of bumping over hard water in the Whaler—would keep him from landing on the cahow islands anyway. "But it all happened so fast when I still had the energy," he says. "Energy I wanted to put into the program."

He also worried that Madeiros hadn't trained long enough for his new job and thought being at Nonsuch would give him an opportunity to continue his mentoring.

When Madeiros had returned to Bermuda from college in 1991, having finished his two six-month stints as Wingate's apprentice, he was slated to become assistant conservation officer, learning the ropes in anticipation of taking over when Wingate retired. But because of government cutbacks, the new post was never created, and Madeiros instead became a superintendent in the parks department. Throughout the '90s, he still worked with Wingate occasionally on a volunteer basis, but, says Wingate, "There hadn't been enough time to pass on my forty years of knowledge."

After the news from Foggo, Wingate began to pursue the possibility of staying in the cottage instead of the main house. The parks department proposed that he become assistant caretaker, with a salary of $400 a month, and rent the cottage for $500 a month. Wingate, speaking to the *Royal Gazette*, called the offer "an insult."

"Critics balked at the original agreement," the newspaper wrote, "which suggested the conservationist would be required to work weekends and public holidays and still pay $100 for the privilege of caring for the island, which he has transformed into a living museum of endemic Bermuda species."

Wingate went over Foggo's head and appealed to the minister of the environment, who asked Madeiros what he would like to see happen. "The minister counseled Jeremy," says Jack Ward, "saying, 'You're not going to be able to express yourself in this job with someone looking over your shoulder like that.'" But Madeiros supported Wingate's petition. "He couldn't stomach the thought that David would be cut out of it," Ward says.

The minister told Wingate he could live in the cottage on a three-year lease but would not receive a salary or an official title. Foggo claimed it was all a misunderstanding. "I thought I left the door open to work to an agreement," the *Royal Gazette* quotes her as saying, "but he chose to [go to] the press."

Wingate was glad when word finally came that he could stay on the island, but the cottage hadn't been used for years and no longer had electricity, since a work crew had accidentally severed the line to it some time before. He could have hooked up a connection to the generator himself but was told the job had to be done by government employees. He waited and waited for Works and Engineering to get the system going again. "I was right back where I started back in 1962," he says, "having to dip water out of the tanks and use Coleman lanterns and candles for light at night." He says he complained about this and was told by the "officious" housing officer, "basically, take it or leave it."

In the six months Wingate remained in the main house while waiting for a decision about where he'd be living, Jeremy Madeiros and his wife, Leila, began to grow impatient with him. "I was separating from Helge at the time," Wingate says, "and they really wanted me out, but I had nowhere to go, nowhere to put my stuff. Government refused to confirm that I could stay in the cottage. I became very bitter, and the Madeiroses became angry with me that they couldn't take over in a clean sweep." Helge and Leila argued, and with the cottage's lack of power and the tension between the two families, says Wingate, "After a while I began to feel that I'm not wanted, I'm not welcome here anymore."

"He was extremely depressed at that point," says Penny Hill, with whom Wingate stayed when he was on the mainland beginning in August 2001, when he had laparoscopic surgery on both knees and needed care as he recovered. "It was his life, Nonsuch and the cahow program, it was all his life. His life had basically, unpleasantly come to an end at that point. I just thought, Why can they not understand what this is doing to David?"

✦

At first, Wingate and Madeiros continued working together, coordinating cahow checks and comparing notes; whatever disharmony surrounded Wingate's move was pushed to the side in their mutual love of the birds. But as time went on, communication began to break down.

The government's heel-dragging, the cottage's lack of electricity, and Madeiros's differing approach to the project on several fronts had Wingate grumbling, not only within his close circle of friends, but also to the tourists and Bermudians who signed up for ecotours to Nonsuch. He couldn't help himself, and some of the talk got back to Madeiros.

"I didn't appreciate him calling the techniques I was using into question constantly," Madeiros says. "I'm just like, 'Well, you know, there were a lot of things he did that were questionable or could have been debated, but people had enough respect for him that they assumed he knew what he was doing.' He wasn't willing to extend the same courtesy in my direction. Each person has their own techniques and style, and you have to trust that they can get on with it. And if not, then it's up to their superiors to deal with it."

"Jeremy came to assume that I was against everything he was doing," Wingate says, "which was not the case at all. I was simply exercising the normal scientific procedure of peer review. He had been my first choice to take over the cahow program eventually because I recognized that for him, like for me, it was a labor of love."

Wingate was also not shy, during this time, about speaking up in his role as an independent environmental advocate, in a way that was "not always highly complimentary to the government," according to Ward. This sort of thing was not new to Wingate; in fact, much of his life was spent precisely in opposition to the government he represented, protesting the dumping of garbage into marshes, arguing against what he saw as fighting nature rather than working with it in parks management, and vocally disputing the sudden rezoning of properties all over Bermuda to favor large developers. But in the past he'd been protected by his exclusive knowledge of the cahows and by popular support of his dedication to Bermuda's ecology. Now, people were beginning to see Madeiros as equally competent, and Wingate's outspokenness was no longer so well tolerated.

In 2002, about six months before he was due to renew his lease on the cottage, Wingate took some volunteers from the Bermuda Zoological Society over to Abbot's Cliff, a high headland on the northern end of Harrington Sound that is significant for its concentration of native and endemic flora. It was on Abbot's Cliff, which became a nature reserve in the 1980s, that Wingate had based many of his planting decisions for Nonsuch, since as of the '60s, he says, "man had never disturbed things enough there to really change it." Thirty years on, though, casuarinas had begun colonizing the cliff side.

That afternoon, after he and his crew had removed about a hundred saplings from the down-cliff base, he decided to tackle the problem where it originated. "The main source of seed for colonizing the base of the cliff was the mature casuarinas that had been planted on Cockroach Island before people realized the casuarina was a problem tree," he says. Cockroach is actually less an island and more a pile of rubble sticking up from the sea at the foot of Abbot's Cliff; it was created, in fact, by a cliff fall thousands of years ago, and was the only nearby source of casuarinas. There was no land registry in Bermuda, so Wingate assumed the island was part of Abbot's Cliff Park, and he and the volunteers cleared away the trees.

Unfortunately for Wingate, the island was not owned by government, but was part of a private estate being managed by an agent who was about to be taken to task by the secretary of environment over an unrelated manner. When the agent appeared for his meeting, however, he "came in with both guns blazing," says Jack Ward, "giving the ministry shit about their people cutting down trees on his property."

When he discovered his mistake, Wingate sent an e-mail to the agent and the secretary of environment "that was as apologetic as it could get in the absence of a land registry," he says. He explained that the casuarinas were taking over the cliff, "pulling great chunks of it down into the water," and also destroying what little remained of Cockroach Island. He had originally planned to go back to tidy up and replant with natives but was stopped before he could finish the job; he offered to do so now. In the end, he finished the work. The estate later leased Cockroach to the Bermuda Audubon for $1 a year and eventually gave it to the organization.

But for Wingate, the damage was done. "Completely naively, I believe," Ward says, "David undermined the ability of the ministry to carry out its duties in such a dramatic fashion that I got called by the permanent secretary, who said, 'No more dealing with this guy. We're dealing with chaos.'" After that, Ward maintains, "It didn't matter whether the electrical system at the cottage was in absolutely perfect nick. He just was not going to get a renewal on that lease."

After Wingate was "kicked off" of Nonsuch—"there's no other word for it," he says—tensions between him and the Madeiroses escalated, in part because of an agreement made between the two men, with Jack Ward as mediator, that Wingate would call in advance whenever he wanted to go out to Nonsuch. To Wingate, this was just another slap in the face.

"Probably since 1968," he says, "it has been a rule that members of the public can't land on Nonsuch or the cahow islands without a permit. But the difference is that's the general public, who could not be expected to know about the sensitivities of the program. To do it to me seems a case of government shooting itself in the foot. My presence would be as an experienced warden, not a threat. But when I'm told I can't land without Jeremy's company or his permission, the implication is that I might pose a threat to the program, which is an absolute insult. That's the rule, but I could not understand why the rule had to be applied to me. I'd started the living museum four years before it even became a parks project."

Wingate was in the midst of a couple of projects on the island,

and he wanted to see them through. "So I ignored the order," he says. "I was out there at night, often when Jeremy wasn't there, and he never would have known I was out there unless I told him. Which is sort of ironic, because if someone had wanted to go out and do damage to the cahows, they could have." More than once when Wingate was conservation officer, vandals destroyed nests, smashed eggs, and killed birds at Spittal Pond.

But the bigger problem for the current residents of Nonsuch was that Wingate was still getting calls from visiting naturalists, conservationists, and others who wanted him to show them the living museum. Complicating the matter was that the calls often came on short notice, and it is considered a given by all who know him that Madeiros, who's usually out in the field, is all but impossible to reach. The end result was that "you might be trying to clean up the house" says Madeiros, "or scantily clad or something like that, and all of a sudden there's a group of people looking at you from five feet away. David would not have tolerated that sort of action when he was out there, so, I think rightly, my wife took exception to him trying to do that."

Wingate counters that that sort of thing happened to him all the time. "My god," he says, "we had such an open house out there. Though the rules of the island were that people should call beforehand, people in Bermuda so often ignore rules, and they'd shyly come up and knock on the door, and I would always welcome them and give them a tour and a cup of tea. I didn't expect Jeremy to do that, but the point is I didn't think it was my private island. It was a government sanctuary."

Both men say that in some ways they are simply too much alike. Neither is an especially good communicator, and nearly everyone involved agrees that lack of communication was at the core of their disputes. "I don't think either one of those guys in their hearts dislikes the other," says Ward. "Things received as personal attacks were attacks on process and methodology, but they were made without verification, and that was probably because they'd both built little walls around themselves and neither understood what the other was so upset about. Jeremy was going, 'I didn't have to tell him [what was going on with the cahow project],' so David says, 'I think this is wrong.' But he couldn't get an audience with Jeremy, the guy he should have been talking to, so he goes off to third parties. Then what Jeremy hears is third-hand and maybe not quite what actually happened."

Madeiros vows that no conflicts will arise when it's his turn to step down. "When I retire," he says, "I intend to walk away. And if they ask for my input, I'll be happy to give it. But otherwise, I'll take a much-deserved rest at that point."

Jack Ward isn't so sure. "We'll see," he says, "we'll see. I quite expect someone's going to have the same problem with Jeremy down the road. To my perspective, these cahows cast some sort of strange spell over people that they go off so deep that their social skills get compromised."

CHAPTER TEN

Loose Ends and Ill Winds

AS HE HAD AFTER Anita's death, Wingate turned to work as anesthetic. "He really said very little," says Penny Hill, "but just flung himself madly into other things."

Though Nonsuch was by now a different island from the denuded rock he first encountered, there were a couple of projects that still nagged at Wingate. First, with the exception of the Bermuda sedge, he had not yet planted an understory. "That's not as surprising as it sounds," he says. "It sounds like I neglected the understory. But the reality is it could only be planted once you had an overstory, and it took forty years to produce a canopy. Only then, when the winter gales could ride over the top, was the habitat becoming right for the more fragile, shade-loving plants."

The planting, when it did begin, in 2001, was "largely inspired," Wingate says, by a young man named Evan Morbey. Morbey had had neurological difficulties as a child, and was a bit of an odd duck who had much older friends and eclectic hobbies, including an obsessive interest in native and endemic plants. Wendy Frith, a friend of Wingate's, had known Morbey's father since they were teenagers and had taken the boy under her wing as he was growing up. She and others who knew Morbey had been telling Wingate about him, and when she finally introduced the two, she says, "it was as though David had found his mirror image. I'd go out to the island and find them just talking and talking and talking."

Morbey, who worked for a landscaping company, lived in a house called Cluster Cottage, which his family leased from the National Trust. On about an eighth of its 2½ acre grounds he'd created a demonstration nursery showing how native plants could be grown together in a home garden.

According to Frith, when Wingate asked Morbey how he'd been so successful with plants that Wingate had been trying to propagate for years, "Evan just sort of shrugged and said, 'I just put them everywhere. I don't choose a spot, the plant chooses. By putting them everywhere, you find where the plant will grow.' He was very intuitive. It was like he trusted that the plants wanted to live."

Over about four years, as plants became available, Morbey and Wingate put hundreds of understory shrubs and grasses like paspalum, turkey berry, and maidenhair fern all over the island. "It was my excuse for going back to stay in the cottage on weekends," Wingate says. "They couldn't very well stop me because it was furthering the living museum project. But it was never officially acknowledged, and no one ever thanked me for it."

After the planting was finished, Morbey and Wingate remained friends, and the young man intended, after serving in the Bermuda Regiment, to go into conservation. "Unfortunately," Wingate says, "Evan left us as mysteriously as he arrived." He died in his sleep in 2010 at age twenty-nine. "The thought was he might have had some fatal flaw in his heart or something," says Wingate, who read the eulogy at Morbey's funeral. "The conservation movement lost a very useful helper, at a time when Bermuda desperately lacks people with those kind of interests."

Wingate recently returned to Nonsuch to do a survey of the understory he and Morbey planted. "Some of the ground-cover plants aren't doing that well," he says. "They're surviving, but they're a bit sickly and not very green. I think they need fertilizing, and my bet is it was cahows that were providing fertilizer for these things in precolonial times. They brought in high-grade nutrients from the ocean that went directly into the roots of the plants." Cahow burrows also provided crucial habitat for skinks and cockroaches, which kept the nests clean and in exchange got high-protein meals in the form of failed or broken cahow eggs. "When the burrows start coming back," says Wingate, "the understory will too."

Before he could even think about one day seeing Nonsuch dotted with natural cahow burrows, though, Wingate had one final project to undertake. Nocturnal *Bufo marinus* toads were introduced to Bermuda from British Guiana in 1885 to help control insects, and for a time were so pervasive and so often squashed by cars and motorcycles that they became known as "road toads." Though the animals are terrestrial, they need fresh water to breed and will go to great lengths to reach it. Wingate suspects they can smell the freshwater pond on Nonsuch from the headland at Cooper's Island, and every now and then, beginning in the late 1970s, one or two would turn up. No breeding took place until 1984, when two males and a female were intercepted in early August. By the end of that month, there were thousands of tadpoles in the water, and even with high predation rates, it wasn't long before the island was hopping with toads.

An intensive culling effort Wingate had started in 1990 coincided with the failure of the PVC liner, and once the pond dried up, he saw no more toads on Nonsuch. But then again, he wasn't looking for them, and the toads can survive without open water; they just can't breed. In June of 1996, after the liner was repaired and the pond reconstituted, he again found the water full of tadpoles.

"When toads breed," he says, "they really breed."

Wingate considered it essential to get rid of the creatures before the cahows arrived, since he believed they could endanger the birds. The toads are protected by glands on their backs that secrete a toxin powerful enough to kill dogs and even humans, who have been known to lick the amphibians for a hallucinogenic high. Wingate worried that if cahows tried to colonize Nonsuch, the toads might compete with them for burrows and, when confronted by an angry cahow, release their toxins, killing the bird and, potentially, its mate or parents. Though no cane toads have ever invaded seabird colonies that Wingate knows of, a 2004 paper in the journal *Biological Conservation* discusses the impact of toads on ground-nesting rainbow bee eaters, a beautiful little near-passerine found in southern Australia. The toads, according to author Christopher Boland of the

Australian National University's College of Medicine, Biology and Environment, have caused a 33 percent decline in bee-eater nesting success. "The possibility that cane toads are having a negative impact on other native, ground-dwelling vertebrate fauna via their role as opportunistic predators," Boland writes, "requires urgent investigation."

But properly removing the toads from Nonsuch would be costly because it would require bringing a trencher over to the island by barge so that a barrier could be erected around the pond to keep the animals from breeding. In 2002, a Bermudian philanthropist provided $8,000 for the job, and Wingate got to work, with help from Madeiros and a handful of volunteers. Because the toads can jump only about a foot and a half off the ground and can't climb smooth vertical surfaces, Wingate chose a UV-resistant black polyethylene similar to the material he had used to re-line the pond but thick enough to keep from sagging. The barrier, a yard high after being sunk two feet in the ground and held in place by steel rods, was placed three to nine feet from the edge of the pond, leaving a strip of dry land within for any birds that might not prefer water landings.

Cane toads spawn after heavy rains, and can only be caught at night; in daytime, they hide in the vegetation, but after dark they're out in the open and can be easily scooped up, since, like deer caught in a car's glare, they're immobilized by the beam of a flashlight. So Wingate, who was no longer supposed to be on the island during much of the project, had to go back and forth at night in heavy swells and gusting winds to try to collect the animals. He'd find them trying to get over the barrier and round them up by the bucketful to be released in distant parts of the mainland. Catching the ones that had been eggs or tadpoles when the barrier went up, not to mention the breeding adults that were hiding in the marsh grass inside the barrier, was more difficult, but on the upside for him—if not the toads—many of them starved to death or were eaten by herons, kiskadees, crows, or one another.

Not counting thousands of tadpoles and toadlets, he eventually bagged more than twelve hundred of the creatures outside the barrier and another five hundred or so inside it; Madeiros's total brought the numbers even higher. There was a little rebound in 2005, but by the following year, the last subadults were captured. The six years it took to remove just a few thousand toads from a six-hectare island, says Wingate, illustrates the challenges of dealing with invasive species on a global scale. "Invasives are now reckoned to be probably only second in importance to human-caused habitat destruction in the extermination of native and endemic species," he says. "It's a problem that is accelerating with globalization, and it reaches its apex on remote oceanic islands like Hawaii and Bermuda because their native floras and faunas are so much more vulnerable, having evolved in complete isolation. Once these invaders become established, it's almost impossible to get rid of them unless they have some Achilles heel you can exploit."

Another invader on Nonsuch is also an amphibian, though so far it doesn't seem to be causing any problems. Wingate had dealt with the whistling frog *Eleutherodactylus johnstonei* periodically during his years on the island. These half-inch-long brown frogs make up for their diminutive individual size with sheer volume, both in terms of numbers and decibels. On all but the coldest nights, the piercing *bleep-bleep* of these creatures, which are almost impossible to spot amid the vegetation they breed in, is incessant.

The frogs were accidentally introduced to Bermuda before the turn of the last century. When Wingate initially started visiting Castle Harbour, its islands were silent. But over the years he would periodically find a frog or two on Nonsuch, probably transported, despite his precautions, in plants he'd brought over himself. Before he became hard of hearing from all the shotguns and military rifles he'd blasted near his ears over the years without protection, he would track the frogs down by their sound, approaching as silently as possible as he combed the forest for them with a flashlight, then shooting them at point-blank range with a BB gun. "It was easier than trying to grab them in dense vegetation," he says, "where they might slip out of your grip. I probably shot about twenty overall and found a nest of eggs, which was incredibly tedious—you think the frogs are hard to find."

One day in the late 1990s, Wingate, bird-watching at Cooper's Island, looked over to Nonsuch and saw a cigarette boat moored at the island's east end, where he hadn't spent much time once the forest had started getting established, and people going into the woods where he hadn't made a path. He sped over to Tucker's Town to get his boat. By the time he reached Nonsuch whoever had been there was gone, but he followed their route and found a small marijuana plantation, about thirty seedlings in buckets, some tools, and a bag of mulch. Several years later, Madeiros started hearing *bleeps*; Wingate had not noticed them because of his increasing deafness. "By the time I realized they'd planted this stuff," he says, "the frogs were probably already over a couple hundred feet of the island. They must have been in the bottom of the buckets they used to bring the plants over." He and Madeiros, after ripping out the plants, spent some time trying to track the frogs down, but quickly realized they were too late and dropped the effort.

Baby whistling frogs are only about a millimeter long—the thickness of a dime—and by the time the animals are big enough to find, they're already breeding. "At this point it's a lost cause," Wingate says. "It's such a shame. Nonsuch used to be so quiet. And of course we have no idea what ecological effect they might have on the living museum. They do build up a tremendous abundance, so obviously they're affecting something, but for the moment the change must be at the micro-invertebrate level."

✦

When Wingate retired, there were fifty-nine breeding pairs of cahows; in the 2011–12 season, Madeiros broke the hundred-pair mark. "If the population continues to grow," the IUCN writes, "the species will warrant downlisting to Vulnerable in due course." But the various threats Wingate battled for half a century might one day seem like trifles compared with what's to come.

Despite politically motivated denials of global warming, the vast majority of scientists agree that it is real and that it is anthropogenic, or caused by humankind. Even Richard Muller, a well-known University of California, Berkeley, physicist, retreated from his skepti-

cism after undertaking a study, funded in part by the archconserva-
tive Charles Koch Foundation, in which he found previous research
was on target.

Polar ice core samples have shown that for at least 800,000 years
before the industrial revolution, carbon dioxide in the atmosphere
ranged from 170 to 300 parts per million by volume; today that concentration is 393 ppmv and rising by about half a percentage point
annually.

The carbon dioxide and other so-called greenhouse gases—water
vapor, methane, nitrous oxide, and ozone—trap heat from the sun
and warm the earth's atmosphere. Since 1880, average air temperatures
have increased by about 1.4 degrees Fahrenheit; between 1850 and
2005, global average sea surface temperature increased by 1.3 degrees
Fahrenheit. That may not sound like a lot, but "if you think about
how big the ocean is, and how deep it is, and how much energy it has,
that's a tremendous source of heat," says BIOS director Tony Knap
in "Ocean Temperatures," a 2011 *NBC Learn* video. "One, one and a
half degrees centigrade in a water column of a hundred meters makes
a massive amount of difference."

All of this has several consequences that could affect the cahows.
First, more CO_2 in the oceans means less calcium carbonate and
iron, both of which are building blocks for certain kinds of phytoplankton that are at the bottom of the birds' food chain. "I guess
nobody knows yet what the effects of that might be," Wingate says.
"There are radical changes occurring. The simple answer is this probably means less life generally in the ocean—a lower biomass—until
evolution can make the adjustments necessary, which of course takes
eons. If everything in the food chain gets scarcer, the cahows would
have trouble finding their rich feeding grounds, so it could be very
serious."

Another effect of global warming is that sea levels are rising, in
part because water expands as it warms, but also because the frozen
surfaces of the earth's Arctic and Antarctic regions are melting like the
rocks in a Dark 'n Stormy on a sultry Bermuda night.

"Who knows?" Wingate says. "The way the polar ice cap is collapsing in Greenland, we could end up with a twenty-foot rise. The best predictions now are three to five feet by the end of the century. But they keep revising it upward." This rise—which is actually expected to be slightly greater in the North Atlantic—is slowly pushing the intertidal zone inland, further shrinking what remains of the islets after cliff falls. "If we have a three-foot rise," he says, "I think Inner Pear and Long Rock will become totally unusable, and Green too, unless we build the burrows higher up. They'll all go under pretty damn quick."

Finally, though scientists don't believe the number of hurricanes in the north Atlantic is growing, the number that have hit Bermuda in recent decades is definitely higher, and their destructive power greater than in the recent past. "We get winter gales up to sixty-five knots," Wingate points out, "so we don't consider a hurricane more than just a storm unless it gets up to ninety or a hundred miles an hour."

There were three major unnamed hurricanes in the late 1940s, the last of which helped spark Wingate's interest in birds by stripping all the hedgerows at Aldie of leaves. "After it passed," he says, "our garden seemed to be blossoming with flowers, but all of the flowers turned out to be brightly colored wood warblers that had fallen out of the eye." Hurricane Edna, passing sixty miles from the island, caused a bit of damage in 1953; then came 1963's Arlene and three storms in the '70s that Wingate calls "fairly routine."

Emily, in 1987, was the first hurricane he considered "significant" in decades. Windspeed reached only 85 miles an hour, but the storm did millions of dollars worth of damage: It was a direct hit, there were many tornadoes in the eye wall, and the forest was ripe for disaster, filled as it was with tall invasives and having no cedars left to divert the wind. In the 1990s came Dean, Felix, and Gert. They were a warning sign for the cahows, Wingate says, causing the first real burrow damage he had seen in his career. But they were nothing compared to Fabian.

It developed off the Cape Verde islands, giving it plenty of time to gain power as it traveled west over the warm open ocean. On September 5, 2003, it slammed Bermuda dead-on as a Category 3, with

120-mile-an-hour winds lasting three to four hours and gusts of up to 164 at the highest elevations. Its storm surge—water pushed along by the hurricane that piles on top of the usual tides—reached eleven feet and waves peaked at thirty-five feet. Power lines were downed, sea walls collapsed, limestone roofs flew off houses, and boats were tossed about like autumn leaves. Four people died when the causeway between St. George's and St. David's was washed out, the first hurricane fatalities in the country in almost eighty years.

When it was over, whole portions of beach were wiped away and, as happens after every hurricane in Bermuda, huge white chunks in the black coastal cliff lines showed where the old rock had been sheared down into the water.

Wingate, who had to navigate a debris-filled golf course to reach his boat the day after the storm, would devote more than thirty pages of his diary to its aftermath over the next few weeks. When he finally got to Nonsuch, he was amazed at how little wind damage the island had suffered, thanks to the native forest; many of the best cedars were unscathed, though a few tilted between 45 and 80 degrees. A rock tunnel leading from the barge to the uplands was scoured bare and its contents washed to sea; the barge itself was later condemned for landing by the government. A window had let water into the house, and its interior had become a kiddie pool. As for the saltwater pond, which he'd thought able to withstand hurricanes, Wingate wrote, "Even in my wildest imaginings I could not have anticipated the scale of destruction."

The entire beach and its backing dune had disappeared, the forest around them was stripped back as much as twenty-five feet, and the pond, he wrote in his diary, "was gone with barely a trace!"

Its loss had divided Nonsuch, and there was another shallow channel across the narrow south neck as well. "One or two more storms like this & Nonsuch will become three separate islands," he wrote, "just as Southampton & Horn are separated!!" What he wouldn't discover until later was what had become of the cahow burrows on the outer islets.

Because the storm hit before the birds returned for the season, none were killed; but 60 percent of the burrows were damaged or filled with storm debris. Divers later retrieved about fifty concrete nest lids from the seafloor.

The worst destruction was on Horn Rock and Inner Pear. Inner Pear's whole center had collapsed and two burrows had vanished completely. Because Horn—which contains the most birds, with about thirty breeding pairs—is the highest of the cahow islands at about thirty feet, it wasn't overwashed, as all of the other islets were. But one burrow was lost in a cliff fall, and five more that were only about five feet above sea level were history. "They were under the sea," Wingate says, "with waves sloshing around on top of them. They all got undermined and eaten away."

Despite some uneasiness in other situations, Wingate and Madeiros still work together cordially, and they and a group of volunteers toiled through September and October to repair the damage, hindered by gales and groundswell—broad, often very high waves caused by earthquakes or tropical storms hundreds of miles off. About a dozen new burrows were built toward the top of Horn, but, Wingate says, "the following year the birds just flew around where their burrows were supposed to be. They couldn't figure it out." Whenever Madeiros found a bird scrabbling around in the rubble, he would pick it up and move it to the newly built replacement burrows on the top of the island, but the disruption affected the following year's crop: The number of breeding pairs declined by five, and there were ten fewer fledglings.

Fabian underscored the urgency of jump-starting a colony on one of the larger islands. "Inner Pear and Horn Rock are young dune-rock islands that could crumble away in a major hurricane," Wingate says. "Inner Pear particularly. If we ever had a Category 5, it would dissolve like a sugar cube."

The possibility that Category 4 or even 5 hurricanes could hit Bermuda in this century is becoming increasingly likely. "The inflow of air at low levels into a hurricane requires lots of heat and moisture," says Florida State University professor of geography James Elsner, who has studied the phenomenon, "so when the temperature of the ocean is warm, storms can, all else being equal, increase in intensity. As the ocean's temperatures rise, in some measure due to global warming, the strongest storms get stronger. It's happening globally, but particularly over the Atlantic."

Some scientists predict a doubling of the number of more violent hurricanes there in the next century. Fabian was a Category 3, which is defined by winds of up to 130 miles an hour. In a Category 4, winds may reach 155; anything over that is a Category 5.

"You have to have a very deep column of very warm water to sustain a five," Wingate says. "The Bahamas are sometimes hit by fives, but by the time they get into our latitude they're getting into cooler water. But I think Bermuda will get into the belt where Category Fives are quite likely." What would a five look like sweeping over twenty-one square miles of low-lying land? "A five is unthinkable," he says. "We'd lose hotels and dozens of houses and long stretches of road along the south shore. It doesn't bear thinking about, really."

Perhaps most frightening for the cahows is that warmer seas mean the hurricane season will extend further into fall than it ever has. The second week of November 2011, Wingate watched from Cooper's Point as Tropical Storm Sean pummeled the cahow islands with gale-force gusts, twenty-foot waves, and a two-foot storm surge. It was too rough to take the boat out, but it had been four days since he'd been to the east end, and he couldn't stay away any longer. "I build up a degree of anxiety about what could go wrong," he says. "It's all part of my sense that I have a responsibility to make amends for all the terrible things man has brought upon the cahow."

His anxiety was not relieved as he stood on the beach with his binoculars, willing them to show him inside the burrows on Green Island. "This is what I always dread," he said, "a late-season hurricane, when most of the cahows are on their nests." As many as eleven burrows on Green could have been affected by Sean, but Wingate wouldn't know until he or Madeiros could get out on the water. "The birds stay in the burrows sometimes for four days at a time at this point," Wingate said. "That's why it's such a vulnerable season, because the pairs are in the burrow. They'll probably leave the burrow when it starts to flood and head out to sea, but that's only if the waves aren't too violent for them to get out. And it might not occur to them. They might think the safety is within the nest. But if the nest drowns, they'll drown with it."

After a few more apprehensive moments, Wingate put down his binoculars. "They're probably all right," he said, as though to convince himself. They were, this time.

CHAPTER ELEVEN

Moving On, Coming Home

FROM THE BEGINNING, WINGATE was "the backbone of every ecological project in Bermuda," says Eddie Wright. "He has always been the voice of the environment." But when his official tenure as conservation officer ended and he was evicted from the cottage, he began to concentrate even more on mainland conservation challenges. "It was a big frustration losing the battle with the whistling frogs," he says. "I still feel if I'd been out there I could have won it. But after that, I understood that the only thing I could do was divert my attention to work elsewhere in Bermuda, where my input was still appreciated and valued, or even welcomed."

Among the projects he's now devoted to are a study he began in 1973 of common terns—now the rarest native bird in the country—to learn more about population bottlenecks, and a program he helped start several years ago called Buy Back Bermuda.

In 1968, Somerset Long Bay Park, in Sandys Parish on the island's western end, became a government-owned public beach; soon after, an adjacent parcel was bought by the Bermuda Audubon Society as a nature reserve. Along the eastern edge of the two properties was three acres of beachfront that a local businessman, Joffre Pitman, had bought in the early 1980s, intending to restore the land—which had been used as an illegal dump site—as a nature reserve and build an underground house there that would blend with the environment. The house was never built, but when the restoration was finished, the lot included a one-acre freshwater pond, native and endemic plantings, and an area for cattle to graze. It became known as Pitman's Pond.

"Right from the word go I wanted it to be protected as it was forever," Pitman says. "I don't know what made me do it. I wasn't a rich person, and from an investment viewpoint, it's got to be the most stupid thing I've ever done in my life."

The Bermuda Audubon Society gave Pitman an honorary membership for restoring the land with his own funds, and for years Wingate—who of course had been a member of the Audubon since its inception and had often served as its president—tried to convince him to donate the property, or sell it at far below market rate, to the organization. Not only was it abutting existing conservation land, but, because it was on the end of the island, it was also the spot hundreds of migrating birds first encountered when flying in to Bermuda. And, Wingate says, "The combination of the pond and the cattle made it irresistible for certain kinds of birds, because the cattle excrement provided food for them. It even had a swan on it at one time."

Pitman liked the idea of selling to the Audubon but couldn't afford to take less than the land was worth. When he finally found a buyer, he expected to see one corner of the lot devoted to a private residence, and the rest left as it was. "Then somebody called and said, 'You're not really going to let them put condos up, are you?'" he says. "They alerted me to the fact."

Two potential schemes for the $1.4 million lot had been passed by Bermuda's planning department. One called for a house with twenty-two horse stables, the other for twenty condominiums. In both, the pond would be partially filled.

When Wingate and Jennifer Gray, who was then president of the Audubon, learned of this, they asked Pitman to give them two weeks to come up to his asking price. At the next Audubon meeting, Gray suggested the organization approach the National Trust about collaborating. "Everyone agreed it was a property worth fighting for," she says, "but we didn't have enough in our reserves to purchase it or even make a down payment."

Wingate represented the Audubon on the trust's council. At the next meeting, he recalls, "I said, 'If we can allow a private nature reserve to be sold for condos without doing something about it, we all might as well pack our bags and leave Bermuda.' In other words, what's the point of a National Trust?" He believed so strongly that one of the two NGOs had to at least bid on the property that he pledged $10,000 then and there. "For me that was a lot of money for a single donation," he says. "I remember after the meeting I thought, Oh, Christ, what have I gotten myself into? Now I really have to do it."

Two other members of the council immediately said they'd double Wingate's offer. "At that point I called up David Saul," Wingate says. "I knew he was the only person who would have any hope of raising that kind of money. He'd worked for Fidelity, and he knew all the wealthy Bermudians and expats, the billionaires, and knew that for them, $100,000 here, $200,000 there would be peanuts. For us, that was unthinkable. We were going to call up our neighbors in the phone book and say, 'Can you spare $10 for this?' That was the level of our fund-raising."

Saul, who had always supported the Audubon and had kayaked in the Long Bay area when he was working in the west end early in his career, met with the two organizations and pledged $20,000 himself. "He gave us the confidence to move ahead," says Wingate. "And then he damn well went out and got the money. Within less than a year, the cash was rolling in, big sums. He even got $300,000 from government."

Pitman had given them two years to close, but well before that time was up, Saul had raised $2.25 million—enough to buy and restore the Pitman property and also start a tidy endowment for future projects under the name Buy Back Bermuda.

By Earth Day 2007, when Deputy Premier Paula Cox cut the ribbon to open the new reserve, the campaign had already set a second goal: to buy a 7½-acre plot in Southampton Parish known as Skroggins Hill. "Now, there's this native plant called *Crossopetalum rhacoma*," says David Saul, "and it is only found in one place on this island, which is on this little plot of land that has never been built on. David Wingate took the owner of this land, Sharon Vesey, and myself, literally on our hands and knees sometimes, through the bushes of nearly eight acres, and said, 'Here before your nose'—and it was denser than a hedge—'is *Crossopetalum rhacoma*. It is found nowhere else in Bermuda but here.'"

Later, when Saul went to make the offer on the property, he says, "Sharon said, 'David, haven't you heard about the world's financial crisis? How much money have you raised so far?' And I said, 'Two million.' And she said, 'Good. Now you go and use that for something else. I'm going to give you this eight acres of Bermuda.' And if hadn't been for Wingate and his enthusiasm, it would be twenty-five condominiums today. And it would be gone."

In the six years since its first acquisition, Buy Back Bermuda has raised more than $5 million and purchased a total of fifteen acres. Wingate says it was a "big blow" when, in early 2011, Saul retired from the organization, but Paul Leseur, a former businessman who was a member of the National Trust and actually came up with the campaign's name, believes it has grown "bigger than any one individual."

Today, schoolchildren, the Garden Club, and even developers contribute to Buy Back, as it's known among conservationists, and corporations have field days for employees to go and volunteer on the properties.

"I've been involved with several capital campaigns on the island," Leseur says, "but this one took on a life of its own compared to the others. We have sixty-seven thousand people living on thirteen thousand acres, and everyone's very concerned that we're chewing up all the open space."

Much of that community involvement, Jennifer Gray maintains, is Wingate's legacy. "I believe David Wingate has done more as an individual for conservation in Bermuda than I think any of us could even imagine accomplishing in a lifetime," she says. "He is one of the most inspiring environmentalists I've ever encountered."

One of Wingate's gifts, she continues, is his ability to "impart his knowledge and wisdom to young people in a way that really does give them hope."

By now, Wingate has influenced generations of young Bermudians. Delaey Robinson is now in his mid-sixties and says his time with

Wingate has had a lasting effect. "I was at university when the environmental movement was taking off," he says, "and was elated to find in David someone who had concerns for the environment in Bermuda as well as considerable knowledge on the ground. He was without doubt my Bermuda environmental guru, and I found it refreshing to be around him since there were not many others sharing his concerns."

As a member of parliament from 1998 to 2003, Robinson says he spoke in support of the environment "whenever matters arose—though my recollection is they seldom did." He still remains an outspoken voice for conservation, most recently joining Wingate and more than a thousand other Bermudians in protesting a proposed development on pristine karst topography in Tucker's Town that would have irreversibly damaged fragile and unique cave-dwelling species.

Twenty-four-year-old Miguel Mejias is one of Wingate's more recent disciples. Every weekend when he was a kid, Mejias's parents would take him to the aquarium, and by the time he reached high school, he knew he wanted to be a marine biologist. He started volunteering at the aquarium, and eventually got a job there, but he soon discovered a problem with his career choice. "I realized I couldn't dive because I couldn't equalize my ears," he says. "When that happened, I felt lost. I spent a year not knowing what to do, and it was frustrating, because I was getting ready to go to university."

The following summer, a friend of Mejias's, Ronald Burchall, introduced him to Wingate, who invited the two young men to start helping him with his field work on the common tern. "David and I went out almost every day," Mejias says, "checking terns and stuff. I felt like I had a purpose again, like life had meaning."

Initially, Mejias couldn't even tie a proper knot to moor the boat, but Wingate just joked about his inexperience and taught him whatever he needed to know. One day, the younger man's hopes were almost dashed again when he and Wingate landed on a tern island and started getting dive-bombed by the birds. "I'm like cowering, kneeling down, covering my head," Mejias says.

"Miguel ducked so hard that he hit his head on the sharp rocks,"

Wingate recalls. "I just sort of laughed and said, 'You're going to do more damage to yourself than the birds are. Just ignore them. They can't really hurt you.'"

Wingate advised his young friend to walk straight ahead and wave his hands over his head to protect his face. "He said, 'Don't be afraid, keep coming with me,'" says Mejias. "They were passing my ears; that's how close they were. But I kept my posture. The last thing I needed was something else to hold me back. I didn't want to have this taken away from me too. That's when I realized I'm here to stay. Nobody's going to take this away from me."

Mejias is now at Trent University in Oshawa, Ontario, majoring in biology with a specialization in conservation.

⚜

Many years ago, Wingate built two artificial burrows on Nonsuch. One, on the point to the west of the house, was used to show tour groups how the structures worked. But he had hoped the other, on the extreme south point opposite Green Island, might be spontaneously colonized. And it was—by tropicbirds. "It was way inland among the sea oxeye," he says. "I never thought the longtails would find it, but it just shows they'll find anything. I left them there. I figured cahows wouldn't colonize until we had some means of attracting them."

Since the early 1980s, Wingate had been following the literature on the use of decoys and sound recordings to lure seabirds to islands they had not yet colonized, and toward the end of his tenure, he began making arrangements to import some weather-resistant sound systems that would play cahow calls every night beginning at dusk. "I was going to build burrows and put sound attraction on Southampton first," he says, "because it's a very manageable island in terms of predators." Southampton is less than three acres—a little smaller than all the cahow islands put together—but it's more isolated from the mainland than Nonsuch, and rats and toads would have to cross Castle Roads, the harbor's natural channel, to get to it. Parts of it are low enough that they sometimes get overwashed during hurricanes, but it's harder to land on than the islets and has no beach, which would keep people from disturbing the birds, and its size makes it safe, for the time being, from major erosion and storm damage.

"Nonsuch is the ultimate habitat," Wingate says, "but my strategy was to get them established on a larger island that is easy to manage first, then on Nonsuch, so if something problematical happened at Nonsuch you'd have a backup. I saw it as a step-by-step process toward the end goal."

Madeiros had another plan.

In 2000, Nicholas Carlile, a seabird project officer in the New South Wales, Australia, National Parks and Wildlife Service (now the Office of Environment and Heritage), visited Bermuda on a Churchill Fellowship to study critically endangered seabirds around the world. He told Wingate and Madeiros about the work he'd been doing with the endangered Gould's petrel, which is very similar to the cahow in both morphology and behavior.

Gould's petrels nest primarily in two gullies about eight hundred feet apart on Cabbage Tree Island, off the coast of Port Stephens, N.S.W. Carlile and his colleague David Priddel wanted to see if they could start a new colony of the birds because, Carlile says, "We literally had all our eggs in one basket."

Historically, fewer than 2 percent of the banded Gould's petrels had changed gullies spontaneously. Carlile and Priddel's plan was to take chicks from one gully to the other before they started leaving the nest to exercise, place them in artificial nest boxes, and hand-feed them for the last week or two. If the birds later returned to the site they fledged from rather than where they were born, the scientists would translocate more of them to nearby Boondelbah Island, where a few pairs had already been seen nesting.

Seabird translocation was first attempted as early as 1954, with short-tailed shearwaters just about to migrate; it didn't work, but ornithologist Dominic Louis Serventy of Perth had some success in the 1960s when he moved 157 of the same species just before they first emerged from the nest. In the 1970s, 90 Newell's shearwater eggs were taken from the mountains on Kauai, Hawaii, to coastal Kilauea

Point and Mokauea Island and placed in wedge-tailed shearwater nests for fostering. The results were not spectacular: By 2003 only a couple of Newell's shearwater nests had been found on Kilauea. But as Manx shearwaters, fluttering shearwaters, Leach's storm petrels, dark-rumped petrels, and other species were translocated in the 1980s and '90s, each try gave scientists a little more to go on.

When the Gould's petrel translocation began, there were about 250 pairs of the birds producing 50 chicks annually; today there are a thousand breeding pairs and 450 chicks a year. But because Pterodromas take so long to return home, when Carlile first arrived in Bermuda, his experiment had not yet begun to show signs of success.

Still, with the islets getting smaller every year, Madeiros thought it was crucial to consider the program for the cahows. In December 2000, he traveled to Australia to spend a few weeks learning the technique.

Carlile's recommendation to translocate half the fledgling crop over a five-year period using an unproven method had Wingate frantic with worry. As early as the 1951 expedition, when Murphy and Mowbray broke an egg while trying to band a brooding adult, he had decided it was best to disturb the cahows as little as possible. Though he calls seeing one of the first cahow eggs found in modern times destroyed by the very people who were trying to save it "quite traumatic," it wasn't the only reason for his hands-off policy. He really had no need to band, since with such a small population, he was able to identify individual birds by behavior and by variations in their tail feathers and coverts, and anyway he had logistical problems with the practice in the early days; getting access to the birds in deep natural burrows wasn't always possible, and the aluminum bands that were in use until the late 1960s were so corrosive they'd last only a year or two on seabirds. Most important, he didn't have time to band; Madeiros was able to devote more time exclusively to the cahows in part because when the Conservation Department was reshuffled around the time of Wingate's retirement, a new position was created to handle planning applications for protectively zoned land. "That used to take half my bloody life," Wingate says.

He had briefly fostered the chick that fell down the cliff, of course, and in 1971 was the first person to successfully raise a baby that had been abandoned by its parents; but those experiences hadn't convinced him the cahows could take a lot of human contact. "I was isolated on Bermuda," he says, "working with birds that are extremely rare. I never had the benefit of working with large colonies. I didn't realize how tough these birds can be."

Madeiros initially banded a small sample of cahows in 2002 and, as he expected, found it caused no ill effects. He has now tagged almost all of the birds. He has discovered, he says, that while some are aggressive and "will draw blood every time you touch them," others are so placid "they almost go to sleep when you're handling them." Over time, the banding will allow Madeiros and his successors to track fledgling returns, nesting and mating habits, any landfalls the birds might make worldwide, their ages at death, and perhaps, in some cases, even the cause of death.

Wingate admits he was wrong about handling the birds. "What I should have realized from the beginning," he says, "is that because they have no understanding of the hazards of mammal predators, they don't think, Oh, Christ, I'm going to be eaten at any minute. And Jeremy's very good with them; much better than I ever was. I'm too keyed up. He tends to be more laid back, and when you're relaxed, it relaxes the birds."

To prepare for his translocation program, Madeiros began putting artificial nests on Nonsuch. In 2004 he also set up a solar-powered, weatherproof Murremaid "music box" on the island. The previous year, at Wingate's suggestion, he'd had the system installed on Horn Rock to try to attract prospecting birds as well as those displaced by Fabian to the new, higher elevation nest complex there. A technician from Cornell University's Macaulay Library of Natural Sounds came to Bermuda to record a wide variety of cahow vocalizations, which were then made into an eighty-minute CD to run on a continuous loop on the Murremaid from 6:30 P.M. to 6 A.M. daily.

"The recorded courtship calls were seen to definitely attract the birds when played back at night," Madeiros wrote in that year's annual report, "with cahows repeatedly swooping low over the location of the speakers singly and in groups of 2 or 3 birds. Loud vocalizations on the sound system were often immediately answered by calls from birds circling over the site. At least one of the new artificial nest burrows . . . was visited twice." But, because the birds he observed were flying around the island before the prospecting youngsters' arrival, in the first week of February, he thought it was probably the newly homeless adults circling overhead, not the prebreeding birds he wanted to get onto Nonsuch.

In the 2004–2005 breeding season, despite Wingate's objections to several aspects of the plan—one of his major concerns was the possibility of disease transfer, as there was much talk in the news at the time of so-called bird flu—Madeiros began translocating chicks. He, Jennifer Gray, and Carlile, who had returned to Bermuda for the event, initially moved a trial group, but by the end of the season, fourteen of the healthiest fledglings had been taken, in waxed-cardboard tomato boxes, from various cahow islands and installed, each with a little of its own nesting material for the scent, into their new homes on Nonsuch. For the next six to eight weeks, Madeiros was totally dedicated to the chicks. To feed them he brought them up to the house in pairs so he could easily sterilize all of the equipment each time. He wrapped each chick in a dishtowel before pushing a fresh anchovy or pilchard from a local fisherman or a small squid from Miles Market—Bermuda's equivalent to Whole Foods—down its throat, wiping away any bits that got onto its feathers with a wet rag and some Dawn detergent. He took daily wing-cord and weight measurements not only of the translocated chicks but also of a control cohort, carefully logging the numbers into his computer afterward.

Over the next five years, Madeiros translocated a total of 105 chicks. All but two fledged successfully. One drowned after falling into the ocean after takeoff—a necropsy showed it had a deformed wing joint—and another died from undetermined digestive problems.

After he found that the first batch of translocated birds weighed less than the controls at the end of the season, Madeiros fed the 2005–2006 cohort a little more, and they fledged at the same weight as their compatriots. Then he realized he could give the translocated chicks an edge. "They go out to sea with no parental supervision," he says. "They might not see another cahow for years, and they have to live on their fat reserves until they learn to feed themselves, first flying to areas that have the type of food they want." Chicks lose eight to ten grams every day they don't eat. Once Madeiros started sending his emigrants out to sea twenty or thirty grams heavier than normal, he saw their survival rates increase from the 30ish percent of previous years to a phenomenal 56 percent, "about the best you can hope for with petrels," he says.

In 2009, Madeiros was amazed to find the first pair of birds that had returned to Nonsuch had reproduced, hatching the chick Somers. "Normally it takes two or three years before a pair would see success," Wingate says, "but this pair just hit it off right from the start, which was part of the miracle—and in time for the quadricentennial of the settlement of Bermuda. It all happened so fast. Not only did a pair establish, but they also succeeded in hatching an egg in the same breeding season."

Wingate read about the achievement in the *Royal Gazette*. "I thought, Well, touché for you, Jeremy, you lucky bugger. I was thrilled for him, to be honest, and it was tremendously satisfying for me as well, because here it's happened in my lifetime." Today there are ten established pairs of the birds on the island—which is ten pairs more than Wingate had ever imagined there would be by now.

By the time the first transplanted fledglings began to come back, Wingate had changed his mind about translocation. "It was a bold thing to do, a massive undertaking," he says. "But it's been a huge success, and an incredibly rapid one. Everything went so slowly in my time. The real action is happening out there now, just when I had to retire." Under Wingate's watch, it was almost a quarter century before the cahow population doubled for the first time; the second doubling took less than twenty years, and he expects that with translocations, that time will become even shorter.

"If one accepts that the adult birds aren't traumatized by the chicks disappearing," he says, "that they simply shrug their shoulders and say, 'Well, he's gone, I don't have to visit anymore,' then it becomes clear there's a spin-off benefit. The adults can go off and molt early, which gives them a head start for the next season. They have more time to fatten up so that they can lay a better egg. Then that chick will have a better chance of surviving. So the benefits go all the way through."

When Wingate was sixteen or seventeen years old, he was invited to lunch at Childs Frick's house. "I'll never forget it," he says. "I was in awe to be with this multimillionaire. And at one point he wagged his finger at me and said, 'Now, David. The real challenge for you is to find out where these birds are going when they're not in Bermuda.' I looked at him and thought, My god, that is a challenge."

Of course, in Wingate's day, the task would have been impossible, even with all the money in the world. But in 2009 Madeiros fitted twelve breeding adults with Lotek archival data tags that record the birds' position on the globe and the sea-surface temperatures whenever they land on the water. The first data loggers weighed almost five grams; the newer version, which he began using in 2011, weighs only two grams and is as big as the nail on Madeiros's little finger. Every single bird he has tagged with them has returned, so he knows the extra weight doesn't cause any harm, and the devices allow him to download information for up to two years. They've shown that the birds feed in much cooler waters than was previously suspected, traveling as far north as Newfoundland; and that about two-thirds of the cahows tracked spent much of their summer breeding season—up to five months—around the Azores. Remarkably, there has even been a record of one nest-prospecting in the Portuguese islands.

Madeiros's discoveries, says Wingate, "make you realize that what we're saving is not a small, localized species, but a major component of the Atlantic ecosystem. The sheer number of the birds in precolonial times and their vast ocean range mean they must have been an important component. Who knows what subtle relationships the presence of the bird might have altered. As the species recovers, if we can ever get it back to an abundant state, the answers to those questions might be revealed."

He is excited to be able to learn more about cahows' lives at sea, but points out that while modern technology can tell researchers a lot about the birds, it isn't necessarily helpful to the birds themselves. "This information might be useful if, for example, you can show they concentrate in an area where someone's proposing to drill oil wells," he says. "You can say, 'No, this is a major feeding ground for an endangered species,' and lobby to stop any development. But the main thing is still to protect them on their breeding grounds from predators and burrow erosion."

Nick Carlile advocates doing away almost entirely with what he calls "nursemaiding" the birds. "Now that Jeremy's got other ways of monitoring them," he says, "he should mitigate his risks as much as he can. Going out at night and coming back at midnight, it's quite amazing but totally unnecessary. He talks about his guardian angel, but he almost got his hand severed a couple years ago."

Even with cell phones and Boston Whalers—the foam-core boats are known as "the unsinkable legend," and can keep bobbing on the surface even after being cut in half—the islets are still jagged rocks isolated in the middle of an often-treacherous sea, and, just as Wingate did, Madeiros lands on them alone in the dark, with no supplies, in a small, cabinless boat. Wingate once narrowly escaped being swept into the open ocean when his engine gave out during a gale in the middle of Castle Roads. He couldn't restart it, and when he threw the anchor overboard, he was startled to find the chain too short to reach bottom. Madeiros himself barely avoided death recently when a storm five hundred miles to the east of Bermuda caused huge groundswells to hit unexpectedly.

"It looked calm enough," he says. "I was out on Horn—that's the one that's trying to kill me, I swear—and dropped anchor. I had just jumped onto the island when I heard a roar behind me and saw twelve or fifteen feet of water coming in like a breaker. So I just ran. When the wave hit me it came up to my waist. It dragged the anchor and pulled the boat back with it, and at the end of this series of waves, the boat was impaled with a big, giant tooth of rock right in the bottom of it with the stern in the water. I'm wondering how I'm going to get this thing off the rocks when another wave came in and did it for me."

Carlile considers this kind of peril crazy and believes the cahows are almost ready to start going it alone in any case. "My advice would be to force the birds onto Nonsuch, where they can breed productively, by blocking the burrows on the outer islands," he says. "In my mind, they should be going into natural burrows. When they run out of space they'll start using the soil. Let the birds dig their own burrows. They are desperate to breed, and those offshore islands are a total loss. It's fairly radical, but it's a radical situation they're in."

Wingate, needless to say, is horrified at this thought, calling the idea "outrageous." Madeiros, too, considers it imperative to keep the breeding population producing as many chicks as possible. "If you close burrows up," he says, "you're going to have a whole pile of birds that will not breed at all for several years. They have to break up and find new homes, and it's quite likely some will never give up on trying to establish new burrows on the same island. It's not like we have thousands or even hundreds of birds on Nonsuch yet. At some point, maybe in the distant future, we'll do that, but only if it looks like the outer islands are on the verge of complete collapse and would be a death trap for the bird."

If Nonsuch ever does reach its saturation point—which Wingate conservatively believes to be about five thousand nesting pairs but Carlile contends could be much higher—there may be other islands in Bermuda that future conservationists could acquire as translocation sites. They include seven-acre Trunk Island—the largest in Harrington Sound—Hall Island, several patches in Hamilton Harbour, and even Daniel's Island off Somerset in the west end. Wingate has developed a new, mass-producible artificial burrow made of the roofing material SKB, which he has been using for years to make the igloo-shaped longtail nests he and Madeiros have placed on cliffs all over Bermuda. The material is light and insulated, and would make installing what the two men call the birds' "government housing" a breeze, since it wouldn't entail 600 to 800 pounds of concrete, as the current burrow design does.

"Between sound attraction, translocation, and these new burrows,"

Wingate says, "you could get cahows on all these islands, and eventually get them back to something like where they should be, even if the outer islands do disappear."

In the 1968 *Sports Illustrated* story, Wingate shared one vision he had of the future. "The islets were gone," he said, "eroded away by geological processes. But the cahows still returned, nesting in artificial burrows fastened to pipes that someone had stuck in the ocean."

It was a fantasy, he says, but "not beyond the realm of possibility." He's cautious about the cahows' future. "I don't want to be too confident," he says. "That would imply we can loosen our guard. But they're survivors, and they've been such an inspiration to humankind that it's hard to imagine we'd ever turn our backs on them."

✦

With every one of the thousands of trees he planted, Wingate pictured cahows some day burrowing under its roots. Today, he says, "I think we're amazingly close to it." The forest on Nonsuch is nearly mature, and the island is easily the greenest in Castle Harbour, with a dense cap of bushy growth crowning its pale gray cliff line. Gone are the days when sky showed through the tree branches; the paths are dark with overhanging vegetation and musty with the smell of composting leaves. To an outsider, the island's apparent wildness would be impossible to square with the idea of one man meticulously hand-planting every tree and shrub.

Wingate can finally envision a time when, even if the islets go under and the mainland is eaten away by rising seas, the cahows could return, in the far distant future, to being one of the few species to dominate whatever land remains. "The bottom line," he says, "is that in the face of all these problems that have been thrown at them, in spite of all these threats, they are surging upward at an exponential rate." He often comments that he is amazed by nature's resilience. "I've seen it firsthand," he says. "If you just give the natural world a little help, it will bounce back. That is the message of hope that I've gotten out of my experience with the cahows."

In 1987, Wingate accompanied Warren Brown, an internationally known blue-water sailor, and his crew as the on-board naturalist for a portion of a cruise Brown took from the Caribbean to Antarctica, with many detours along the way. For eight weeks, they sailed aboard Brown's 61-foot yacht *War Baby*. They started in Jamaica and passed through the Panama Canal before putting in at Cocos Island, 345 miles from the Pacific shore of Costa Rica. Cocos is about the size of Bermuda, and Wingate was on a dawn watch when it rose out of the darkness as *War Baby* approached. The wildlife coming and going from the island, he says, was like nothing he'd ever seen, with countless birds swirling around the boat as it came in, dolphins at its bow, whales a bit out to sea, and a preposterous number of fish visible under the glass-clear surface. The scene took him back to the accounts of the early settlers to Bermuda, who wrote of a land swarming with life. "As we approached," he recalls, "I thought, This is my dream, to get at least a part of it back there, to give the cahows back a small piece of their original habitat."

It has been his dream in a literal as well as figurative sense. Always plagued by anxiety about the birds, Wingate has often fallen asleep at night only to find himself on the verge of a great discovery, an amazing experience, that's just beyond his grasp. "I'm always reaching for the next bird and that hoped-for explosion in the population," he says, "but I usually wake up before I get the magic breakthrough."

That breakthrough finally came November 2011, almost exactly six decades after he witnessed the birds' rediscovery in Castle Harbour. The English seabird expert Bob Flood was visiting Bermuda to see the cahows and, not knowing Madeiros had taken over the project, wrote to ask Wingate to take him to Nonsuch. Wingate explained the situation, and Flood contacted Madeiros, who agreed to meet both men on the island. "That's how I came to have one of my rare, rare night watches out on Nonsuch," Wingate says.

Around dusk, Flood and Wingate motored out into Castle Harbour, where they saw a few cahows off in the distance, flying low over Horn Rock. As darkness fell, they met Madeiros at the main house, and the three men positioned themselves on the ground just above the cliff nearby. "As soon as it got dark, cahows came whizzing in,"

Wingate says. "It was just incredible. I could not believe how the population has surged since I last had a night watch. Before we knew it there were about ten birds scudding back and forth overhead, calling in response to the Murremaid."

Wingate was mesmerized. It was exactly like the experiences of the early settlers. He and Madeiros called to the birds, and four subadults began to take an interest in them, fluttering and hovering over the men's heads before pairing off again and then zipping away. Eventually one of the four dropped out of the sky and landed between Wingate and Madeiros, close enough that the younger man could easily have reached out and picked the bird up.

Madeiros later told Wingate he'd been checking the bands of returning cahows earlier in the day and still had their scent on his clothing, but Wingate saw the bird's actions in a different light. "It was as if it was coming to say, 'Gee, guys, thanks for saving us,'" he says. "'As you can see we're having quite a party here.'"

Acknowledgments

WITHOUT THE KINDNESS and generosity of Jim and Debbie Butterfield, this book might not have been finished; the Bermuda Zoological Society also provided support.

I wish to thank all of those mentioned in the book who gave so generously of their time and memories—particularly, of course, David Wingate, who opened his life and home to me, shared his encyclopedic knowledge, and patiently endured countless questions.

In the first, tentative stages of this project, when people were wondering who this American was wandering around their country asking questions, the names Michael Heslop and Philippe Rouja were the only introduction needed.

Librarians Ellen Hollis and Alison Green, National Museum of Bermuda curator Elena Strong, Bermuda historian Kristy Warren, and Andrew Baylay of the Bermuda Archives offered invaluable research assistance. I also want to thank the many Bermudians who helped with my work or simply welcomed me as a friend—among them Alistair Border, Tony Brannon, Andrew Dobson, Chris Flook, Rachel Fuhrtz, Robin Gilbert, Richard Lowry, Blanche Marshall, Tony McWilliam, Aileen Morrison, Louis K. Mowbray, Thad Murdoch, Gil Nolan, Timika Olden, Drew Pettit, Tim Petty, Perry Robinson, the Simpson family of Crawl Hill, Robbie Smith, Wolfgang Sterrer, Maria Trott, Wendy Tucker, Jahdal and Tamika Williams, Stella Winstanley, and the staff and researchers at Shorelands and the Bermuda Aquarium, Museum and Zoo. Thanks also to Bruce Adams, Heather Bottelli, Mike Flaherty, Rosalind Grenfell, Jay Gulledge of the Washington, D.C., Center for Climate and Energy Solutions,

Julian Hume, Vern Lochausen, Tristram Pough, Florence Shepard, Ingrid Skousgard and Miles Cowan, Katharine Wingate, and Peter Wingate.

It is with regret that I note the passing of Dick Thorsell in April 2012. I feel privileged to have met him and learned about his experiences in Bermuda.

I recommend that those interested in the cahows and David Wingate track down copies of the documentary films *Rare Bird* by Lucinda Spurling and *Bermuda's Treasure Island* by Deirdre Brennan.

Special thanks to the *Boston Globe Magazine* for assigning me a Bermuda story in the first place; to my early readers, Don MacGillis and Joe O'Brien, both of whom saved me from embarrassment more than once; to my agent, Kitty Cowles, for her wisdom and for always being there; to my editor, Alexis Rizzuto, whose insightful comments vastly improved the finished product; and to John Lombardo for his unique brand of encouragement and good humor.

References

Adams, Robert P., and David Wingate. "Hybridization Between *Juniperus Bermudiana* and *J. Virginiana* in Bermuda." *Phytologia* 90, no. 2 (August 2008).

Bartram, John Tavernier. See David Wingate, "John Tavernier Bartram."

Beebe, William. *Nonsuch: Land of Water*. New York: National Travel Club, 1932.

———. "Rediscovery of the Bermuda Cahow: An 'Extinct' Bird Is Still Breeding Somewhere Along the Rocky Coast." *Bulletin of the New York Zoological Society* 38, no. 6 (November–December 1935).

Bent, Arthur Cleveland. "Life Histories of North American Petrels and Pelicans and Their Allies: Order Tubinares and Order Steganopodes." *Smithsonian Institution*, bull. 121 (1922).

Boland, C. "Introduced Cane Toads *Bufo marinus* Are Active Nest Predators and Competitors of Rainbow Bee-eaters *Merops ornatus*: Observational and Experimental Evidence." *Biological Conservation* 120, no. 1 (2004).

Brassey, Lady Anna. *In the Trades, the Tropics, and the Roaring Forties*. 1885; repr., New York: Cambridge University Press, 2010.

Bried, Joël, and Maria C. Magalhães. "First Palearctic Record of the Endangered Bermuda Petrel *Pterodroma cahow*." *Bulletin of the British Ornithologists' Club* 124 (2004).

Butchart, Stuart H. M., Alison J. Stattersfield, and Nigel J. Collar. "How Many Bird Extinctions Have We Prevented?" *Oryx* 40, no. 3 (2006).

Butler, Nathaniel. See Lefroy et al.

Campbell, Lord George. *Log Letters from "The Challenger."* London: MacMillan and Co., 1876.

Cardwell, D. S. L. "Science and World War I." *Proceedings of the Royal Society of London* 342, no. 1631 (1975).

Challinor, David, and David B. Wingate. "The Struggle for Survival of the Bermuda Cedar." *Biological Conservation* 3, no. 3 (April 1971).

Cunningham, G. Storm. *The Restoration Economy: The Greatest New Growth Frontier*. San Francisco: Berrett-Koehler Publishers, 2002.

Department of Environment and Conservation, New South Wales. "Gould's Petrel (*Pterodroma leucoptera leucoptera*) Recovery Plan," white paper. Hurtsville, N.S.W.: Department of Environment and Conservation, 2006.

Fabry, Victoria J., et al. "Impacts of Ocean Acidification on Iron Availability to Marine Phytoplankton." *ICES Journal of Marine Science* 65 (2008).

Gummer, Helen. "Chick Translocation as a Method of Establishing New Surface-Nesting Seabird Colonies: A Review." *DOC Science Internal Series* 150. Wellington, New Zealand: Department of Conservation, 2003.

Hall, Fred T., Davenport, Iowa, to Arthur A. Allen, Ithaca, New York, March 8, 1951. Personal files of David Wingate.

Hall, Fred T., Davenport, Iowa, to Robert Cushman Murphy, New York, January 5, 1951. Personal files of David Wingate.

Hughes, Lewis. *A Letter Sent into England from the Summer Islands*. London: William Welby, 1625.

———. *A Plaine and True Relation of the Goodnes of God towards the Sommer Ilands, Written by Way of Exhortation, to Stirre Up the People there to Praise God*. London: Edward All-de, 1621.

Hurdis, John L. *See* Reid, Savile.

Jones, John Matthew. *Contributions to the Natural History of the Bermudas*, vol. 1. Washington: Government Printing Office, 1884.

Jourdain, Sylvanus. *A Plaine Description of the Barmudas, Now Called Sommer Ilands*. London: W. Stansby, for W. Welby, 1613.

Kennedy, Jean. *Isle of Devils: Bermuda under the Somers Island Company, 1609–1685*. London: Collins, 1971.

Lang, Daniel. "Letter from Bermuda." *New Yorker*, July 20, 1943.

Lefroy, John Henry, John Smith, and Nathaniel Boteler, *The Historye of the Bermudaes or Summer Islands*. London: The Hakluyt Society, 1882.

Lever, Sir Christopher. "Conservation Success for Two Bermudian Bird Species." *Oryx* 18, no. 3 (1984).

Madeiros, Jeremy. "Breeding Season Report for 2005/2006. Cahow Recovery Program." Annual report. Bermuda: Department of Conservation Services, 2005–2006.

———. "Cahow Recovery Program Update: 2003/2004 Nesting Season." Annual report. Bermuda: Department of Conservation Services, February 2004.

———. "Cahow Recovery Program: Breeding Season Report for 2006/2007 and Update on the Cahow Translocation Project." Annual report. Bermuda: Department of Conservation Services, 2006–2007.

———. "Cahow Recovery Program: Breeding Season Report for 2008 and Update on the Cahow Translocation Project." Annual report. Bermuda: Department of Conservation Services, May 2009.

———. "Cahow Recovery Program: Breeding Season Report for 2010." Annual report. Bermuda: Department of Conservation Services, 2009–2010.

May, Henry. "Narrative of the First Voyage, Sir James Lancaster." In *The Voyages of Sir James Lancaster, Kt., to the West Indies, with Abstracts of the Journals of Voyages to the East Indies, During the Seventeenth Century, Preserved in the India Office*. New York: Burt Franklin, 1877.

McDowall, Duncan. "Mr. Mowbray's Fish House, Part I." *Bermudian*, Fall 2009.

Meyers, Ron A., and Eric F. Stakebake. "Anatomy and Histochemistry of Spread-Wing Posture in Birds. 3. Immunohistochemistry of Flight Muscles and the 'Shoulder Lock' in Albatrosses." *Journal of Morphology* 263, no. 1 (January 2005).

Mowbray, Louis S. "Believed Extinct for 300 Years, a Rare Oceanic Bird Reappears." *Bermudian* (April 1951).

Murphy, Robert Cushman, New York, to Albert E. Parr, New York, February 13, 1951. Personal files of David Wingate.

Murphy, Robert Cushman, and Louis S. Mowbray. "New Light on the Cahow, *Pterodroma Cahow*." *Auk* (July 1951).

Murphy, Robert C., and Grace E. B. Murphy. "The Cahow Still Lives." *Natural History* (April 1951).

Nelson, Richard J. "On the Geology of the Bermudas." *Transactions of the Geological Society*, 2nd series, vol. V, part I (London, 1837).

Nichols, John T., and Louis L. Mowbray. "Two New Forms of Petrels from the Bermudas." *Auk* (April 1916).

Nightline. "Nightline in Primetime: Brave New World." Transcript. ABC News, August 26, 1999.

Oviedo y Valdés, Gonzalo Fernandez de. *See* Purchas, Samuel.

Parker, Ian. "Digging for Dodos: Hunting an Extinct Bird." *New Yorker*, January 22, 2007.

Pollard, J. A. "Paradise Regained: Bringing an Island Back to Life." *Oceans*, no. 4 (July 1985).

Pough, Richard, New York, to Childs Frick, Bermuda, n.d. Personal files of David Wingate.

Pough, Richard, New York, to Fred Hall, Rochester, New York, January 16, 1948. Personal files of David Wingate.

Proceedings of the Royal Society of London. See Cardwell, D.S.L.

Purchas, Samuel. *Hakluytus Posthumus, or Purchas His Pilgrimes*, vol. 19. 1625; repr. Glasgow: James MacLehose and Sons, 1906.

Ramirez, Diego. *See* Wilkinson, Henry.

Ratcliffe, D. A. "Decrease in Eggshell Weight in Certain Birds of Prey." *Nature* 215 (1967): 208–10.

Rattenborg, N. C. "Do Birds Sleep in Flight?" *Naturwissenschaften* 93, no. 9 (September 2006).

Reid, Savile. *The Birds of the Bermudas*. Hamilton, Bermuda: Royal Gazette Office, 1883.

Rogin, Gilbert. "There Are Problems When Man Plays God." *Sports Illustrated*, November 4, 1968. http://vault.sportsillustrated.cnn.com/.

Shepard, Paul, Jr. "Can the Cahow Survive?" *Natural History*, September 1952.

Shufeldt, R. W. "The Bird-Caves of the Bermudas and Their Former Inhabitants." *Ibis* 58, no. 4 (October 1916).

————. "A Comparative Study of Some Subfossil Remains of Birds from Bermuda, Including the 'Cahow.'" *Annals of the Carnegie Museum* 13, no. 3–4 (1921).

Smith, John. *The Generall Historie of Virginia, New England & the Summer Isles.* 1629; repr. Glasgow: Robert Maclehose & Co., 1907.

Strachey, William. *See* Purchas, Samuel.

Thorsell, Richard S. "Report on Cahow–Long-Tail Activities During March and April 1954." Unpublished typescript, June 20, 1954.

Twain, Mark. *See* Wallace, Elizabeth.

van Wissen, Ben. "Eyewitnesses." In *Dodo Raphus cucullatus (Didus ineptus)*, Ben van Wissen, ed. Amsterdam: ISP/Zoologisch Museum-Universiteit van Amsterdam, 1995.

Verrill, Addison E. *The Bermuda Islands: An Account of Their Scenery, Climate, Productions, Physiography, Natural History and Geology, with Sketches of Their Discovery and Early History, and the Changes in Their Flora and Fauna Due to Man.* Published by the author, 1902.

————. "The Cahow: Discovery in Bermuda of Fossil Bones and Feathers Supposed to Belong to the Extinct Bird called 'Cahow' by the Early Settlers." *American Journal of Science.* New Haven, CT: Tuttle, Morehouse & Taylor Co., 1908.

————. "The 'Cahow' of the Bermudas, an Extinct Bird." *Annals and Magazine of Natural History* 9, no. 7 (1902). London: Taylor and Francis.

Wallace, Elizabeth. *Mark Twain and the Happy Island.* Chicago: McClurg Co., 1913.

Wilkinson, Henry, ed. "Spanish Intentions for Bermuda, 1603–1615, as Revealed by Records in the Archives of the Indies, Seville, Spain," *Bermuda Historical Quarterly* 7, no. 2 (1950).

Wingate, David B. "Attracting Longtails to Artificial Nesting Holes with Decoys." *Monthly Bulletin* (Bermuda Department of Agriculture and Fisheries) 48, no. 10 (October 1978).

————. "Bermuda Petrel (Cahow) *Pterodroma Cahow* History, Rediscovery, Conservation Strategy and Recovery Plan: The First 50 Years." Unpublished typescript, 2009.

————. "Cahow, Living Legend of Bermuda." *Canadian Audubon* 22 (1960).

————. "The Cahow: Saga of Survival: Disappearance and Re-discovery." Souvenir program, Bermuda Festival (1982).

————. "Discovery of Breeding Black-Capped Petrels on Hispaniola." *Auk* 81 (April 1964).

————. "Frigate—What an Invasion!" *Critter Talk, Newsletter of the Bermuda Zoological Society & Friends of the Bermuda Aquarium* 29, no. 1 (2006).

————. "From Oceania to Suburbia: 400 Years of Dramatic Change for Bermuda's Bird Community." Speech presented at Bermuda Audubon Society's Fiftieth Anniversary, Bermuda, 2004. Personal files of David Wingate.

_____. "John Tavernier Bartram (1811–1899): Naturalist of 19th Century Bermuda." *Bermuda Historical Quarterly* XXI, no. 4 (Winter 1964).

_____. "Restoration of Nonsuch Island as a Museum of Bermuda's Pre-Colonial Terrestrial Biome." *International Centre for Birds of Prey (ICBP) Technical Publication*, no. 3 (1985).

_____. "The Restoration of an Island Ecology." *Whole Earth Review* (Fall 1988).

_____. "Successful Reintroduction of the Yellow Crowned Night-heron as a Nesting Resident on Bermuda." *Colonial Waterbirds* 5, no. 106 (1982).

_____. "Terrestrial Herpetofauna of Bermuda." *Herpetlogica* 21, no. 3 (September 24, 1965).

_____. Untitled essay. In *Birds and People*, edited by Mark Cocker and David Tipling. London: Jonathan Cape, forthcoming.

_____. "Update on the West Indian Top Shell Re-introduction in Bermuda." *Re-introduction News*, no. 25 (April 2006).

_____. "The West Indian Top Shell in Bermuda—A Conservation Tragedy." *Monthly Bulletin* (Bermuda Department of Agriculture, Fisheries, and Parks) 60, no. 4 (April 1989).

Wingate, David B., et al. "Identification of Bermuda Petrel," *Birding* (February 1998).

Wingate, David, to Richard Pough, New York, April 15, 1959. Personal files of David Wingate.

Wingate, Janet. *Nonsuch Summer*. Published by the author, 2005.

Wurster, Charles F., and David B. Wingate. "DDT Residues and Declining Reproduction in the Bermuda Petrel." *Science* 159, no. 3818 (March 1, 1968).

Zimmerman, David. *To Save a Bird in Peril*. New York: Coward, McCann & Geoghegan, 1975.

Index

Printed in the United States
By Bookmasters